PROMOTING READING COMPREHENSION

Edited by
James Flood, *San Diego State University*

For the IRA Cognitive Psychology

and Reading Comprehension Committee

Published by the
INTERNATIONAL READING ASSOCIATION
800 Barksdale Road, Box 8139
Newark, Delaware 19714

INTERNATIONAL READING ASSOCIATION

Copyright 1984 by the
International Reading Association, Inc.

Library of Congress Cataloging in Publication Data
Main entry under title:

Promoting reading comprehension.

　　Bibliography: p.
　　1. Reading comprehension—Addresses, essays, lectures.
2. Teacher-student relationships—Addresses, essays, lectures.
I. Flood, James.　II. IRA Cognitive Psychology and Reading
Comprehension Committee.
LB1050.45.P76　1984　　　　428.4'3　　　　83-22740
ISBN 0-87207-737-3

Contents

Foreword

In 1979, the IRA Cognitive Psychology and Reading Comprehension Committee began compiling a manuscript delineating the most important and authoritative research and theory dealing with reading comprehension and prose analysis. Comprised of some of the leading researchers and theorists in the country, the committee was headed by James Flood. The results of that committee's work are embodied in this volume, *Promoting Reading Comprehension* and in a companion volume, *Understanding Reading Comprehension.*

The first volume dealt with developing an understanding of the term "comprehension." World reknown educators, linguists, psycholinguists, and cognitive psychologists explained the process from various vantage points.

In this volume, *Promoting Reading Comprehension*, Flood has assembled an equally reknown group of scholars who examine how reading comprehension can be promoted and how various factors enhance or inhibit this comprehension in youngsters.

The first section of the volume examines instructional research dealing with the social environment in which reading comprehension takes place. And, in the concluding chapter, Nancy Roser provides a historical overview of the teaching and testing of reading comprehension.

The second section of *Promoting Reading Comprehension* concentrates on the interaction between reader and text. Again, the leading authorities examine the constraints and aids afforded the reader by the actual text. A unique chapter in this section is the last in which Roselmina Indrisano and Joanne Gurry compare the underlying structure of popular TV shows to those structures generally found in printed material. Suggestions are included for the use of TV in improving reading comprehension.

Finally, in the last section of this volume, Flood has assembled a group of scholars who examine the role of the teacher in promoting reading comprehension in children. In some cases, the teacher is the parent in the home; in other cases, the teacher is the more traditional classroom instructor. In the last chapter of this book, Flood and Diane Lapp outline a plan which helps ensure that all students do indeed comprehend.

Certainly, any reader of this volume and its companion book cannot help but be impressed with the synthesis of research theory and practice evident on these pages. Flood and his colleagues are to be commended for the tremendous scholarship which went into the production of these volumes. No teacher or researcher can afford to ignore this monumental collection.

Jack Cassidy, President
International Reading Association, 1982-1983

Acknowledgement

The editor would like to express appreciation to Jacqueline Collins for her thorough and diligent work in proofreading this manuscript.

IRA PUBLICATIONS COMMITTEE 1983-1984 Joan Nelson-Herber, State University of New York at Binghamton, *Chair* • Phylliss J. Adams, University of Denver • Janet R. Binkley, IRA • Nancy Naumann Boyles, North Haven, Connecticut, Board of Education • Faye R. Branca, IRA • Martha Collins-Cheek, Louisiana State University • Alan Crawford, California State University at Los Angeles • Susan Mandel Glazer, Rider College • Jerome C. Harste, Indiana University • Nelly M. Hecker, Furman University • Roselmina Indrisano, Boston University • Douglas Inkpen, G.B. Little Public School, Scarborough, Ontario • Eleanor Ladd, University of South Carolina • Jamet R. Layton, Southwest Missouri State University • Irving P. McPhail, Johns Hopkins University • Caroline Neal, West Virginia College of Graduate Studies • P. David Pearson, University of Illinois • María Elena Rodríguez, Asociación Internacional de Lectura, Buenos Aires • Betty D. Roe, Tennessee Technological University • S. Jay Samuels, University of Minnesota • Ralph C. Staiger, IRA • Sam Weintraub, State University of New York at Buffalo.

Introduction

Promoting Reading Comprehension celebrates our past and our future. The challenge of the past, developing literacy among all students, has become the promise of the future. This collection of papers presents an historical accounting of instructional approaches to the teaching of comprehension as well as insights into effective approaches for the present and the future.

The volume consists of three parts: 1) Instructional Research in Reading Comprehension, 2) The Reader and the Text, and 3) The Reader and the Teacher. Each paper discusses critical issues in comprehension instruction and recommends strategies for effective teaching.

Four chapters are presented in Part One, Instructional Research in Reading Comprehension. Pearson proposes a framework for conducting research in teaching reading comprehension. Mosenthal discusses his findings on how teaching is conducted based on his research in the classroom. Harste and Carey remind practitioners that the social context of instruction affects teaching and learning. Roser traces the history of teaching and testing reading comprehension.

In Part Two, The Reader and the Text, the authors discuss text-related issues in reading comprehension instruction. Drum examines children's understanding of texts, reviews past research on text comprehension, and offers recommendations for teaching. Marshall explains how the findings of discourse analysis can be used in assessing children's comprehension. Bruce and Rubin discuss the ways children hypothesize during reading and suggest ways in which teachers can intervene to improve instruction. Meyer discusses organizational aspects within the text that can be taught to enhance students' understanding of the text. Tierney, Mosenthal, and Kantor specify the ways in which an understanding of discourse analysis can be used to improve text selection and use. Indrisano and Gurry discuss the text structures found in popular television shows and offer suggestions on the ways teachers can use television to positively affect reading comprehension.

The Reader and the Teacher is the focus of Part Three. Interactions between teachers and their students are discussed, and recommendations for instruction are presented. Based on the findings of their studies with young children during prereading lessons, Mason and Au make suggestions for teaching the young child. Goldfield and Snow explain ways in which parents and young children can interact with positive effects during reading episodes. Bransford and Vye studied successful comprehenders in an effort to isolate the variables that have the most effect on developing comprehension skills. From their studies they offer a set of teaching recommendations. Nelson and Herber discuss a unique, positive approach to assessing and teaching reading comprehension strategies to middle and secondary school students. Their approach is consonant with the most recent findings in instructional research in reading comprehension. Graves suggests methods for selection and teaching important vocabulary to secondary school students. Chapman summarizes the findings of current research in teaching reading comprehension in his paper on the teacher of reading. In the final paper, Lapp and Flood present a plan for teaching reading comprehension. Their plan is a synthesis of the varied, complex, and effective ideas presented in this volume.

JF

PART ONE   Instructional Research in Reading Comprehension

A Context for Instructional Research on Reading Comprehension

P. David Pearson
University of Illinois at Urbana-Champaign

When the history of reading research is written for this century, the decade of the seventies will be regarded with irony. During the past decade, our knowledge of the basic cognitive processes involved in reading comprehension grew dramatically, as did our knowledge about basic instructional processes. Nonetheless, our knowledge about teaching reading comprehension advanced very little, if at all.

This ironic state of affairs can be pardoned, perhaps, on grounds that we had to learn about the basic processes of comprehension and instruction before we could combine knowledge about these two areas in order to make any advances in applied knowledge about teaching reading comprehension.

The time has come to begin a vigorous program of research that directly addresses the issue of how we can improve the reading comprehension of our students. Our knowledge of basic processes, while not complete, is sufficient to allow us to begin to apply knowledge about comprehension *and* instruction to issues of reading comprehension instruction. Even if we did not have the benefit of basic process knowledge, we should still begin the applied effort. Literacy is too important a concern to allow us the luxury of waiting for further advances in basic research. Besides, the argument for waiting reveals an elitist fallacy about the relationship between basic and applied research. There is no reason why applied research cannot and should not inform basic research in the same way that basic research has informed applied research.

In this paper I will briefly summarize important conclusions from research on basic cognitive processes involved in reading comprehension, and from research on classroom instruction. I will discuss what we have learned about how reading comprehension *is taught* (or is *not* taught) in today's schools. I will discuss the experimental studies in which researchers have tried to intervene in the ecology of the school to improve students' reading comprehension. Finally, I will speculate about promising directions that such research might take.

Basic Cognitive Processes in Reading Comprehension

The first thing to note about the cognitively oriented research of the 1970s is that it was not so much directed toward reading comprehension as it was toward understanding how information of any sort, including graphic symbols, is processed. In other words, the research has been as much about attention, encoding, inference, memory storage, and retrieval as it has been about reading comprehension. This is as it should be. It would be counterintuitive and counterproductive to focus exclusively on reading comprehension, as if separate mechanisms and processes were necessary for processing print, as opposed to auditory or other visual information. A unified theory of cognitive processing seems a more reasonable possibility than does a set of separate theories.

The most basic conclusion of this research is that reading, and especially reading comprehension, is a complex interactive process (Rumelhart, 1977; Stanovich, 1980) in which a reader varies his focus along a continuum from primarily text-based processing (concentration on getting the author's message straight) to primarily reader-based processing (concentration on predicting what the author's message ought to be). This variation in focus is determined by a number of intertwined factors: reader purpose (What do I have to do with this information once I've read it?), familiarity (How much do I already know about the topic addressed in the text?), interest and motivation (How much do I care about learning this body of content?), and discourse type and complexity (How much do I already know about the conventions involved in this particular mode of discourse?).

It is at once a curse and a blessing that the reader's focus, or type of processing, is determined by so many factors. The curse is that this inherent complexity makes it difficult for us to understand, let alone improve, reading comprehension processes. The blessing is that with so many factors involved, the likelihood increases that we will find a small subset of factors—or even one factor—that we can manipulate systematically to achieve improved comprehension. Our hope, therefore, may lie in being able to select those factors most amenable to amelioration.

A second conclusion to be drawn from basic research in cognition is that both *content* and *process* factors are involved in reading comprehension. Content factors are the knowledge structures residing in our long term semantic memory that determine how well we understand and integrate a particular text. They resemble what computer scientists call data structures. To put it simply, the more we know about the topic addressed in the text, the greater the likelihood we will understand, integrate, and remember the information contained in the text (Anderson, Reynolds, Schallert, & Goetz, 1977; Pearson, Hansen, & Gordon, 1979). But there is another type of content, besides knowledge of topic, that influences comprehension: knowledge about the text structure or text genre in which the topic is embedded. The work on story structures (Neilsen, 1977; Omanson, 1978; Stein & Glenn, 1977; Thorndyke, 1977) and typical rhetorical structures found in expository writing (Meyer, 1977; Meyer, Brandt, & Bluth, 1980) indicate that familiarity with structure influences comprehension. Neilsen, for example, found that even when topical information (as defined by the characters and activities) was controlled, subjects were better able to recall and recognize information presented in a causally organized structure, than presented in a sequentially organized structure. Several studies (Mandler, 1977; Stein & Glenn, 1977; Thorndyke, 1977) have indicated that violations in what might be labeled canonical story form result in decreased recall of information. The point is that both topical and structural content have identifiable influences on comprehension.

Process factors are comparable to what are called control procedures in computer processing. They refer to *how* data are processed instead of *what* data are processed. The two types of factors are not independent. In fact, process factors may be but different facets of the same amalgam under consideration when content factors are discussed. I refer to attention, encoding, inference, and retrieval, as well as executive monitoring of these procedures (metacognitive processing—knowledge about the procedures or how they are "proceeding").

That these processes undergo developmental improvement seems intuitively obvious. In fact, empirical researchers have indicated such a trend for inference (Paris & Lindauer, 1976; Paris & Upton, 1976); encoding of information into memory (Pichert & Anderson, 1977); retrieval of information from memory (Pichert, in press); and metacognitive monitoring (Baker & Brown, 1983). What is not clear in most of these studies is the cause of this improvement—a sheer developmental increase in cognitive capacity, an increase in subjects' world knowledge, instructional history, or a growing awareness that the processes are available and ought to be used.

For example, regarding inference, Paris and Lindauer (1976) seem to argue for an awareness of strategy availability, while Trabasso et al. (in press) and Chi (1978) present evidence favoring a growth in world knowledge. Alternatively, recent studies by Hansen and Pearson (1980) and Gordon (1980) suggest that inference performance increases with direct instruction and/or practice.

The point that can be made to conclude this section is that both content and process factors have been shown to influence comprehension. (I have omitted reference to the influence of textual manipulations on comprehension, not because they are unimportant, but because they can be accounted for by including a cognitive factor such as knowledge of textual organization. I prefer this latter approach since it suggests that meaning resides in the reader rather than on the printed page.)

Classroom Instruction Research

In the past decade researchers have spent a great deal of time observing what goes on in classrooms. The general paradigm for the research is based upon the assumption that observation techniques will allow us to identify management, material, design, and verbal interaction patterns that discriminate between successful and unsuccessful classrooms and/or schools. This is typically accomplished by identifying, in advance, successful and unsuccessful schools, teachers, or classrooms. Then, depending upon the degree to which one accepts the tenets of the ethnographic tradition, the researcher conducts controlled observation (preplanned, systematic, and theoretically determined), or uncontrolled observation (no predetermined scales or protocols). Then the researcher examines the observational data, looking for factors which differentiate successful and unsuccessful sites.

The logic of this paradigm is similar to the good/poor reader paradigm used in descriptive reading research: Give similar tasks to readers with widely different reading ability, looking for cognitive or behavioral correlates that discriminate between good and poor readers. The assumption in both cases is that those factors which discriminate between the good and the bad will be likely candidates for subsequent experimental research in which those variables are systematically manipulated to determine whether or not improvement occurs.

The research conducted under the auspices of the California Beginning Teacher Evaluation Study (Fisher, Berliner, Filby, Marliave, Cohen, Dishaw, & Moore, 1978), by Brophy and Evertson (1976), and reviewed by Rosenshine (1979) and Rosenshine and Berliner (1978) all represent variations on this paradigmatic theme. Also, the debate centering on the follow-through reports (Becker, 1977; House, Glass, McLean, & Walker, 1978) provides some provocative data regarding effective aspects of instruction. Finally, the work of Stallings (1978) is relevant to this set of issues.

Summarizing (and hence oversimplifying) the situation, we get the following scenario. First, the greater the proportion of time students spend on a task, the better their performance on the task. Academic engaged time, to use Rosenshine's term (1979), is a reasonable predictor of reading achievement gain, ranging in magnitude from correlations of .30-.59 (e.g., Fisher, Silby, Marliave, Cohen, Dishaw, Moore, & Berliner, 1978; Samuels & Turnure, 1974; Stallings et al., 1977; Stallings & Kaskowitz, 1974).

Second, while related to engaged time, a separate variable which could be labeled "content covered" or "content mastered" (the two tend to be confounded) tends to be positively related to achievement gain (Anderson, Evertson, & Brophy, 1979; Barr, 1973-1974; Brown, 1979; Good, Grouws, & Beckerman, 1979; Harris and Serwer, 1966). This relationship seems to hold, according to Rosenshine (in press) across a wide range of content: Number of books read, number of words taught, number of basal levels completed, or number of computerized modules mastered.

Third, error rate seems to add a significant amount of power in predicting achievement above and beyond engagement and content covered. The California Beginning Teacher Evaluation Study (BTES) (Berliner et al., 1978) examined the additional predictive power of error rate over simply engagement and time allocated for reading. They found that error rate increased the correlation with reading achievement in 7 of 10 predictions. Interestingly, the data suggest that lower error rates (about 80-90 percent correct) are successful with low achievers whereas somewhat higher error rates (about 70 percent correct) are more effective with high achievers. These data derive from a variety of settings for teacher-student interactions (words correct, answers to questions correct, etc.). Also, the combined predictions (combining allocated time, engagement rate and error rate) suggest that time spent on decoding is correlated with achievement in grade 2 to a greater degree than is time spent on comprehension, while the reverse is true in grade 5. Of course, this may reflect little more than the differences in test items across grades.

Fourth, group instruction, particularly small group instruction is consistently associated with positive gains in achievement while individualized instruction is associated with negative or negligible gains (Berliner et al., 1978; Kean, et al., 1979; Soar, 1973; Stallings & Kaskowitz, 1974). Granted neither is as effective as one-to-one instruction; however, assuming a normal student-teacher ratio (15-1 to 30-1), group instruction appears more effective than individualized seat work oriented instruction. Note, however, that grouping is confounded with engagement, which may be the operative variable; for example, in the BTES Study (Fisher et al., 1978) engagement rates averaged 84 percent in group situations and about 70 percent in individualized situations. Even more dramatic is the data for conscious nonattendance to task: 16 percent when students worked alone versus 5 percent when students worked in groups.

Taking all these findings together, the conclusion emerges that traditional instruction consistently wins out over innovative instruction. One is tempted to conjure up a picture of a hard-hearted taskmaster of a teacher drilling students mercilessly on boring skills, using choral recitation as a major response mode. This is not the case. Studies that have examined qualitative and affective variables in successful and unsuccessful classrooms tend to have difficulty discriminating between classrooms on these sorts of variables. In fact, most studies have found very little in the way of direct student criticism or harshness to students (Anderson et al., 1979), and such teacher behavior either correlated negatively with achievement (Soar, 1973; Soloman & Kendall, 1976; Stallings, Needles, & Staybrook, 1979) or was positively related to achievement only when the criticism specified desirable alternative behaviors. Remember that these same studies found positive relationships between the four previously reviewed variables and achievement; thus it must be the case that this traditional cluster of teacher strategies does not lead to cold or harsh teacher/student interactions.

I cannot leave this realm of research without commenting on the research evaluating direct instructional models. Most of the debate about the efficacy of direct versus incidental instruction has centered on Follow Through comparisons between DISTAR and other more humanistically oriented programs (Becker & Carnine, 1978; House et al., 1978; Stallings & Kaskowitz, 1974). Hence the research has been confounded in the sense that it has compared direct instruction in decoding using a fairly regimented group oriented program (DISTAR) with incidental instruction emphasizing comprehension in a humanistically oriented program (for example, the language experience programs in Follow Through). In short, the direct instructional model (after Engelman, 1977), which emphasizes rules, minimal contrasts to elicit discrimination of distinctive features of the rules, and lots of practice *after* instruction, has not been fairly tested. We do not know from the Follow Through research which aspect of the DISTAR program direct instruction, decoding, or regimentation—leads to superior decoding performance in high risk populations.

The systematic application of direct instructional approaches in the area of comprehension instruction has lead to superior comprehension performance in several studies (Day, 1980; Gordon & Pearson, in press; Hansen & Pearson, 1980; Raphael & Pearson, in press; Tharp, 1980). The Tharp study is important because it has evaluated a frontal assault on comprehension instruction over a several year period. What is remarkable about the results of Tharp's research is that groups of high risk native Hawaiian children have moved from mean comprehension test scores hovering near the 20th percentile to near the 60th percentile.

Rosenshine and Stevens (in press) characterize this gestalt of variables as an overall academic orientation to teaching and learning. Success seems to be characteristic of warm but task-oriented classroom environments where students are expected to and do complete work related to reading and reading skill development. The teachers working in these classrooms might well be labeled hard nosed humanists.

Current Practices in Teaching Reading Comprehension

The research surveying current practices for *teaching* reading comprehension is limited to a single study (Durkin, 1978). Durkin observed approximately 300 hours of instruction in both reading and social studies classes. She developed a scheme for classifying teacher behaviors. Comprehension instruction was limited to lessons on how one goes about doing comprehension tasks—finding main ideas, paraphrasing, determining sequence, and so forth. Comprehension assessment was represented by teachers quizzing students about stories they had read (and focusing on right answers). Comprehension assignments consisted of mentioning to students how they were to go about completing a workbook ditto, or other written assignment. There were many other categories, but these are most relevant for our purposes.

Of the total of 17,997 minutes of observation, Durkin found that less than 1 percent of the total time was devoted to activities that met one of her definitions of instruction. What were teachers doing in the classes she observed? First, they were giving lots of assignments for students to do on their own without teacher supervision. Second, they were asking students lots of questions about stories they read and focusing on getting the right answer. Third, they answered a fair number of individual questions about assignments. What was going on in the name of comprehension? Put simply, assignment giving and question asking. The prevailing wisdom concerning comprehension instruction seems to be that if students get enough exposure to a skill or kind of question, they will eventually get better at it. While such a position may be consistent with the engaged time on task argument derived from Rosenshine and Steven's review, it is not consistent with arguments emanating from the direct instruction or grouping findings. Furthermore, simply on common sense grounds there is something suspicious about a position whose implicit rationale is that if students have trouble with X, what they need is to practice X more often. Such a position probably works fine for students who can perform the task at a moderate error rate; however, for students who hover near chance level on the task, the additional practice may only reinforce their already misguided strategies. In other words, what Durkin found in our schools in the name of comprehension may be a practice that promotes a "the rich get richer and the poor get poorer" syndrome.

In a sequel to her classroom observation study, Durkin (in press) examined the teachers' editions of five currently popular basal reading programs looking for instances of comprehension instruction, defined in terms that were comparable to the criteria used in her earlier study. While the sheer incidence of comprehension instruction was higher than in her previous study, the general pattern of a dominant reliance on assessment and mentioning was replicated.

Durkin's two studies, taken together, reveal a picture of virtually no direct instruction in comprehension. Instead, teachers seem to spend most of their classroom discussion time asking students questions about stories they have read and giving assignments. Regarding comprehension skills—such as main idea, sequence, cause-effect, fact-opinion—manuals provide little guidance concerning how the skills ought to be presented to students. Teachers apparently provide little guidance to students about how they ought to solve problems and/or answer questions exemplifying these skills. The prevailing wisdom is to provide massive doses of unguided practice. Nor is there much evidence, either in manuals or classrooms, that students receive substantive feedback that would allow them to evaluate how well they were performing a task or, more important, what inappropriate strategies they might be adopting. The student who is not doing well on a particular comprehension skill seems to have little help to look forward to, save additional opportunities to improve performance on his or her own through practice.

Research on Comprehension Instruction

Durkin's two studies tend to engender an atmosphere of pessimism, and well they should. Perhaps, however, they have done the reading profession a definite service. If nothing else, they prompt the question, What is the alternative to practice and assessment? As an antidote to that pessimism, let me turn to a review of a few recent studies that have evaluated the effects of direct conscious attempts to help students develop heuristic strategies (if not rules) for dealing with a range of typical comprehension tasks.

These studies share a set of features in common. First, all of them are derived directly from basic research on the reading process; that is, they represent attempts to bridge the gap from basic research to a real instructional issue. Second, all have evaluated the efficacy of their instructional treatments by using transfer tasks. They have asked the question, What happens to student performance when instructional crutches are removed? Third, all have obtained positive results; they have shown that the intervention at issue elicits positive gains in some aspects of comprehension. Fourth, all have attended, at least in some way, to the question of control processes. They have included, directly or by implication, techniques that allow students to monitor for themselves whether or not they understand task demands or know when they are performing the task appropriately.

In this first study, Hansen and Pearson (1980) were interested in improving children's ability and predisposition to draw inferences. Beginning with the observation that children were best at answering the kinds of questions teachers ask most often, i.e. literal recall of story details, they wondered whether this observation represented a robust developmental trend, an accident of children's instructional history (i.e., they have more practice at literal questions), or a fact about the world (literal questions are inherently easier).

They devised three instructional treatments. In the first, a business as usual approach, average second grade students were given a traditional diet of questions accompanying their basal reader stories—about 80 percent literal to 20 percent inferential questions. In the second, a practice only treatment, literal questions were removed from these children's basal reader lives altogether; they received only inferential questions. In the third, students received the traditional question diet but were confronted lesson after lesson with a massive set toward inferential story comprehension. Prior to each story, they were asked to predict what they would do and what the story protagonist would do when confronted with 2 or 3 critical situations (actual situations from the to-be-read story). They then read the story to compare their predictions with what actually occurred (Directed Reading-Thinking Activity). In addition they were provided with a visual model of comprehension as a process of relating the new to the known.

Four kinds of dependent measures were analyzed, using pre-test story understanding tasks (answering literal and inferential probes) as a covariate in a multivariate ANACOVA. On the first measure, literal and inferential probes from the last five stories in which the instruction was embedded, both the practice only and the inference training group outperformed the traditional group on both literal and inferential probes. In addition, where differences existed between the two experimental groups, they favored the inference training group. The data suggest that a set for inference induces a level of processing affect that generalizes to both inference and literal tasks, at least in a local environment.

On the second measure, literal and inferential probes from totally new and unaided stories, the two inference oriented groups exceeded the traditional group only on inference probes for the familiar transfer story. These data suggest that whatever heuristic developed could not overcome the strong influence that prior knowledge has on inference performance (i.e. no differences on the inference probes for the topically unfamiliar selection).

On the third measure, free recall of a totally new story, there were absolutely no differences, arguing for a transfer of identical elements phenomenon. In short, since the students never practiced free recall, their ratio of intrusions (inferences) to text reproductions was not influenced.

On the fourth measure, a posttest only standardized reading test, there was a treatment by subtest interaction. On the vocabulary subtest, there were no reliable differences among groups, strengthening the argument that there were no pre- or postexperimental general verbal ability differences among the groups. On the comprehension subtests, however, there were strong differences favoring both experimental groups over the traditional group. At first blush this may seem surprising, since standardized tests are typically insensitive to specific instructional treatments. However the standardized test used was the Stanford Achievement Test which uses a modified cloze (fill-in-the-blank) response format. Such a format, if it does anything, places a premium on inferences from prior knowledge; how else would anyone determine the best fit for the cloze blank? Hence the transfer is not so surprising.

The primary conclusion one can draw from these data is that inference ability, even for young students, is amenable to direct training and monitoring; however the local and task alike transfer effects are more impressive than the broad transfer effects.

Gordon (1980) extended, at least in part, the inference training hypothesis to older children (grade 4). Over a period of 8 weeks, she contrasted the effects of an even more explicitly trained inference group with a placebo control group that received fun language experience and immersion activities and a second experimental group whose instruction focused on activating and fine-tuning pre-existing content schemata (the topics addressed in the stories) and structure schemata (helping students develop an abstract framework for what is entailed in a story) before and after reading.

Five dependent measures were used: 1) Comprehension of literal and inferential probes summed over the eight stories in which the instruction was embedded, 2) comprehension of literal and inferential probes on transfer stories read immediately following the eight week experiment, 3) same as #2 only delayed two weeks, 4) a standardized comprehension test measure, and 5) free recall protocols from the last story read in the training period.

While the results are not quite so dramatic as in the Hansen and Pearson study, the patterns of significant results are consistent. There were no significant differences between groups on the standardized test or on the immediate comprehension test, again suggesting that broad transfer is difficult to obtain. However, there were statistically reliable differences favoring the inference training group on inference items derived from the instructional stories. Also, high achieving students in that group did better than other groups on the inference items on the delayed posttest. The most remarkable differences favored the content and structure schemata activation group on the free recall protocols; their scores were often two or three standard deviations above the inference group and the placebo control group, particularly on recall measures which were sensitive to the development and use of a story schema. Apparently these students developed an abstract story "map" which served them well in encoding and retrieving information structurally important in a story schema. As with the Hansen and Pearson study, one is more impressed with the local than the broad transfer effects. Also, one is struck by the specificity of the transfer that does occur. The principle of transfer of identical elements suggests itself (i.e., the greater the similarity between training and transfer tasks, the greater the likelihood of transfer). One is tempted also to invoke Rosenshine's engaged time on task principle in explaining these data.

Raphael (1980) carried the inference training paradigm directly into a metacognitive realm. Over four 45 minute sessions, she trained average fourth, sixth, and eighth grade students and low, average, and high sixth grade students to monitor their allocation of resources (text versus head) in generating answers to questions that invited textually explicit comprehension (derive an answer from the same text sentence from which the question was generated), textually implicit comprehension (derive an answer from a text proposition different from the one from which the question was derived), or scriptally implicit comprehension (derive an answer from one's store of prior knowledge). She modified this scheme, taken from Pearson and Johnson (1978), for students by labeling the three response types RIGHT THERE, THINK AND SEARCH, and ON MY OWN, respectively.

Using a "model → guided practice → independent practice → direct feedback" instructional design, she guided the students to apply the strategy to increasingly larger text segments (one paragraph to a 600 word passage) with an increasingly larger number of questions per lesson and increasingly fewer feedback prompts from the instructor. In the strategy, students read the relevant text and the question, generated an answer, and then decided which of the three strategies they had used to generate the answer.

In the transfer test, students read entirely new passages on their own, answered questions and decided on the strategy they thought they had used to generate the answer. The performance of the training group was contrasted not with an untreated control but with a control group that received a 20-minute orientation to the response classification task.

Four dependent measures were analyzed: 1) *Hits* (students gave their response strategy the same category rating as the experimenter gave); 2) *Matches* (students actually did what they said, regardless of response quality); 3) *Appropriate Responses* (students gave responses that could be scored correct given a complex set of scoring protocols that allowed for considerable deviation from the expected response), and 4) *Correct Hit Matches* (given that students achieved Hits and Matches, they got the items correct).

On all of these response measures, reliable differences were found favoring the training group over the orientation group; that is, trained students got better at discriminating task demands of different types of questions (Hits), evaluating their own behavior (Matches), and giving quality responses (Appropriate Responses). On the conditional measure, which requires discrimination, *and* evaluation, *and* response quality, training/orientation differences were magnified even further. Apparently, students changed both their response strategies and their response monitoring strategies. Raphael concluded that they had developed both new comprehension and comprehension monitoring heuristics that gave them more control over a traditional question answering task.

Working with low ability community college students, Day (1980) contrasted approaches to training students to write summaries for prose passages. The treatments differed systematically from one another in terms of how rules for writing summaries were integrated with self-management strategies designed to help students monitor their own progress in summary writing. Treatment 1 consisted of self-management alone (a fairly traditional self-checking procedure to determine whether the summary conveyed the information the student intended to convey). Treatment 2 was rules alone; subjects were trained to use van Dijk and Kintsch's (1978) five rules for summarizing narratives (delete redundancies, delete irrelevancies, subordinate sub-topics, select topic sentences, create topic sentences). Treatment 3 simply put Treatments 1 and 2 together in sequence. First do one, then the other. Treatment 4 integrated the rules and self management strategies into a single coherent routine. One might say that the four treatments varied along a continuum of integration of explicit training and explicit monitoring devices. A "model → feedback → practice" instructional design was used.

The dependent measure was the proportion of time students used each of the five summarization rules (number of actual uses/number of potential opportunities to use). Day found that from pretest to posttest, there was a ceiling effect on the two deletion rules; that is, almost all students could already apply them. On the subordination rule all but Treatment 1 students made significant gains, with the greatest gains accruing to the integrated group (Treatment 4). On the selection rule, again Treatments 2, 3, and 4 exhibited greater gain than did Treatment 1; however, there were no reliable differences among Treatments 2, 3, or 4. Also, average ability students gained more than low ability students. On the creation rule a pattern emerged similar to that found for subordination. The greatest gains accrued to the integrated group (Treatment 4). Furthermore, posttest performance indicated that while gains were similar across rules, absolute performance levels were conditioned by rule complexity; rule 3>rule 4>rule 5.

Day's data suggest that with different tasks and with slower students, "...explicit training in strategies for accomplishing a task coupled with routines to oversee the successful application of those strategies is clearly the best approach" (p. 15).

This summary provided by Day could well serve as a summary for the four studies reviewed in this section. All point to the direction of making clear what the task requirements are, providing heuristic guidelines for task completion, allowing substantial massed practice along with substantive feedback, and insuring some provision for self monitoring. The data are encouraging. It looks as though we can teach comprehension skills after all.

Future Directions for Comprehension Instruction Research

The last section clearly reveals my own biases about the direction instructional research on reading comprehension ought to take. Research should focus on explicit attempts to help students develop independent strategies for coping with the kinds of comprehension problems they are asked to solve in class. One could infer that such research was needed by examining the gaps in instruction found by Durkin (1978) and the positive correlations between existing instructional practices and achievement noted by people like Rosenshine and Stevens (in press). That the few instructional studies on reading comprehension also support such a line of research is encouraging.

As a general model for how we might proceed, I close with a set of guidelines paraphrased from Brown, Campione, & Day (1980):

1. The trained skill must be instructionally relevant.
2. Training should proceed from simple to complex.
3. An analysis of training and transfer tasks should provide evidence of where breakdowns occur.
4. There should be direct instruction concerning when and how to use the strategies.
5. Feedback should be given during class discussions and for independent work.
6. A variety of passages (or other materials) should be used in order to facilitate transfer to new situations.
7. Self-checking procedures should be used as an inherent part of the training strategy.

In reflecting upon this model and the studies reviewed in the previous sections, I am struck by the consistency of this perspective with what we might call common sense. The question then becomes: How did we stray from the common sense course, and how do we get back to it?

Reading Comprehension Research from a Classroom Perspective

Peter Mosenthal
Syracuse University

How do children learn to read in classroom lesssons? This question is important because classroom lessons are the primary means by which society passes on literary skills from generation to generation (Mehan, 1979). It is in classroom lessons that children learn the various strategies for decoding and comprehending (Barr, 1973-1974), and children develop attitudes about themselves and about reading (Labov, 1977; McDermott, 1976). In classrooms, children learn how to negotiate academic and behavior tasks in learning to read (Doyle, 1979). And it is in classrooms that children are judged, classified, and assigned to different reading groups, which entail different teacher expectations and different instructional emphases (Allington, in press).

Classroom lessons serve a second important function as a means for cultural transmission. It is largely through classroom lessons that our society assimilates children into its cultural ideology. As Resnick and Resnick (1977) and Walmsley (in press) have noted, instructional methods and materials, and tests of literacy always presuppose a cultural ideology. This ideology determines what we teach, how we teach, and how we evaluate in classroom lessons. In addition, this ideology determines how we define good students and poor students, good readers and poor readers (McDermott, 1974). Finally, it is often by way of classroom lessons that our society acculturates minority children (Dumont, 1972; McDermott, 1977; Simons & Gumperz, 1980).

Despite the immense importance classroom lessons have on children's reading acquisition, very little is known about how children actually read and learn to read in the classroom. In part, this stems from the fact that the classroom has been a "missing link" in reading comprehension research. For the most part, researchers have overlooked the classroom as an important variable. Researchers have tended to offer pat solutions to complex classroom problems on the basis of simple studies conducted in formal experimental situations (see Bronfenbrenner, 1977, and Mishler, 1979, on this point). While this is not to deny the contributions formal experimental studies have made towards education (Getzels, 1978), it does raise the question of ecological validity and context specificity: Can the question of how children read and learn to read in classroom lessons be answered outside the classroom in formal experimental situations?

The purpose of this paper is to address this issue. In particular, this paper challenges the assumption that the results from formal experimental situations provide us with valid explanations of how children read and learn to read in classroom lessons. First, it is argued that while reading researchers have tended to define reading comprehension primarily in terms of text, task, and subject contexts, the most important context influencing reading comprehension in classroom lessons may be the interaction between the teacher and the students. Second, it is argued that because the contexts of learning to read interact in a dynamic, evolutionary fashion, one must supplement quantitative methods with qualitative methods to adequately understand the reflexive and recursive patterns in children's acquisition of reading comprehension in classroom lessons.

The Contexts of Reading Comprehension

Although reading comprehension has been defined many ways, one can represent the range of these definitions in terms of a Context Pyramid (see Jenkins' "Problem Pyramid," or "Theorist's Tetrahedron," 1979, p. 432). This Contexts Pyramid is presented in Figure 1. Each vertex of this Pyramid represents the variables researchers have used to define reading.

The significance of the Contexts Pyramid is that it illustrates that reading comprehension is a multicontext phenomenon. In formal experimental situations, the Situation Organizer Context is usually represented by the experimenter. The Text Context is usually represented by a carefully constructed set of linguistic stimuli whose structures are either well formed or not well formed as defined by some grammar. The Reader Context, more often than not, is represented by a college sophomore of above average intelligence, nineteen years of age. The Task Context is represented by a set of precisely stated instructions and procedures which readers, as subjects, must follow in order to

Figure 1. The Context Pyramid of reading comprehension. Following Jenkins (1979, p. 432), each vertex represents a cluster of variables of a given type shown to influence reading comprehension. Each degree represents a two-way interaction between Contexts; each plane calls attention to a three-way interaction, and the entire Figure represents the five-way interaction of all the variables that could possibly influence reading comprehension.

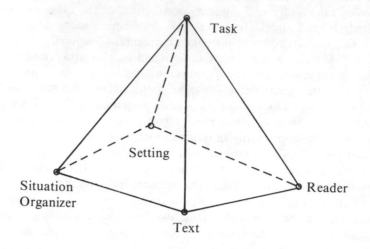

demonstrate that they have "comprehended" the text stimuli. Also included in the Task Context is the modality in which the stimuli are presented. The Setting Context is represented by either a formal laboratory or an adjunct conference room in a school.

In classroom lessons, the configurations of the Contexts are quite different. In classroom lessons, the Situation Organizer Context is represented by the teacher and the pupils in the lesson. In the younger grades, the Text Context is represented by the teacher's basal reader lesson guide, the students' basal reader texts, students' workbooks, and other teacher prepared stimuli such as flash cards, dittos, word charts, and blackboard exercises. The Reader Context is represented by children, representing a broad range of age, intelligence, background experience, and maturation. The Task Context is represented by a variety of instructions and procedures generally defined in the lesson outline in the teacher's basal reader manual. The Setting Context is the classroom in which students usually gather in some specified location apart from other students in order to participate in reading lessons.

Although no experiment could be conducted without involving all the contexts in the Context Pyramid, quantitative reading

Mosenthal

researchers have assumed that not all these Contexts contribute equally to reading comprehension. Operating in traditional Campbell and Stanley (1963) fashion, these researchers have tended to apply the following algorithm to the Contexts Pyramid:

1. Identify a favorite Context as a Causative Context of reading comprehension.
2. Identify an Effect Context which is acted upon by the Causative Context.
3. Describe or explain the relationship between the Causative Context and Effect Context. (This completes the descriptive definition of reading comprehension.)
4. Define the Causative Context in the operational definition of reading comprehension as the Independent Variables; define the Effect Context as the Dependent Variables.
5. Verify, using statistics, the syllogism:
   a. If descriptive definition is valid, then operational definition is valid;
   b. Operational definition is valid, therefore descriptive definition is valid.

What this algorithm means is that, in informal experimental studies, researchers begin by constructing a descriptive definition of reading comprehension (Rudner, 1966). If this study is at the level of merely discovering Causative Contexts, one may identify a broad range of variables from within and/or between Contexts as representing examples or features of comprehension (Davis, 1968; Graesser, Hoffman, & Clark, 1980). In such cases, one is more concerned with discovering Causative Contexts than with explaining the relationship between some well defined Causative Context and Effect Context. On the other hand, if the study is at the level of explaining the relationship between the Causative Context and the Effect Context, one may establish a descriptive definition of reading comprehension by presenting a model or a theory (Clark & Haviland, 1977; Kintsch & van Dijk, 1978; Thorndyke, 1976; Vipond, 1980).

Once one has arrived at a descriptive definition of reading comprehension (steps 1-3 in the algorithm), one then establishes an operational definition of reading comprehension. In so doing, one attempts to link factors in the descriptive definition to observable variables in the operational definition (see Bridgman, 1978, on this procedure). In most instances, Causative Context variables are represented as independent variables; Effect Context variables are represented as dependent variables. In descriptive studies, the extent to which Causative Context variables are shown to significantly influence

Effect Context variables represents the extent to which one has successfully isolated a Causative Context in the descriptive definition of reading comprehension. In theoretical studies, the extent to which the Causative Context variables significantly influences the Effect Context variables according to a model's or theory's predictions represents the extent to which one has successfully explained the relationship between Causative Context variables and Effect Context variables.

The important thing to note here is that in formal experimental situations, researchers have tended to descriptively and operationally define reading comprehension in terms of three primary Contexts: Text, Reader, and Task. Of these three Contexts, Text and Reader Contexts have been the most popular Contexts from which to draw variables to describe reading comprehension (Olson, 1977). There have been attempts to define reading comprehension by defining the Causative Context as the Task Context and the Effect Context as the Text and/or the Subject Context (Bransford, Franks, Morris, & Stein, 1979; Craik & Lockhart, 1972; Frederiksen, 1972; Graesser, Higginbotham, Robertson, & Smith, 1978; Stein & Bransford, 1979). For example, in the levels-of-processing framework proposed by Craik and Lockhart (1972), researchers have debated whether tasks involving semantic processing are more beneficial for retention than tasks that involve nonsemantic processing. There have been attempts to define reading comprehension by defining the Causative Context as the Text Context and the Effect Context as the Subject Context (Frederiksen, 1977; Glenn, 1978; Goetz, 1979; Kintsch, Kosminsky, Streby, McKoon, & Keenan, 1975; Mandler, 1978; Meyer, 1975; Omanson, Warren, & Trabasso, 1978). Most of this research has attempted to demonstrate how the structure and/or the content of text influence how and what people remember from text. There have been attempts to define reading comprehension by defining the Causative Context as the Subject Context and the Effect Context as the Text Context. For example, researchers have shown that how readers comprehend text varies as a function of readers' developmental level (Ackerman, 1978; Hildyard, 1979), reading ability (Perfetti & Lesgold, 1977; Spiro, 1979; Tierney, Bridge, & Cera, 1978-1979), cognitive style (Spiro & Tirre, 1980), schema structure and background knowledge (Anderson & Pichert, 1978; Chiesi, Spilich, & Voss, 1979; Mosenthal, 1979b; Pearson, Hansen, & Gordon, 1979; Spiro, 1980), and metamemory ability (Brown, 1978, 1979). There have been those attempts to define reading comprehension by defining the Causative Context as the interaction between the Text Context and the Subject Context (Rumelhart, 1977) with the Effect Context being either the Text Context and/or the Subject Context. Finally, there have been those attempts to define reading comprehension by defining the Causative Context and the Effect Context within a single Context and sometimes even within and between Contexts. For example, there have been those studies investigating the effect of background knowledge or use of schema structure on reading ability (Grabe & Prentice, 1979; Meyer, Brandt, & Bluth, 1980) and the effect of one level of language processing on another (Cirilo & Foss, 1980; Graesser, Hoffman, & Clark, 1980). An example of a within-and-between Contexts study is one by Vipond (1980) investigating the importance of micro- and macrolevel text processing in the comprehension of good and poor readers.

In attempting to apply their research to practice, comprehension researchers (Anderson, 1977; Baker & Stein, 1981; Meyer, 1977; Pearson & Johnson, 1978; Walker & Meyer, 1980) have assumed that the theory relating the Causative and Effect Contexts in formal experimental situations can be generalized to explain the cause-and-effect Context relationship in classroom reading lessons. In terms of the principles of general scientific methodology (Hempel, 1966), this practice is untenable given the enormous mismatch between the way Contexts in formal experimental situations and the way Contexts in classroom reading lessons are represented. As noted earlier, this mismatch is significant. Yet, despite this mismatch, one often finds researchers operationally defining comprehension in terms of a few precisely stated operational tasks and procedures, using above-average college sophomores, reading artificially constructed text stimuli in laboratory settings, with the reader performing before an unknown experimenter. From this, these researchers generalize their definition of comprehension to classroom situations in which the tasks are varied and many, the readers are children representing a broad range of individual differences, the text is a complex narrative, the setting is a familiar reading group area, and the audience is a teacher and fellow pupils. It seems strange that although such experimenters are often careful not to generalize their findings much beyond their operationally defined Causative and Effect Contexts in the formal experimental Contexts Pyramid, they fail to demonstrate such restraints in generalizing their findings to classroom situations (Marshall & Glock, 1978-1979).

The inappropriateness of generalizing from formal experimental situations to classroom lesson situations has been discussed by Blatt and Garfunkel (1973), Bronfenbrenner (1977), and Mishler (1979). The danger of such cross-contextual generalization has been noted by Venezky (1979):

> I want to return for a moment to the studies by Elkonin (1963), Zhurova (1963), Bruce (1964), and others to discuss the limits on what we can learn from a laboratory. Elkonin, Zhurova, Bruce, and various others proved conclusively that children before some magic age—6 in Bruce's study, 7 in Zhurova's, and so on—could not perform certain tasks that involve manipulating abstract sounds. The children in these studies couldn't segment words, or repeat the first sound of a word, or do other sound processing tasks before 6 or 7 years of age. Here was quite convincing evidence from reasonably well designed studies. However, most of these studies involved 15 or 20 training trials on some small set of stimuli and 15 to 20 transfer trials. And from that evidence, the authors generalized to whole theories about reading, or about sound segmentation, or about the development of certain abilities in children.
>
> The great shock comes when you take these tasks, or slight modifications of them, into a classroom with the same age children and start doing these things day after day. You soon discover that almost all kids from kindergarten up can be taught all these tasks without tears or frustration, given repeated practice and appropriate sequencing of tasks. There is a world of difference beween the ongoing, day-by-day activities of the classroom and the laboratory. (p. 280)

Research in the Contexts of Comprehension

In failing to consider how readers comprehend and learn to comprehend in classroom reading lessons, it may be the case that researchers have overlooked significant Causative Contexts not necessarily represented by variables in the Task, Text, and Reader Contexts. One such important context may be the interaction between the teacher and students and between students themselves (Au, 1980; Cazden, 1979; Cherry, 1978; Heap, 1978; McDermott, 1976, 1977; Mehan, 1978; Morine-Dershimer, Galluzzo, & Fagal, 1980; Simons & Gumperz, 1980; Wilkinson & Dollaghan, 1979). In pursuing this possibility, Mosenthal has attempted to demonstrate the influence the interaction between a reader and an audience has on children's comprehension. In one study, Mosenthal (1979a) attempted to examine how third and sixth graders, when confronted with contradictory story information, resolved the contradiction under two types of audience conditions. First, five types of strategies were identified which people typically employ to resolve text contradictions when old information in a story setting is incompatible with information in a story ending. It was found that third graders tended to shift their strategy preferences so as to minimize the amount of text restructuring when reading and recalling a story for a teacher vs. second graders. Sixth graders, on the other hand, tended to shift their strategy preferences so as to maximize the amount of text restructuring when reading and recalling a story of second grader versus a teacher.

In a second study, Mosenthal (Mosenthal & Na, 1980b) demonstrated that the manner in which fourth graders chose to devise their text recall was a function of the type of response register these students maintained with their teacher. In this study, three principal groups of children were identified by the type of verbal interaction pattern, or "register" (Halliday, 1978), these pupils most often maintained with their teacher. One group of pupils was identified as using an "Imitative Response Register." This was a verbal interaction pattern in which children added no new information to a teacher's preceding utterance. When these students read and recalled a series of stories for their teacher during a normal reading lesson, they tended to "reproduce" the stories; i.e., they recalled the stories literally, more so than did the other two identified register groups.

A second group of students was identifed by their use of a "Noncontingent Response Register." This was a verbal interaction pattern wherein pupils identified a new topic of conversation having little, if any, relation to the topic in the teacher's preceding discussion. In this sense, these children introduced new information without acknowledging old information. When these students read and recalled a series of stories for their teacher, during a normal reading lesson, they tended to "embellish" the stories they read; i.e., they introduced many elaborations and distortions (Steffensen, Joag-Dev, & Anderson, 1979), more so than did the other two register groups.

Finally, a third group of students was identified as using a "Contingent Response Register." This was a verbal interaction pattern wherein children added new information that clarified or added to the old information in the teacher's preceding utterance. When these students read and recalled a series of stories for their teacher during a normal reading lesson, they tended to "reconstruct" stories; i.e., they used many text-structured inferences, more so than the Imitative and Noncontingent Response Register groups.

These findings emphasize the importance the interaction between the Audience and Reader Contexts plays in how students comprehend during classroom reading lessons. The results of this experiment were more or less duplicated in another experiment (Cohen & Mosenthal, 1979) using a slightly different scheme for scoring pupil-teacher interactions.

In a fourth experiment, Mosenthal (Mosenthal & Na, 1980a) examined the relationship between type of pupil-teacher interaction, task type, and reading ability. In this study, the "informal task Context" represented children's reading and recalling text for the teacher as part of the normal reading lesson activity. This task was assumed to be low in risk (or consequence of failure), since no grade was assigned or no classification of students by performance outcome was proposed. In contrast, the "formal task Context" represented pupils' reading and recalling text for the teacher as part of the yearly standardized teaching procedure. This task was assumed to be high in risk, since the teachers told the students that grades were to be assigned and that students would be classified by ability based upon performance outcome.

In the low-risk condition, individual differences among students appeared as a function of the type of response register students most often maintained with their teacher, thereby replicating the findings in the Mosenthal & Na (1980b) and Cohen & Mosenthal (1979) studies. However, in the high-risk task condition, individual differences among students appeared as a function of reader ability rather than register pattern; average and low ability readers tended to reproduce the text more often than did the high ability readers; high ability readers tended to reproduce and embellish the text more often than did the average and low ability readers.

These findings suggest that how pupils integrate text information in reading comprehension depends, in part, upon how children perceive the risks and ambiguities of different tasks. In informal routine classroom reading lesson tasks, where risks and ambiguities are low, children have different expectations of what constitutes appropriate behavior in interacting with a teacher (Cherry, 1978; Mehan, 1979). These different interactions arise because teachers have different performance expectations for each student (Brophy & Good, 1970; Rosenthal & Jacobson, 1968). These different notions result in different uses of meaning (i.e., referential, text-structured inference, and pragmatic inference) in the classroom. These different notions of appropriateness correspond to the different response registers children adopt in interacting with their teacher. In using classroom meaning differently in informal classroom lesson tasks, children consequently integrate text differently in completing the task for a teacher.

In formal testing tasks, where risks tend to be high and ambiguities numerous (Doyle, 1979), children appear to adopt recall strategies reflecting their ability, rather than the registers they typically maintain with the teacher in informal tasks. In the study under consideration, poor and average ability readers appeared to minimize risk and ambiguity by reproducing the information (Spiro, 1977). In other words, they tended to recall more referential, or literal, but less inferential meaning (i.e., text-structured and pragmatic) than the high ability readers. High ability readers, on the other hand, tended to minimize risk and ambiguity by more fully processing the text, i.e., bringing more schema to bear on the text (Anderson, 1978; Spiro, 1979); in other words, by more thoroughly processing the text, better readers may be better able to fill in gaps of new knowledge by inferring from schema knowledge.

In addition to the studies cited above, Mosenthal has demonstrated the influence of response register type on how children adopt perspectives while comprehending and recalling stories (Mosenthal & Na, 1980c) and on how children compose expository and narrative text during routine classroom reading lessons (Mosenthal, Davidson-Mosenthal, & Krieger, in press; Mosenthal & Na, in press).

Implications for Comprehension Research

In sum, the findings of the previously cited studies have two important implications for comprehension research in classroom reading lessons. First, the demonstrated effect of the student-teacher interaction pattern during informal classroom reading lessons suggests that comprehension researchers need to look beyond the Text and Reader Context if they are to explain how children comprehend in classroom reading lessons; this is particularly true in instances where researchers attempt to explain comprehension in terms of integrating information from text (e.g., Walker & Meyer, 1980). In comprehension research in the classroom, one needs to determine how student-teacher interaction patterns develop during the course of reading lessons, how these patterns change over time, and how these changes concomitantly influence pupils' comprehension. The one-time interaction between an experimenter and subject in a formal experiment in a laboratory will shed little light on this question.

A second important implication of the previously mentioned studies—and particularly the study involving good and poor readers—is that they highlight the difference between routine classroom reading lesson tasks and formal testing tasks. The formal task of taking a standardized test in the classroom resembles the formal task of comprehending in a formal experiment; both are high in risk and ambiguity. Spiro (1977) has noted this when he suggests that in formal social situations, such as in an experiment, people will reproduce text in order to minimize distortion and to maximize correct literal recall of the text. In informal or routine social situations, such as in a daily classroom reading lesson, people will reconstruct text, integrating new knowledge with existing knowledge, in an attempt to "update" knowledge. In short, the tasks in formal experiments provide us but with the one view of the chameleon, comprehension; the chameleon changes color in the tasks of daily classroom reading lessons.

Reflexive and Recursive Interactions in the Contexts Pyramid

It has been argued that in order to define comprehension in classroom reading lessons, one must be able to determine how student-teacher interaction patterns develop and change during the course of reading lessons and how changes in interaction patterns produce concomitant changes in pupils' comprehension. While this statement appears to be justifiable in light of the response register findings cited, there is an assumption in this statement that needs to be questioned. It is an assumption peculiar not only to this statement but characteristic of all statements deductively derived from quantitative studies.

As was noted earlier, quantitative studies in comprehension research, fashioned in the spirit of Campbell and Stanley (1963), generally assume that there is a definable Causative Context and a definable Effect Context in the Contexts Pyramid. In addition, such studies are based on the assumption that this cause-and-effect relationship is reliable and will hold over time. This represents the *recursive*, or Contexts constancy, assumption of quantitative research. Once we have identified a recursive relationship between two or more variables in the Contexts Pyramid, we are given the power to predict contextual outcomes in relation to contextual inputs.

This assumption of quantitative researchers has been seriously challenged by many qualitative researchers. For example, proponents of phenomenology and symbolic interactionism (see Bogdan & Taylor, 1975; Eddy, 1980; Mehan & Wood, 1975, for detailed discussion) have emphasized that behavior is *reflexive* rather than *recursive*. What this means is that behavior is a function of all the interactions of the Contexts Pyramid and because these interactions are constantly changing, people are forever creating new meaning, thus continually changing their concept of reality. In this sense, meaning is reflexive, or constitutive (Mehan & Wood, 1975), rather than recursive. Hence, argue qualitative researchers, to explain behavior in terms of a cause-and-effect model is to overlook the dynamic, ever-changing interactions between Contexts in the Contexts Pyramid.

Qualitative researchers often cite a second major limitation of cause-and-effect models. These researchers emphasize that all social organizations, such as classroom reading lessons, consist of actors who develop definitions of a situation, or social schema, *through the process of interpretation*. These actors then act in terms of these definitions. While people may act within the framework of an organization (such as the one provided by an experimenter in a formal testing situation), it is the person's interpretation and not the organization which determines action. While contextually explicit situations, as defined by some model or theory, may set conditions and consequences for action, they do not determine what a person actually does.

Models and theories of some hypothetical cause-and-effect relation in the Contexts Pyramid represent researchers' attempts to impose a fixed interpretation of how people interpret meaning. For example, a researcher may have carefully selected a task, designed materials and identified readers in such a way as to suggest that readers remember text in a hierarchical manner. Of course, these manipulations will have some influence on how the subjects will comprehend. Yet readers will also act according to the meanings the experiment's organization holds for them, and not just according to what some researcher thinks these meanings should be, as specified by some model or theory. Hence, some readers may interpret the experiment as an organized exercise in minimizing errors; other readers may interpret the experiment as an organized exercise in maximizing correct answers (Mosenthal, 1979; Mosenthal & Na, 1980).

In order to understand the reflexive interactions of all the Contexts in the Contexts Pyramid and in order to understand the individual meanings people assign to these ever-changing reflexive interactions, qualitative researchers have adopted a different approach to understanding the Contexts Pyramid than have quantitative researchers. This approach is generally referred to as "ethnomethodology" (see Bogdan and Taylor, 1975; Mehan and Wood, 1975, for a detailed explanation of this approach). Using this approach, qualitative researchers have attempted to describe how people apply abstract rules and common sense understandings to situations (which are assumed always to be ambiguous and problematic) in order to make actions appear routine, explicable, and unambiguous. Thus, in this approach, meanings are viewed as practical accomplishments on the part of members of a society. Applying this approach to classroom reading groups, reading comprehension is viewed as a practical accomplishment on the part of a reader as a member of a reading group (McDermott, 1976).

As it stands now, there has been little attempt to synthesize cause-and-effect and ethnomethodological approaches to describing classroom reading comprehension. In terms of general developmental models of growth (Brown, 1978, 1979) and classroom competence, it would intuitively appear that both approaches are both right and wrong. On the other hand, one must be able to account for discernible cause and effect patterns in classroom reading comprehension (Mosenthal & Na, 1980a, b). No doubt, there are certain behaviors in classroom reading comprehension that lend themselves to Gardner and Riegel's football analogy (noted by Brown, 1979). In football, behavior is characterized by a sequence of sudden quick actions each leading to a new structural state where the action appears to be temporarily frozen.

Similarly, in the acquisition of classroom competence, there will be certain times when different Contexts exert more influence on children's classroom competence than other times. In terms of the Contexts Pyramid, one might argue that over time, different Contexts will emerge as Causative Contexts and as Effect Contexts. To represent these different structural states, one will need to use a cause-and-effect approach to describing classroom reading comprehension acquisition. However, to represent the sudden quick actions in which no Causative Context predominates, one will need to use an ethnomethodological approach to describing reading comprehension acquisition.

On the other hand, one must also be able to account for those classroom behaviors which never evolve into cause and effect relationships. In this regard, one might argue that certain behaviors in classroom reading comprehension best lend themselves to Riegel's soccer analogy (also noted by Brown, 1979). In soccer, unlike football, behavior is characterized by ceaseless action which depends on continuous interactions between the individual members and in the transaction between the members of the opposing team.

Similarly, in the acquisition of classroom comprehension competence, there will be instances where behaviors of reading comprehension represent the total interaction of all the Contexts; even over time these behaviors will never evolve into a relation where one Context is clearly a Causative Context and where one Context is clearly an Effect Context. To represent such instances, cause-and-effect approaches will be of little value; only an ethnomethodological approach will be of use here.

In sum, researchers who wish to understand reading comprehension in classroom reading lessons may be confronted with a version of Heisenberg's Uncertainty Principle (Mosenthal, 1978). Heisenberg noted that in order to adequately describe an electron in the context of an atom's orbital paths, one needs to account for both the speed of the electron and its position on the atom's orbit. Unfortunately because electrons travel at such a high speed, one is never able to assess an electron's characteristics by position when it is traveling at full speed. If one slows an electron down to assess its characteristics by position, one is unable to assess its characteristics by speed.

Heisenberg argued that the only way one could resolve such a dilemma was to use a series of observations, one in which the electron was assessed in terms of speed, one in which the electron was assessed in terms of position. Only by combining facts from these observations would one be able to adequately arrive at a definition of an electron.

In investigating reading comprehension in classroom reading lessons, researchers are faced with the problem that the acquisition of reading comprehension is both a recursive and reflexive phenomenon which changes over time. It will only be by combining cause-and-effect approaches to account for the recursive aspects of reading comprehension acquisition and ethnomethodological approaches to account for the reflexive aspects of reading comprehension acquisition will researchers arrive at an adequate definition of reading comprehension in the classroom.

Classrooms, Constraints, and the Language Process

Jerome C. Harste
Robert F. Carey
Indiana University

Because of our involvement in teaching and supervision within reading practicum experiences, we have constant entry to a number of public school classrooms. One exciting dimension of this experience is exploration of the teacher's role in assisting written language growth and development. What has become both readily apparent and surprisingly persistent concerning the relationship between written language instruction and the language process is that: 1) the constraints which operate in one language setting may be different or not present in another setting, and 2) what constraints are established strongly affect both the process and product of language learning. Considered together, these tenets support the premise that written language growth and development is, first and foremost, a sociopsycholinguistic process.

To add credence to this position, observations made of pupil and teacher behaviors are presented. This paper includes a conceptual model for the continued exploration of this premise, and is intended to refocus inquiry in the area of written growth and development, and to point out needed directions for the development of a theory of written language instruction.

Understanding the Premise

Before defining by example what is meant by the thesis that written language growth and development is a sociopsycholinguistic process, some more general discussion seems warranted. What this statement implies, quite simply, is that in order to understand the cognitive and linguistic processes involved in reading and writing, one must consider the linguistic and situational context in which that processing occurred. From an instructional perspective, this thesis reiterates the importance of the teacher, saying, in effect, "What we do does make a difference." From an empirical perspective, this thesis cautions the researcher by suggesting that many of the behaviors which are observed and mapped as stages of cognitive growth and development are but artifacts of instructional history, or the research setting, or both; in short, artifacts of sociocognitive constraints operative in the setting itself.

With this discussion in mind, we will restate our findings: the cognitive processing behaviors displayed by pupils in alternate instructional and research settings are a function of the contextual constraints which operated in those settings.

Conceptualizing the Premise

Figure 1 illustrates what this thesis means conceptually. This model presents a transactional view of the process involving both a language setting and a mental setting. Each, in a sense, provides an environment for the other (Carey & Harste, 1979; Harste & Carey, 1979; Rosenblatt, 1938, 1978). "Language Setting" as a concept is meant to suggest that any instance of oral or written language contains multimodal cues (both linguistic and situational) available for processing (Neisser, 1976). Where print is found (newspaper, library book, textbook, basal reader), under what conditions it is encountered (as a reading lesson, a test, an English lesson on style), and the relationship between parties involved (a student reading an assignment for his teacher, a little brother reading to a little sister), modify not only what schema are accessed, but direct strategy utilization and hence sampling of the print setting itself. In writing, similar elements of register operate to establish what strategies will or will not be utilized. Given this perspective, strategy utilization in reading and writing may well differ under different contextual constraints—i.e., one teacher as opposed to another, a formal language period as opposed to an informal one, a school as opposed to a nonschool situation, and so forth.[1]

We term the corpus of available linguistic and situational constraints in a language setting (Figure 1, Circle A) "contextual constraints." In reading instruction, for example, what the teacher believes about language (whether language is perceived as a sequential

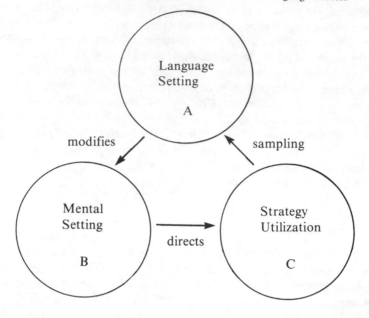

Figure 1. A Sociopsycholinguistic View of the Language Process

set of skills to be mastered or as a transaction in meaning) and about learning (whether learners are viewed as having linguistic information on which a program can be built) strongly affects what instructional strategies are employed and what language information is featured (Harste & Burke, 1977). Thus, teacher beliefs operate as situational constraints becoming operationalized through instructional decisions. Such instructional constraints are readily perceptible in classrooms as teacher prompts (Harste, in press), classroom behavior (DeFord, 1979), and other tangible results of instructional decisions (Barr, 1973-1974; Rhodes, 1978). Linguistic constraints are apparent in those instructional settings which fail to provide whole instances of language. For example, words listed on the blackboard for introduction deprive the student of the syntactic and semantic information which would have been available had a complete text been used.[2] Because any instance of print provides *both* linguistic and situational cues which are not only interactive but available for processing and modifying schema access (Figure 1, Circle B), we might best think of print perception as robust (Harste, 1978).

Harste and Carey

In process, "contextual constraints" (Figure 1, Circle A) become "cognitive constraints" (Figure 1, Circle B) by modifying anticipatory schema, or by being (because of past encounters) part and parcel of the anticipatory schema which was accessed on the way to the process. We refer to the complex set of relationships between contraints in the language setting, and their past and present effect on the mental setting as the 'sociocognitive constraints' operative in the setting.

Figure 1, then, presents reading and writing as dynamic, multifaceted events as opposed to monolithic skills which, once learned, can be universally applied.[3] It is important to understand that the process depicted in Figure 1 is cyclic and highly interactive, with each encounter providing opportunity to alter constraints and hence affect not only what anticipatory schema are accessed, but what strategies are utilized by students.

Before leaving this model, it should be noted that our field research has shown that teachers, through the instructional decisions they make, establish instructional constraints which are readily observable in the reading and writing behaviors of their students.

Exploring the Premise

To examine the practical differences which a sociopsycholinguistic view of the language process offers, the remainder of this paper will discuss some instances of pupil behavior in reading and writing where instructional constraints were known or signaled. For clarity, a psycholinguistic and sociopsycholinguistic analysis of each instance will be given. Though the phenomenon illustrated in these examples is apparently not very well understood or not recognized by teachers, researchers and theoreticians, we believe that it is universally true.[4]

Some Examples

Instance 1 ● (Reading) Andrew, a first grader, when asked to read a selection entitled "The House" (Scott Foresman Basics in Reading, 1978), produced the text illustrated in Figure 2.

A psycholinguistic analysis of Andrew's response indicates that it is in part graphophonemically based. "Black" for *duck* suggests that Andrew saw the letter "d," extracted key distinctive features, but misidentified it as a "b." Similarly in the same word, the grapheme cluster "ck" elicits the phoneme cluster /ck/. Even further, Andrew's substitutions of "purple" for *puppy*, "that" for *the*, and "yellow" for *yard* reflect a utilization of initial letter-sound relationships.

Figure 2. Reading Sample (Andrew, age 7)

```
                        ( The House )

   blacK                  purple          that yellow
A duck, a pig, (and) a puppy (are) in the yard.
```

```
┌─────────────────────────────────┐
│  Key:                           │
│  blacK                          │
│  duck  = substitution           │
│                                 │
│  (and) = omission               │
└─────────────────────────────────┘
```

Because Andrew's production of both *black* and *purple* follow this recognition of the noun marker "a," and because the phrase "in that yellow" is a legitimate English grammatical structure (as far as it goes), we can also say of Andrew's reading strategies that they reflect a partial, though not particularly effective, utilization of the syntactic cue systems in reading.

While it is less clear whether the semantic system of language is being utilized, some involvement is apparent when one views partial structures produced ("a black," "a pig," "a purple," "in that yellow") from semantics-of-syntax perspective (de Beaugrande, 1979).

Utilization of contextual cues available in the print setting is less apparent, though data relative to Andrew's use of these cues is equally available in the sample, once the research and instructional context preceding the collection of this reading sample is explained.

To correctly interpret Andrew's omission of *and*, for example, it seems important to understand that this data was collected in an uninterrupted oral reading setting. Specifically Andrew was told:

> "I'd like you to read for me today. I'm not going to help you. If you come to something you don't know, I'd like you to try to get it, but if you can't, guess at it, or skip it, but just go on. Okay? Here's the story. I'd like you to read it orally. Just pretend I'm not here."

These directions operate as one set of contextual constraints governing Andrew's processing of the text. His omission of the "and" and his willingness to go on is not only reflective of his understanding of these constraints, but illustrative of how these constraints affect perception and strategy utilization.

Harste and Carey

In this regard, it is important to understand that this "skipping-it-and-going-on" may not be a strategy which Andrew would normally employ (although it could be). All we know is that these constraints were present in the language setting, and behaviors which reflect operations within these constraints cannot be assumed to reflect the pupil's general mental setting or schema of what would normally be done when reading. In this instance, the constraints which operate in the setting interfere with our getting a "true" picture of what Andrew's real reading strategies are.

Similarly, because the language setting in this instance is rich, i.e., a whole text having not only graphophonemic, but syntactic and semantic cues available as well, it follows that the constraints set up in the directions given to Andrew allow him a strategy which could make him look better as a reader than he normally might look. In other words, the constraints set up allow Andrew to skip and go on, thus affording him opportunity to pick up alternate available cues from the text. Such cues might operate proactively (setting up better prediction) and retroactively (via conformation and correction), and may not in fact represent what Andrew would normally do in an alternate reading setting. While there is no direct evidence that this is the case, it is important to understand that in an uninterrupted oral reading setting such as the one set up for Andrew, the constraints which operate in the setting itself allow the reader to use better strategies than he may normally use.[5]

Instructional constraints too were operative. Andrew's teacher, like many first grade teachers, begins formal reading instruction by building what she called a "basic" sight vocabulary. Later, specific lexical items sharing similar graphophonemic relationships are pulled from this vocabulary for study and analysis. Materials to be read contained only those words which previously had been introduced as sight words, under the assumption that such a procedure increases the likelihood of success. Operating from this theoretical orientation, Andrew's teacher had just prior to the collection of this reading sample conducted a unit on color words.

Given this information, it is interesting to reanalyze Andrew's reading behavior. In light of the instructional constraints operating within the print setting, salient features of Andrew's reading behavior (e.g., his calling of color word names) becomes clearer. The constraints set up by instructional procedures, namely a belief that words encountered in print will have been previously introduced as sight words, operate as parameters on cognitive processing. Instead of monitoring story meaning, Andrew is monitoring reading instruction.

From a sociopsycholinguistic perspective, Andrew's reading behavior reflects utilization of both linguistic and situational cues. The latter is apparently a general parameter governing linguistic cue system processing. It is interesting to note that any analysis less than the total sociopsycholinguistic analysis which we have done is only a partial analysis and, in fact, could lead one to misconstrue the relationship between key variables operative in this instance of language processing.[6] For example, one might conclude that Andrew had not effectively used the syntactic and semantic systems of language in conjunction with his utilization of the graphophonemic system. While not necessarily incorrect, this conclusion misconstrues the fact that Andrew's predominate concerns were pragmatic in nature, and as such these concerns both overshadowed and directed Andrew's processing of the available linguistic information in this setting.

Instance 2 • (Reading) Matt, another first grader, when asked to read the same selection that Andrew read, produced the text illustrated in Figure 3.

Figure 3.   Reading Sample (Matt, age 7)

T-H-E H-O-U-S-E
The House

T D-Y-C *
A duck, a pig, and a puppy are in the yard.

Key:

T-H-E
the = substitution; instead of
      reading "the," the child
      responded by spelling out
      the word.

y   = corrected; the child first
      said "y" and then corrected
      to "u."

✳   = reading terminated at this
      point.

Harste and Carey

From a psycholinguistic perspective, this response provides few insights into what Matt knows about how the systems of language operate in reading. About all that one might say is that Matt has some letter name knowledge.

Some might even conclude that Matt is not ready for formal reading instruction. This is especially so if access to the process is seen as hinging on the breaking of an abstract linguistic code (Mattingly, 1972, 1979).

Matt's response to print is curious, especially in light of the fact that a growing body of research supports the notion that children as much as three years younger than Matt approach print with the expectation that it be personally meaningful (Baghban, 1979; Bissex, 1979; Clay, 1975; Goodman, 1976; Harste, Burke, & Woodward, 1979; Hill, 1978; Ylisto, 1967).

From a sociopsycholinguistic perspective, however, Matt's behavior seems less curious. Matt's teacher, unlike Andrew's teacher, began reading instruction in her classroom emphasizing letter name knowledge. Each letter of the alphabet was systematically introduced and studied. Each letter had its day. On "T day," children talked about the letter T, identified what sound it made, conducted auditory and visual discrimination exercises, and cut out pictures of "T words" from catalogs to enter into their growing "Personalized Alphabet Books."

Given this instructional history and the fact that this reading sample was collected from Matt while he was in a classroom situation, it does not surprise us that Matt's perception of the reading process is one of letter name calling. This perception of the process (the net result of a complex set of sociocognitive constraints) not only affects what strategies he uses, but also his sampling of the print setting.

In the cases of both Matt and Andrew, a "situational ceiling effect" is exhibited, i.e., the level of cognitive processing exhibited paralleled that specified and stressed in the instructional setting. The relationship between contextual constraints and cognitive processing operations exhibited by these students' responses is striking. While these examples have been selected because they illustrate this relationship, it is our contention that a similar sociocognitive relationship exists in any instance of language processing. In these examples, this relationship is only more marked in that the constraints identified here are negative. Instruction in these instances is the greater mediator, delineating cognitive potential, rather than releasing it.

Instance 3. • Jeff, age 6½, was in first grade when the writing sample illustrated in Figure 4 was collected.

Figure 4. Writing Sample (Jeff, age 6 1/2)

This sample was collected under an uninterrupted writing condition:

> "Here's a piece of paper for you, and here's one for each of us. Let's write stories. We'll write a story on our pieces of paper, and you write a story on your piece of paper. Then, when we get done, we'll share our stories with one another."

Jeff looked at his piece of paper for a long time, and then began by drawing the picture which you see illustrated. After completing his drawing, Jeff announced that he was done with his story. We shared our stories with him, and then asked him to share his story with us. His story involved himself and his sister and the things they liked to do at home.

We said, "But, Jeff, we wanted you to write your story."

He responded, "But I don't know how to write. I can't even read yet."

We returned, "Oh, I'll bet you do; why don't you go and write the names of what some of the things are that are in your picture?"

"But I can't spell."

"Just spell them the way you think they are written."

Jeff gave us a look of incredulity, but returned to his seat and wrote the words you see written. In writing *tree*, Jeff spelled it J—R—E, transforming the /d/ sound into a /j/, a writing miscue readily

Harste and Carey

explainable in terms of Charles Read's observation that sounds produced at the same point of articulation are often interchanged in transcription (Read, 1971). As Jeff wrote J-R-E, one could observe his simultaneous oral pronunciation of /tree/.

When he finished, he said, adding the letter Y, "I'll bet there's a silent Y on the end of that word."

In writing *house*, Jeff spelled it H-O-S, again following functional spelling rules previously identified by Read (1971).

When he completed his handiwork (H-O-S), he looked up and said, "I'll bet there's a silent E on the end of that word," adding the E which you see.

Jeff did the same for T.I.E.-Fighter (t-i-f-o-f-o-r-e), sun (s-u-e) and x-wing rocket fighter (s-w-i-g-r-o-g-i-t-f-o-r-c), always stopping and speculating about the existence of a possible silent E and then, in each case, adding it to his functional spelling of that word.

In spelling *cloud*, Jeff wrote K-L-D, then stopped and said, "I bet there's a silent L on the end of that word."

Now we ask: Can there be any doubt what Jeff's instruction had been?

Jeff had been working on silent letters at the ends of words in school. This observation, apparent in Jeff's writing, was readily confirmed by observation of a reading lesson in which the teacher, fellow students and Jeff continued to work on silent Es, studying their effect on vowel sounds.

What is unfortunate, of course, is that rather than assist Jeff in understanding how print operates, the instructional setting, in this instance, has had an opposite effect, convincing Jeff that print is unpredictable, full of silent Ys and Es and Ls. As such, Jeff's response provides clear evidence for support of the thesis that in order to understand the cognitive operations involved in writing, one must do so in light of the context in which that processing takes place.

If one were to analyze Jeff's writing devoid of such contextual constraint information, one might correctly deduce that Jeff was engaged in language hypothesis testing, but erroneously map this level of hypothesis testing in the course of natural development. Rather than reflective of "true" cognitive development, Jeff's behaviors, like Matt's, are best seen as instructional artifacts.

Jeff shows no evidence of testing other hypotheses relative to how the syntactic or semantic systems of language operate. One cannot assume, however, that he does not possess such written language information. All one can say is that given the set of sociocognitive constraints under which Jeff is currently operating, other types of written language information which Jeff may possess are not being accessed.

One has some evidence that Jeff does, in fact, possess better written language information than this performance indicates. Jeff elects to draw instead of to write. Later, he clearly demonstrates that this decision was based on a conscious awareness of what processes each of these labels stood for (e.g., his oral story was indeed a story, and his drawing was a response to his perception that he doesn't know how to write). While at first blush some might interpret Jeff's problem as being one of "metalinguistic awareness" (Downing, 1970, 1979), or "linguistic awareness" (Mattingly, 1972, 1979),[7] in point of fact such conclusions are neither supported by Jeff's functional spelling behaviors, nor his ability to comprehend and transfer the set of contextual constraints which instruction has convinced him are applicable in this language setting.

Equally important is the fact that, even by changing the constraints, we were able to get him to display only a portion of what he knew or what we suspect he knows. In this regard, there appears to be a "residual instructional effect" which could only be explored if one were to work with Jeff over a longer period of time. It may be that such past instructional effects can never be completely overcome.[8]

This, of course, is a rather pessimistic note, mentioned only in passing to illustrate the importance of more indepth study of the socioconstraints which operate in language settings and their immediate and long term effects on cognitive processing operations.

Instance 4. • (Writing) In response to our request to write a story (same conditions as described in Instance 3), David (age 7) hesitated, watched us writing our stories a moment, and then elected to write the set of words seen in the upper left-hand corner of his paper: *beat, seat, heat, beach, ball, tall, hall, pall, call, mall, saw.*

Once David tired of his list-making, he chose, like Jeff, to draw a picture rather than to write a story. Upon completion, he brought his picture to us and we shared stories. His was a marvelous story about spaceships and rockets and man-eating plants.

When he finished, we said, "We really wanted you to write a story."

David responded, "But I don't know how to write my story."

"What do you mean? You already showed us you could write by writing these words up on the corner."

Figure 5. Writing Sample (David, age 7)

"Well, yeah, but...I don't know how to spell the words for my story."

"Well, that's okay. We're not interested in your spelling. We're interested in your story."

"But I can't spell the words like you!"

"We don't care about that. Just do the best you can. You're only in the second grade. Your spelling ought to look like a second grader's, not like ours. If your spelling looked like ours, what would you have to learn? Just do the best you can."[9]

At this point, David proceeded to write the words you see in his picture. As you can see, David was extremely good at spelling with the only deviation being "tinefighers" for T.I.E. Fighters (a spelling which we had to check out ourselves).

When David finished, he asked, "Did I spell anything right?"

We responded, "You did beautifully. Now will you please turn your paper over and write your story for us?"

David's story is illustrated in Figure 6.

Figure 6.   Writing Sample (David, age 7)

> Once there was two SpaceShips Fighting together and one of them got killed.
> and then a Rocket blasted ots in The sky.
> and then a tine Fighter came in.
> and then I came out To see what was The matter,
> and then I saw a maneating plant behind me.
> Then anther plant was there and the
> The maneating plant came out

David was overly concerned with spelling (though one must ask why, as his story is almost letter perfect). His oral version was a cohesive, well-formed story (Halliday and Hasan, 1976; Stein, 1978). His written version seems by comparison to be a set of relatively discrete statements, more descriptive than story-like. We can only speculate how David's overconcern for spelling might have hindered him from placeholding the message he wished to convey.

When one examines this entire sequence, a number of interesting and important aspects surface. First, David's initial response to the task is to limit what he writes to those items of language which have been introduced instructionally, rather than to write a story. These items reflect, in David's estimation, what he knows about written language.

Tiring of this list-making task, David moves to pictures and drawing. Rather than engage in further written language hypothesis testing, David plays it safe by moving to an alternate communication system to placehold his message. The issue of spelling seems to be key in this decision, as well as in David's perception of himself as unable to write.[10]

In this regard, it is particularly interesting to note that the instructional method used with David stressed recognition of spelling pattern consistencies. Rather than facilitate David's confidence, this instructional focus has seemingly made David unsure of his own ability to figure out how words are spelled. David reluctantly engages in the process and does so only after we assure and reassure him that the constraints operating in this situation are different from his normal instructional setting.

Step by step, as constraints alter, David demonstrates that he not only knows how to spell, but that he knows much more than this about how language operates. Upon completion of the last line, when rereading the story to us orally, David said, "There's something wrong with that last part, but I can't find it." David read and reread his last line, making editorial changes, but never was able to get it just the way he wanted.

David's behavior here, too, is significant, as it shows that David is continuing to alter his initial perceptions of the process; whereas before he was meticulously involved in spelling, now his focus appears to have shifted to a concern for semantics.

David's overall performance vividly illustrates not only negative, but positive effects of the sociocognitive constraints. When constraints challenge students to assume responsibility and rise to new expectancies in an open-ended and risk-free environment, positive effects are charted as they demonstrate those kinds of cognitive processing and hypothesis testing which more clearly reflect their abilities and development. At the end of this session, David begins to test alternative ways of saying what he means. At this point in the process, David's writing behavior more closely parallels that of the proficient writer (Emig, 1976): a conclusion which almost certainly never would have been reached had initial constraints operating in this language setting not been altered.

Conclusions

This paper has attempted to capture some of the field data and thinking which led us to our present interest in and exploration of sociocognitive constraints which operate in language settings.

It is our belief that the issues raised in this paper merit widespread exploration and have much utility for the profession. An experience we had while involved in teacher preparation illustrates this point most vividly.

We asked preservice teachers in our college methods class to collect uninterrupted writing samples from elementary-aged children during a field practicum experience. One classroom teacher recommended we use Leslie, a fourth-grade girl, saying, "I find her interesting, but frustrating. She knows how to spell, but she'll spell a word correctly in the beginning of her paper and then turn around and misspell the same word later on."[11]

Our practicum student decided to follow the lead provided by the teacher, assuming Leslie might indeed be a real find by providing interesting data to discuss in class. Leslie's story is illustrated in Figure 7.

In part because the teacher had called attention to Leslie's spelling, her handling of *turn* (initially spelled both with an "e" and a "u" in line 4, spelled correctly in line 5, and then spelled T-E-R-N throughout the rest of the paper—see lines 12, 16, 17 and 19), and *light* (initially spelled correctly in lines 4, 7, 9, and 12, but misspelled in line 17), became particularly noticeable.

After complimenting the student on her fine story, our practicum student, also somewhat bothered by Leslie's behavior now that it had been pointed out, asked, "Leslie, do you ever reread what you have written to find the mistakes you've made?"

Leslie paused a moment in a state of incredulity and responded, "Oh, no. My teacher does that!"

This response is almost a benediction, providing clear evidence of the instructional constraints which were perceived by Leslie, and which guided her written performance in this setting.

The constraints present in this instance of language instruction worked against the attainment of the teacher's instructional goal, that of making her students independent writers. The unwritten message of past instructional behavior, i.e., the teacher's careful correction of the children's writing, became a powerful force altering instructional intent. Rather than insuring corrective feedback, it short-circuited the process of growth toward proficiency. Thus, a procedure intended to facilitate written language development actually hinders it.

Harste and Carey

Figure 7. Writing Sample (Leslie, age 10)

The Mistry of the
Lightbulb.

One day a man got out of
bed he turned on the light
it said turn me Off the
man said no!no!no,NO!
the light said yes, and
reached out and pulled the svich
the light shouted the man
and he ran and slammed the
door! help! help! "someone help"

"The light ternd it self off"
and he ran so far he ram
into the peshen and got
bite by a shark. And that
night a rober came and terned
on the light terned it off
and ran out the door to its
house. The robber ternd on the
light and it said "dont do tha"
the rober jumped out the went
dow and his mom came and
Took the light and it said
"leave me alone" the robers mom
said "help me" and jumped out
the wendow and the light jumped
out to. And no one now about
it ever agen.

Based on this experience and others like it, we believe that
analyzing the language process from a sociopsycholinguistic perspective
provides a more cogent and accurate insight than looking at the
language process abstractly, devoid of situational context. Obviously a
good deal of work still needs to be done in identifying, specifying, and
mapping those sociocognitive constraints most useful in furthering our
understanding of the language process. Our research raises issues which
have important implications for teachers, researchers, and theoreticians.

Language and language learning is inherently social. Written language is a necessary but not sufficient condition for understanding language processing or for designing language instruction.

Notes

1. Current insights into language as a sociopyscholinguistic process have largely been confined to oral language situations where the phenomena are best known as "register switching" and "language variation." Hymes' work (1967, 1978) is particularly noteworthy, as is Halliday's adaption of this work (1975) captured in the notions of *field, mode,* and *tenor.* Cicourel's studies (1974) of oral language from the perspective of cognitive sociology do much to describe how such constraints operate and evolve in oral language settings. Vygotsky's work (1978) on cultural constraints operative in language settings is equally suggestive. Coraso's work (1977) in young children's acculturation in classrooms and Cook-Gumperz's (1977) study of children's use of persuasive argument have moved these concepts well along toward educational application. Sinclair and Coulthard (1975), McDermott (1977), Greene and Wallat (1978) and Cazden (1972, 1978) have applied such insights to the analysis of oral classroom discourse. Grice's Cooperative Principle (1975), Searle's work in speech act theory (1969, 1975, 1979) and Pratt's application of these works to literary analysis (1977), provide still other bases for extending our understanding of the constraints which operate in oral and written language settings and for studying their effect on cognitive processing.

2. In fact, the issue is more subtle than this. Rhodes (1978) found, for example, that texts used for beginning reading instruction varied in the availability of syntactic and semantic cues, depending upon the theoretical orientation from which they were constructed, and that such variations strongly affected print perception and processing.

3. Our position here is very much like Smith's (1978):

> In its specific detail, the act of reading itself depends on the situation in which it is accomplished and the intention of the reader. (p. 176)

H. Alan Robinson (1978), too, has long expressed an interest in the reading demands of alternate print setting, though this concern leads him 1) to suggest multiple reading processes, and 2) to approach instruction in each from a skills perspective.

While the model we present does not argue for more than one reading process (here, we argue with the position taken by Goodman, 1967), it would suggest that positions which see the acquisition of language skills as a separate issue from written language proficiency or proficient written language use (and hence support a model of instruction which differs from a model of proficient reading or writing) are conceptually faulty (see for example the recent position taken by Pearson, 1979). This position, of course, is widespread and is most readily evidenced in the stance taken by some reading educators that in the elementary grades one is "learning to read," after which time one uses "reading to learn."

4. See, for example, current models of the reading process. Some completely ignore the social dimension of language (Gough, 1976; LaBerge and Samuels, 1976), while others make only a passing and token reference (Rumelhart, 1976; Adams & Collins, 1977). Goodman (1976), Bransford and McCarrell (1974), de Beaugrande (in press), and Kintsch and van Dijk (1978) have models which give more adequate coverage, but like most extant models of reading are too restricted in terms of what components of the process they are willing to explain to act as instructional models. This is not to demean such models (for any theoretician has not only the right but the responsibility to delimit what aspects will be explained), but to suggest that language instruction encompasses other variables which must be understood if a model of reading is to act as an instructional model.

Harste and Carey

Researchers, too, seem to underplay or ignore the social nature of language and language learning. Mishler's criticism of the "context-stripping techniques used in language research" (1978) addresses this issue directly. Even very recent research in reading comprehension has confounded this variable in the research design. See, for example, Anderson, Reynolds, Shallert, and Goetz's highly significant study entitled "Frameworks for Understanding Discourse" (1977). While we do not wish to suggest that this research has not provided important insights into the process (our own thinking, as is evident in this paper, has been highly influenced by this work), we do wish to suggest that the portrait painted of the language user duped by his schema is inaccurate and fails to capture the dynamic give-and-take of language processing. What relative influence contextual constraints play in relationship to cognitive constraints is of course an empirical question and is currently a topic of investigation (Carey, Harste, & Smith, in progress).

5. This is true, of course, of all miscue research (Allen & Watson, 1976), though it is a point seemingly not very fully discussed and may, in fact, be why many teachers and researchers see much of the data collected under these conditions as being atypical in comparison to that data which they have available from similar readers.

6. This data supports the power of current miscue analysis data collection procedures (Goodman, 1967; Goodman & Burke, 1971, 1976) in that data collected under these conditions provide information from which not only a psycholinguistic, but a sociopsycholinguistic analysis can be made. Reading miscues, like writing miscues are, in this sense, "windows" to the sociocognitive constraints which operate in the language process.

7. Mattingly, himself, may in fact object with this example in that the "linguistic awareness" which he sees as key to control is morphophonemic awareness. Many others (DeStefano, 1979; Johns, 1979; Williams, 1979), however, who seem to find this notion of "linguistic awareness" cogent, have moved, or suggested moving, far beyond the bounds initially discussed by Mattingly.

8. Our thanks to Carolyn Burke who initially made this observation when examining some adult reading data which we had collected.

9. Our thanks to Vera Milz, a classroom teacher from Bloomfield Hills, Michigan, who suggested this response as a way of encouraging functional spelling with those children who are reluctant to engage in the process because they have already learned that it is safer not to engage in this kind of risk taking. Carolyn Burke (Indiana University) has found the response, "Well, then, you can just pretend to write," also to be effective in getting children to move into functional spelling.

10. There is nothing inherently wrong with David's move to an alternate communication system. Writers (even very young ones) often make such moves to increase their "communication potential" (Harste, 1979; Harste, Burke, & Woodward, 1978), as is evident by the number of models and illustrations which accompany most texts, including this one. The issue here is not David's move to an alternate communication system but what motivates this move. (Readers interested in further exploring the notion of "communication potential" should also see Halliday's notion of "meaning potential" (1974)—a term which he uses to refer to a language user's power to mean using what he knows about how oral and written language works.)

11. It is equally significant that this teacher's perception of what constitutes good writing (i.e., good spelling) did not permit her to even tender the hypothesis that as this student really got into writing (communicating what she wanted to say), placeholding the message took precedence over control of the form. If we were obliged to write our manuscripts under the constraints established in most classrooms, most of us would find the process so ridiculously difficult that we, like many students, would opt out whenever we could.

Teaching and Testing Reading Comprehension: An Historical Perspective on Instructional Research and Practices

Nancy L. Roser
University of Texas

In order to tell a story of the history of reading comprehension as it has been defined, taught, and tested, I sampled a literature so rich in information and so diverse that I gained renewed appreciation for educational researchers in our field who have attempted to compile it . As I approached the tasks of search, analysis, and synthesis, I had a keen sense that, despite the fact that reading educators and researchers have held changing, conflicting, and even competing views of reading comprehension (with the most current being a scholarly sense of uncertainty), many of the ideas that fall so fresh upon untried ears have quite ancient origins.

Ironically, reading comprehension has not changed. Whatever children and adults did as they read in ancient Egypt, Greece, or Rome, and whatever they do today in order to derive or apply meaning to print is the same process.

What has changed then? Current theories have been built with an influx of knowledge from the fields of linguistics and psychology. Theorists have begun to separate the *process* of comprehension from the *products* of comprehension (Simons, 1971). The process refers to the cognitive operations that the reader engages in as he reads, generally thought to be unobservable; the products of comprehension are the observable behaviors that take place because a reader reads. For the most part, researchers and educators alike had been concerned with comprehension products: answers to questions, answers to tests, copious skills lists, overlapping taxonomies—reflecting an unsatisfactory, sometimes confused description of the process. Dealing with observable behaviors is a defensible act when there is some assurance that the process can be inferred by viewing the product. But most experts believe we have not yet completely described the process of reading comprehension. Most of us are continuing to learn about reading comprehension—and rightly so. Far less tangible, less neatly packaged, less easily measurable than word recognition (which had assumed a majority of the reading literature), reading comprehension was overdue for scrutiny. The most recent literature focuses on the two ingredients that are essential for this study of the process of reading comprehension: The reader and the text. Robinson wrote, "If the significant characteristics of each could be identified [reader and text], then the interaction of the reader and the material could be interpreted" (1975, p. 11). And it is this interaction—these "inside-the-head/outside-the-head" factors (Pearson, 1978; Smith, 1971)—that are so intriguing to us now as we attempt to construct testable theories of reading comprehension.

This article opens with its conclusion, or rather its "to be continued," and with a reminder that reading comprehension has not changed. What have changed are: 1) *awareness* of issues, of confusion, of complexity, and this awareness has been heightened by the approaches which we have used to study, describe, and measure the process; and 2) *instructional procedures* as reflected in historical accounts and in published series. But the latter changes (the instructional ones) are surprisingly few—and are mainly perceptible by analyzing centuries rather than decades. Comprehension assessment has begun to reflect some changes, but some of those changes are actually "returns" to earlier practices. Thus, two avenues of historical consideration are traced from 1915 to the present: the teaching of reading comprehension and, concurrently, the measurement of comprehension.

The Teaching of Reading Comprehension: Has it Changed?

Mitford Mathews in his *Teaching to Read: Historically Considered* would have us conclude that learning to read as the Greeks and Romans did was not particularly troublesome. The teaching of reading for early Greeks and Romans was something anyone could do.

> Those who taught children to read and write were regarded with great disdain and contempt. Whenever possible, slaves were assigned to this monotonous, unimaginative task. In old Athens there was a saying of one who was missing that he was either dead or had become a school master and was accordingly ashamed to appear in polite society. It was thought that kings and others of high rank who had lived evil lives would, in the next world, be forced to maintain themselves by teaching reading and writing. (Mathews, 1966, p. 9)

The Greeks had achieved (or nearly achieved) what some scholars called "alphabetic writing"—in which every letter represents one, and only one, speech sound. More than two and one-half thousand years ago, a native user of the language, well-versed in its sounds, could, according to Mathews, learn to read expediently—and one assumes that this means the students could comprehend the written word. Interestingly, the term *comprehension* doesn't enter Mathews' historical review, appear in his index, or affect his fascinating interpretations of teaching and learning to read through the centuries. (Later his explanations of the 18th century word and sentence methods describe a system for bringing reading to children in wholistic fashion, thus one "assumes," with a meaning-emphasis.)

The Greeks had borrowed letter forms from their neighbors, the Phoenicians, and experimented until they achieved a complete set of symbols or letters with which they could represent every sound in their language, then ordered the symbols in a fixed fashion. As soon as there was a body of written discourse, there was reading instruction. Boys learned to read by first thoroughly mastering the names and forms of letters and then by learning the syllables which combined consonants and vowels in two- and three-letter combinations. Learning to read by this predictable syllabic method continued for more than 2,000 years. In 20 B.C. Dionysius of Halicarnassus wrote:

> When we are taught to read, first we learn the names of the letter, then their forms and their values, then in due course syllables and their modifications, and finally words and their properties, viz. lengthenings and shortenings, accents, and the like. After acquiring the knowledge of these things, we begin to write and read, syllable by syllable and slowly at first. And when the lapse of a considerable time has implanted the forms of words firmly in our minds, then we deal with them without the least difficulty, and whenever any book is placed in our hands we go through it without stumbling and with incredible facility and speed. (Mathews, 1966, p. 7, citing W. Rhys Roberts in *Dinosysius of Halicarnasses*, London, 1910, p. 269.)

Even though borrowers of the Greek alphabet (the Romans and Etruscans) did not take the names of the letters the Greeks had given them, Roman boys learned just as the Greeks did. Roman teacher Quintilian in the first century wrote that in learning to read a child must not be rushed:

> It is incredible how much retardation is caused by reading haste; for hence arise hesitation, interruption, and repetition, as children attempt more than they can manage; and then, after making mistakes, they become distrustful even of what they know. (Mathews, 1966, p. 12, citing John Selby Watson [ed.] *Quintilian's Institutes of Oratory*, London, 1875-76, I, 16.)

Here we gain one of the first pictures of a less-than-perfect system for learning to read—and notably, the first attempt to categorize miscues.[1] One can only speculate as to how the above mentioned interruptions affected the comprehension process.

When the Romans invaded England in the first century they took with them the Latin language and literature. It is thought that perhaps sometime in the seventh century English was written for the first time by Christian missionaries who knew both English and Latin. As soon as English was written—albeit in a different alphabet than we use today—people began to read. Unfortunately, very little is known about how reading was taught for seven or eight hundred years—except of course that the earliest responsibility for the teaching of reading fell by edict of the Pope to the secular priests and monastic institutions (Davies, 1973).

After the Norman Conquest, the times were hard for the common people, and because the people of power and position spoke Norman (a form of French) there must have been little interest in learning to read the English language. But there are records that by the thirteenth and fourteenth centuries, there were "petty schools" in England, staffed by poorly prepared teachers whose job was to teach the alphabet, the syllables, and if the child progressed, the primer, or prayerbook.

The name for the petty schools seems to have been derived from the status of such learning among the scholars in the community (Davies, 1973, p. 34). By the time of the Reformation (1517) grammar schools and universities had developed. The 400 grammar schools in England so jealously guarded their status as feeder schools for the universities that they were unwilling to deal with rudiments—like teaching a child to read. Learning to read continued to be defined as learning the letters, learning the Catechism, and the primer. Sometimes older students oversaw this learning which apparently went on through drill with the children reciting from their horn books.[2]

An educator, Charles Hoole, noted at the time that the usual manner of teaching letters was to have the child go over all the letters forward and backwards until he could name each of them. He described this as very effective for the "ripe-witted" children, but others faced with the same treatment, "have been thus learning a whole year together (and though they have been much child and beaten too for want of heed) could scarce tell six of their letters at twelve monts' end" (Mathews, 1966, p. 29). Observations such as these help us to understand that reading comprehension was probably not considered—at least at the beginning stages of reading.

It was not until 1779 when a Prussian educator, Friedrich Gedike, who deplored the drudgery of the whole dreary learning-to-read process, spoke out sharply against the "...shockingly slow, inflectionless, uncomprehending manner in which pupils read." He described pupils who were able to pronounce words but had no interest in them, for they were beyond the pupils' abilities to understand. This seems to reflect one of the earliest shifts of interest to comprehension, but the instructional community wasn't ready for these radical ideas that would have the learner be immersed in oral instruction in "practically everything," listening, speaking, singing, and opportunities to express in a variety of ways. Gedike and some of his colleagues and followers felt that through immersion in one's own rich cultural heritage, it would be a given that all children would read by the ages of ten to twelve (Mathews, p. 37). These ideas, over 200 years old, seem to come from the pages of the educational journals that arrived in the mail today.

The Puritan colonists had brought with them to America the Hornbook, and later the *New England Primer*. The Primer was still a "church" book, full of moral injunctions, prayers, and catechisms, but with the prevailing secular instructional materials included—the alphabet, the vowels, consonants, and syllables (Huey, 1973, p. 244). It was used in America for 150 years and sold over 3 million copies. So emphasis in early American reading instruction appeared to be on learning to read in order to be equipped with the skills to read the Bible in order to lead a religious life. Memorization and recitation were the instructional modes that allowed "induction into the reading process through the alphabetic method" (Smith, 1965, p. 34). We have no notion that meaning was considered: success with reading still meant success with pronunciation.

Both Edmund Huey and Smith describe Noah Webster's American Spelling Book (1783), the "Old-Blue-Back Speller," as the book which finally surpassed the Primer in popularity. The Blue-Back, first published in 1783, sold 100 million copies and served as the major literacy tool for four to five times that many children (Mathews, 1966, p. 101). Yet, apart from its emphasis on a moral rather than a religious catechism, and inclusion of rules for correct reading and speaking, the little Blue-Back followed its predecessors by representing the alphabet, 197 syllables, and then long lists of words divided into syllables. There were, however, 10½ of its 158 pages devoted to literature and that was a step, if not a leap, toward meaningful reading (Smith, 1965, p. 48). And the Blue-Back also included emphasis on sounds as well as letter names. The emphasis had as its roots, according to Smith, the new country's perceived need for its citizens to be able to articulate and to pronounce. The art of elocution was of extreme importance to a burgeoning democratic, representative government.

Instructional emphasis provided for this inference: A reader who could orally interpret with style and flair must understand what he reads. Until the middle of the nineteenth century, it seems safe to conclude that for the most part instruction in reading did not focus on whether the reader understood what he read. The task was still one of fluent and accurate pronunciation. Comprehension, it must have been felt, was a byproduct.

The first use of the term "comprehension" appears in the third reader (1856) of J. Russell Webb's *Normal Readers* (Smith, 1965). Webb emphasized as an instructional goal a "full comprehension of the matter to be read"—an indication of a trend toward attention to meaning, at least for more advanced readers. Webb's nephew credited him with both the birth of the "word method" and the resultant changes in instructional methodology that gave attention to meaning. (Real credit for the emerging changes should probably belong with such educators as Pestalozzi, Herbart, Froebel, Mann and, later, the progressive Colonel Francis Parker, who advocated radical changes in education, pioneering a movement toward child-centered and more meaningful learning.)

The famous McGuffey Readers, written by William H. McGuffey, appeared as one of "the new graded series" between 1836-1844. The prevailing emphasis on elocution was still evident but comprehension can also be detected:

> Brief notices concerning the various authors represented have been inserted; the more difficult words have been defined, and their pronunciation has been indicated by diacritical marks; and short explanatory notes have been given wherever required for a full understanding of the text (*McGuffey's Fourth Eclectic Reader*, Revised Edition, 1879, Preface, p. ii).

In addition, stories are accompanied by a series of questions that ask for retelling, for interpretation, and for reader judgment—about what can be expected from any current fourth-level book in a reading series.

Beginning with the mid-nineteenth century, Smith describes a period of emphasis on reading as a cultural asset—reading for a citizenship with enough leisure time to pursue and appreciate literature. Instructional texts spoke not just to what the young reader should know and *understand* as a result of reading, but to the *interest* and *involvement* that the reader should have with the stories. I found the background information, and the establishment of a purpose for reading "Franklin's Whistle" (American Book Company, 1895) not unlike the background materials and preparation for reading that is still a part of directed reading lessons in current teachers' editions.

> The child should never be permitted to read for the sake of reading as a formal process or end in itself. The reading should always be for the intrinsic interest or value of what is read, reading never being done or thought of as "exercise." Word-pronouncing will therefore always be secondary to getting whole sentence meanings, and this from the very first. (p. 380)

And he has a prescient suggestion:

> School readers, especially primers, should largely disappear, except as they may be competent editings of the mother tongue, presented in literary wholes; or, as they may be records of the child's own experiences and thoughts, or as they may be books needed for information in the everyday life of the school. The children should learn to read books, papers, records, letters, etc., as need arises in their life, just as adults do, and they should be trained to do such reading effectively (p. 381).

Measurement of Reading Comprehension Begins to Affect Instruction

The other strand of the comprehension story begins in the first decades of the 20th century and so I will try to begin to weave the two strands—testing and teaching together from about 1915 to the present. Following the advent of an age of scientific measurement came the first reading tests. While the "roots" of comprehension measurement are shorter than those of teaching, they are by no means more distinct.

The advent of "exact measurement" did not follow a long period of "reading involving aesthetic appreciation," as we have just seen. Rather, it had been only a few decades earlier that emphasis had shifted from correct pronunciation to proper elocution and then at last toward the child and the consideration of his literary interests. Farr wrote in 1971:

> Reading comprehension, before the scientific advent of measuring instruments, was probably determined by how well a reader achieved his purpose when using print as a medium (p. 187).

We can hypothesize that the reader may have estimated his *own* comprehension by how well he achieved his *own* purposes, but we have seen that instruction in purposeful reading had had a brief history.

In 1924, William S. Gray had called for a new emphasis in reading instruction, and he labelled it "intelligent silent reading." But he was describing comprehension when he wrote:

Not many years ago the problems of reading instruction were discussed largely in terms of oral reading and effective expression. Such matters as pronunciation, inflection, emphasis, and force received constant attention. Oral reading exercises were so prominent in the daily program that many teachers gave little or no thought to other phases of the subject.

During recent years, however, a different view has become very prominent. Progressive teachers now think of reading primarily as a means of extending experience and of stimulating the thinking power of boys and girls. In this connection they recognize the importance of *intelligent silent reading* [emphasis added]. They emphasize thoughtful assimilating by the reader rather than oral interpretation. (Gray, 1924, p. 348)

Gray chose descriptors (his own and others') that dealt with "ideas," "motives," "action," and "knowledge."

By the second decade of this century, then, we know that reading comprehension was topical and that the search was on for the psychological construct necessary to measure it. The earliest formal and informal measures of reading comprehension were based on how well a reader could reproduce in writing what he had read (Pintner, 1913). Although the *Gray Standardized Reading Paragraphs* (1915) was probably the first published reading test, the first published comprehension measure was the Kansas Silent Reading Test (1916), resembling a group verbal intelligence test of today.

Other silent comprehension tests followed. Most of the early instruments presented sentences and/or paragraphs to read in timed settings and required identification of correct responses to items. Most early comprehension tests, then, dealt with rate of reading and how well an examinee could understand a written communication, as judged by response to questions, ability to select an inappropriate word in a paragraph, to complete a sentence, to identify true and false statements, and so forth. It seems we have not come very far in producing tests that vary from these early formats.

During the 1910-1920 decade, reading research proliferated, mostly because the means to measure were proliferating. In the 1920's, the instructional focus on silent reading continued, and teachers were urged to check comprehension through whatever means could be devised. The *Pathway to Reading Primer* (1925) was probably designed to be read silently. Children dramatized, drew, or otherwise *demonstrated* comprehension of what they had read.

From the 1930s onward, investigations were conducted concerned with isolating factors related to comprehension. Criticism of various reading comprehension tests appeared in Buros' 1939 *Mental Measurements Yearbook*:

Although the authors state that they seek to measure the ability of pupils to interpret what is read and to make inferences, it appears that the questions used for this purpose require the reproduction of facts stated directly in the reading text rather than inferences made from these facts....

However, if the tests on comprehension are broken down, it will be shown that comprehension of the paragraphs is measured by asking for: (a) details directly stated in the content, (b) details implied in the content involving multiple-choice techniques, (c) "yes" "no" answers, (d) total meanings, (e) central thought, etc. These techniques have long been proven good, but this application to the paragraphs in either of the forms is not consistent. Some paragraphs are followed by only one type of question; if the two forms are compared, the inconsistency is increased more than ever. Another way of putting this point is to inquire, What is paragraph comprehension? Is it something that is to be measured only through details in one instance, and a combination of several different techniques in another?

Farr (1971) called the period of the 1940s until recent times a period of subskill proliferation. One of the early attempts to isolate specific reading comprehension skills employed factor analysis of the results of nine comprehension tests administered to a group of college freshman. Five statistically significant skills that contributed greater than chance variance to reading comprehension scores were found:

Knowledge of word meaning

Reasoning in reading

Concentration on literal sense meaning (without consideration of implications)

Following the structure of a passage
and

Recognizing the mood and literary techniques of a writer.

The first two of these—word knowledge and reasoning—accounted for 89 percent of the total variance (Davis, 1944). There were criticisms of factor-analysis studies at the time and later—critics who questioned the tests used, the overlap between the measures, bias of passages, etc. Davis' later work, however (1968), continued to point out that reading comprehension is not a unitary trait.

Attempting to compile and organize the myriad skills that were identified, labelled, and that needed to be categorized under reading comprehension resulted in some confusion for educators, researchers, and test developers alike. One list of 50 standardized reading subtests which purported to measure reading comprehension was compiled. Simons (1971) noted that some reading "skill" checklists contained several hundred or more reading comprehension skills.

Finding a systematic organization for these skills has been one way in which the complexities have been handled, with some of the lists organized into taxonomies. But these lists and taxonomies, and the instructional materials, tests, and instruction that they influenced, suffered some common ailments:

1. The lists and taxonomies appeared more scientific, "suggesting a greater precision" than they possessed (Clymer, 1968).
2. A given skill could exist under a variety of labels from one source to another (Pearson & Johnson, 1978).
3. There was confusion as to what the items in the list were describing: the uses of comprehension, the instructional procedures, or the cognitive processes involved in comprehension.

Teachers' editions for basal reader programs and "workbooks" seemed to have had their origins in the period of silent reading and burst of measurement. A particular author's views on comprehension were no longer easily gleaned by examining the child's reader: With the advent of teachers' editions and workbooks, texts no longer included questions, directions, and activities within them.

When Smith considered the contributions of the 1950s she wrote: "Comprehension is no longer treated as a lump sum; the emphasis at present is upon the higher thinking processes of interpretation and critical reading" (1967, p. 10). The relationship between reading and thought had been emphasized by Thorndike (1973) over sixty years ago, but pragmatically, Kingston (1961) countered that the linking of reading and thought confused issues further by linking two complex and abstract terms. He called for an operational definition of reading comprehension, one that would allow for some direction to the teaching, research, and assessment while the Great Truths were being searched for.

More recently, criterion-referenced assessment techniques have attempted to "operationalize" comprehension still further. States, school systems, and basal reader publishers have begun to provide their own tests. But when reading comprehension is formally measured (by whatever means—norm-referenced tests, criterion-referenced tests, cloze), the test selector is implicitly agreeing that valid decisions about readers' "comprehension" can be made with the results. We have found ourselves stuck with a definition of reading comprehension as "that which the reading comprehension test tests." And the tests continue to assess a variety of things. Concerns with assessment of comprehension have grown:

1. Difficulty with defining the construct of comprehension.
2. Difficulty in achieving valid and reliable measurement of that which is not adequately defined.
3. Inability to deal with a proliferation of "subskill" titles, which have developed to further pin down comprehension.
4. Concerns related to making diagnostic or instructional decisions on the basis of tests of reading comprehension.

5. Confusion over how comprehension should be assessed and with what types of instruments, e.g., how can one demonstrate "mastery" of an ongoing process?
6. Concerns with dealing with complex text variables that affect comprehension or comprehensibility
7. Concerns with the effects on comprehension of such elusive reader variables as background knowledge, interest and purpose.

Summary

One of the first ways to measure comprehension was described by Pintner (1913) as having the student "write down as much as he could of the matter read." As tests proliferated, and instructional emphasis moved toward silent reading, "skills" of comprehension became important bases for both testing and teaching. Tests attempted to tap these skills by providing questions over text segments, questions designed to "get at" literal comprehension and all the skills it subsumed. Other questions tapped inferential comprehension—requiring the reader to move beyond that which is stated literally. Within this century, then, measurement of comprehension has received form, been refined, encountered controversy, and prevailed in its paragraphs-and-questions format until the present day—when comprehension researchers are applying more sophisticated variations of Pintner's methods. The sophistication stems from knowledge of language, learning, and learners. Valid measurement in the future will depend upon application of a theory of comprehension that will account for the effects of reader differences, text variables, and perhaps the instruction that has occurred.

Within the past decade, educators have also been demonstrating more concern about teaching reading comprehension. When Austin and Morrison described reading practices in more than a thousand of the nation's public schools (1963), they concluded that, on the basis of classroom observations, it appeared that practices which William S. Gray considered undesirable in 1937 had become firmly entrenched: two notable examples were emphasis on word calling without "corresponding emphasis on word meaning" and "comprehension drills which scarcely begin to probe into the child's understanding. . ." (p. 3). The great majority of educators reported recognizing comprehension at the heart of the reading process and indicated that they spend over 75 percent of their reading time devoted to developing comprehension skills (pp. 36-37). Yet, both administrators and teachers acknowledged the teaching of "comprehension skills" as one of the most persistent problems. One of the Austin-Morrison recommendations was

> emphasis in the beginning and continuing reading programs be placed on the concept that understanding the meaning of the printed passage and not mere word-calling constitutes reading (p. 222).

When Dolores Durkin (1978) observed classrooms for the purpose of finding, timing, and describing comprehension instruction, she found that less than one percent of 24 teachers' time during the reading period went to comprehension instruction (p. 21). While comprehension instruction may have had a narrow definition in this study, it was nonetheless evident that assessing comprehension, making assignments, and monitoring those assignments received much greater proportions of time.

The story of comprehension instruction, then, has moved from no awareness; to a period of rhetorical emphasis; followed by a published flood of texts, guides, packages, workbooks, and kits; leaving little impact on teacher behavior. Perhaps comprehension has been described with so many dimensions and become so complex that teachers are no longer certain *what* to teach; they are fully occupied by the task of discerning whether there is life in the coals. There is only time for prodding reader retention.

In any event the story of reading comprehension instruction is nearly as complex as the construct itself; the path through educational history is bumpy, not clearly marked, and seems to double back on itself. As Pearson and Johnson (1978) have suggested, reading comprehension may be at once a "unitary process" and a set of "discrete skills." Acceptance of that practical explanation would further endorse the efforts of both the cognitive psychologists as they search for ways to explain the unity, as well as the efforts of practitioners who must interpret the whole into transferable goods.

> Reading comprehension must also be regarded as a set of discrete processes. The simple fact is that you cannot deal with the universe of comprehension tasks at once...[recognizing]...that for the sake of instructional convenience and sanity, you have to start somewhere and move toward something else. (Pearson & Johnson, 1978, p. 227)

Where that "somewhere" is and what that "something else" entails aren't yet clear. Some current researchers (Anderson, 1977; Rumelhart & Ortony, 1977) lead us to believe that the "somewhere" is within the reader. The "something else," then, is the reader's increased comprehension and the path between the two is instruction—the teaching skills that strengthen the reader-text interaction and bridge the known with the new. "Something else" is the goal of research, instruction, and measurement of comprehension. Authors in this volume point the way.

Notes

1. Reading for the Greeks and Romans was an oral process. Even into the Renaissance period, reading meant oral reading. Monks of the Middle Ages devised a devil named Titivillus whose job was to "...collect fragments of words mumbled, or skipped, or read silently in the recitation of the divine office. These he carried down to hell in bagfuls where they were duly registered against the offender" (Mathews, p. 13), heralding, *I* believe, the birth of the "diagnostic reading record sheet."

2. Paddle-shaped pieces of wood on which letters had been written in the shape of the cross onto skin which was then fastened to the wood and covered with a sheet of transparent horn to prevent smudging.

PART TWO   The Reader and the Text

Children's Understanding of Passages

Priscilla A. Drum
University of California at Santa Barbara

After a decade of research on comprehension of extended language passages, what have we learned about children's understanding of these passages? The effects of age, of ability levels, of different tasks, and of passage characteristics have been considered. The results of these studies are examined here to look at possible educational implications.

First, characteristics of passages will be discussed as related to selection of materials and expectations for learning at different grades. Second, the task demands, such as recalling the information, analyzing the structure of texts, and recognizing inferences, will be scrutinized for differences by grade. The intent here is to determine what activities children can reasonably be expected to perform as a result of exposure to passages.

Passage Characteristics

To study what information people learn from passages, the content must be described in order to match the content retained to that of the passage. The method for analyzing the passage can either be content specific, such as event narratives (Warren, Nicholas, & Trabasso, 1977) and propositional hierarchies (Kintsch, 1974); or a generalized model of abstract categories of passage information which can then be applied to similar type passages, such as Meyer's logical structure (1975) and the story grammar work (Rumelhart, 1975; Mandler & Johnson, 1977; Thorndyke, 1977; Stein & Glenn, 1978).

Brief passages, similar to ones used in many research studies, can be classified into two general organization patterns: those whose information is clustered around topics and those whose information is presented in a temporal order representing a narrative sequence (Thorndyke, 1979). Stories are most often used with young children. Therefore, story analyses will be described before that of description. The two do overlap; some of the same manipulations have been used with both types of passages, and the distinction between stories and time-sequenced social studies passages is more ephemeral than real (Gentner, 1976).

Stories

Chronological narratives reflect the temporal order of real life events in which motives, actions, results, and reactions occur in sequence, and the episodes in the main character's life are integrated by goals and subgoals. Time from first to last thus provides a natural structure for remembering episode information.

Story grammarians (Rumelhart, 1975; Mandler & Johnson, 1977; Thorndyke, 1977; Stein & Glenn, 1978) specify the necessary category components for simple stories, those with one major character and one or two episodes. The categories include a setting that provides the time, the place, and the protagonist; and an episode that includes an initiating event, a goal or desired outcome, actions taken to reach the goal, the eventual result, and the reactions to this result. Those who have developed and used story grammars in research believe that listeners and/or readers will use their knowledge of story structure to understand and to remember specific stories. Stories that fit this description will be more easily understood than those stories that either delete components or do not represent the information in the prescribed order.

Story passages have been used most commonly with young children, ages four to ten. The assumption is that narration is easier than description, that events are remembered best and description is seldom retained (Gomulicki, 1956). According to Baker and Stein (1981), children have less exposure to exposition in primary schools and therefore do not recognize the structure of descriptive texts. As Mandler states, "Story schemata are acquired through experience with listening to stories as well as experience with typical kinds of causal and temporal event sequences in the world" (1978, p. 15). In any case, the belief is that children use their knowledge of real life events as a guide in understanding stories and in recalling them later.

Events are better recalled than description in grades five and above (Drum, 1978), but there have been few research comparisons for the type of passage below this age. One study by Christie and Schumacher (1975) examines memory for actions central to a story versus descriptions of the characters or the setting. The children listened to a story about two children and a boat that gets loose into a lake. Children of kindergarten age retained more action information than descriptive information as did the older second and fifth graders. The descriptive material such as hair color, added nothing to the actions of the story, and seemed gratuitous interruptions; so the results do not truly speak to differences between topic-clustered information and narrative.

Within most story experiments, the material has been comparatively simple, a moral or fable with one or two episodes, generally one setting and one character, and both the goals and feelings stereotypical of what most people would feel or want given a similar problem. With stories like this, both adults and children remember the event information best and generally include some reference to the main character. The internal responses, such as feelings or thoughts, are less often stated by both young and old relative to the other story grammar categories (Mandler & Johnson, 1977; Baker & Stein, 1978; Stein & Glenn, 1979). This result may be due to the recall situation in which the re-teller implicitly assumes that the listener is aware of common human reactions to events. What happened is what is unique; the consequent emotions can be expected unless they are unusual. When direct questions about inner emotions are included (Stein & Glenn, 1979), even first graders are aware of feelings; they just don't often include them in recall.

Deleting category information, such as setting, from the story presentation does not decrease recall of the remaining information unless the category is part of the main episode. College students are also bothered by deletion of this information (Bower, 1978; Thorndyke, 1977). Subjects make more additions in stories with deleted categories; they seem to infer the missing categories and try to fill them, indicating that it may be requisite information for a well-formed story. Even second graders are more likely to construct inferences if there is very little information (Glenn, 1978).

If the story is well-ordered chronologically, then recall sequences are well-ordered, reflecting the "ideal" story—the story schemata. Two-episode stories where the first episode is complete before the second is initiated produce more second grade recall than one-episode stories of the same length (Glenn, 1978). However, interweaving two-episode information causes a decrement in recall for children in grade two and beyond (Mandler, 1978; Glenn, 1979). Mandler (1978) found that the youngest children, grades two and four, were most likely to reorder the interleaved material into sequential episodes; sixth graders did somewhat less reordering, and adults generally maintained the interleaved input order. However, the grade two children recalled comparatively little under either condition. Thus, we have the youngest children unable to cope with listening to two-episode stories (or perhaps with retelling them—a verbal report deficit rather than a comprehension one), and the adults unaffected by the structural reorganization of simple stories. When materials are selected for elementary children that present deviations from chronological order, some children will likely need direct instruction on the clues for organizing time; others will learn to reorder such materials themselves through exposure alone.

Story differences have had only slight effects on recall for young children, for they retain or retell little of the content. Poulson, Kintsch, Kintsch, and Premack (1979) found that four year olds recalled very little under any condition, but they did somewhat better on a normal order, simple picture based story than they did on a more complex set of pictures. Brown (1975) also presented an ordered and a random group of pictures. Kindergartners could not recall much of the stories they made up for the pictures while second graders could. First graders did mention 46 percent of the units in four stories presented without pictures (Stein & Glenn, 1979). Thus, there is a somewhat ordered pattern of materials for young children if one is examining their ability to recall what they have heard. For preschoolers, use simple chronologically ordered narratives accompanied by equally simple pictures. By first grade, the pictures are no longer necessary but chronological stories with few episodes and commonplace themes are.

Bartlett's "War of the Ghosts" (1932), Kintsch's "Tar Baby" (1978), Waters' subject-generated passages without editing as listened to by other subjects (1978), Bransford's "Robot's Washing Windows" (1980), all indicate that without some context that provides an advance structure for the story, the ability to retain the information is diminished at all ages. With ordinary or commonplace content appropriate to the age tested, only minimal passage structure is needed, but with technical or unusual content, the structure must also be in the head of the listener or be provided through analogy by the instructor. A method (or methods) for ascertaining in advance who has the requisite knowledge frame needs to be developed so that the preceding statement can be tested; at present, it is just assumed.

Another aspect of children's story knowledge is shown in the child's ability to tell stories and to evaluate them. Applebee (1978) tried to trace the child's concept of story from 1) Weir's study (1979) of her son's crib monologues, 2) the examples presented in the Pitcher and Prelinger (1963) two to five year olds' stories, 3) the 145 six and seven year old stories collected by Willy (1975), and 4) his own studies. He examined the quality of the stories by the age of the children and the years of education, noting increased use of openings ("Once upon a time")—inclusion of titles, closing ("that's what happened") and more consistent past tense. The younger children accepted stories as facts and were likely to use everyday, home events in their telling of stories. Naturally, amount of production (words, t-units) increases with age, but story structure also seems to follow a somewhat systematic path. Using Vygotsky's stages for ordering collections (1963), Applebee found that children's stories could be characterized as a listing of nouns, to sequences with one character doing a series of unrelated things, to primitive narratives where there is a cause and an effect, to unfocused chains where several primitives are brought together, to focused chains similar to radio serials, to true narratives where motivation grows out of results. Most preschool children do not tell true narratives until after school entrance, but there is a general evolution toward the narrative form. The content seems to move from the facts of immediate life into the unknown. The evaluation of six year olds, "I like to 'cause it's good," is most common; by age nine, usually some reason is given.

Applebee points out the elaboration of story structures in production and increasing knowledge of the bases for stories: An appreciation of fiction versus fact, of thematic value, and of the interdependence of style and meaning. But the time for the appearance of each type of knowledge varies; one three year old told a true narrative and 24 five year olds could not. The signals which indicate where a child is on the continuum of story knowledge have not been explored sufficiently. What a particular child can learn to do will depend on the present state of knowledge, but the language used and the physical actions must be understood by the observer for appropriate instruction to be provided.

Description

Descriptive passages where information is clustered around a topic have a more abstruse structural pattern. Here, exposition is confined to information about things and ideas, rather than actions that lead to a change of state for a main character. It is much harder to specify necessary components and/or organizational structures for the descriptive passages used with school children. Once a topic has been selected, there are no rules for decisions about the amount and type of information to include. The choice and elaboration of details seemingly depends upon the purpose, what a reader is supposed to know after reading, and the intended audience, the age and their expected content sophistication.

Researchers have used various means in describing the content of expository passages in order to note what pieces of information the better or older readers remember. Some form of referential coherence (Halliday & Hasan, 1976) determines whether a multiple sentence unit is a passage or a list of unrelated sentences. Then, by means of common references, the passage is analyzed into propositions. "We establish a linear or hierarchical sequence of propositions in which co-referential expressions occur. The first (or superordinate) of these propositions often appears to have a specific cognitive status in such a sequence: They are recalled two or three times more often than other propositions" (Kintsch & van Dijk, 1978, p. 365). Thus, the first rule used is that a full proposition rather than the name of the most frequent noun delineates the topic of a sequence of sentences (van Dijk, 1979). Second, the order of appearance in the passage, as long as there is no change of topic, establishes the order of importance of a propositional unit.

The first proposition likely brings forth memory for similar topic information and clears the mind of other conflicting or interfering information, at least it does in experimental situations where subjects are usually cooperative in attending to the task. Also, co-reference either explicitly or implicitly repeats some part of the original proposition so that it predominates throughout the passage. However, propositional hierarchies do not specify "good" structures for exposition generally, but instead try to determine what will be retained from a specific passage.

The most common finding for expository passages is that both adults and children of all ages, whether high or low in verbal ability, remember the most important information within the text, if they remember anything (Christie & Schumacher, 1975; Drum, 1978, 1981; Evans, 1978-1979; Kintsch, 1974; Meyer, 1975, 1977). Poorer readers do remember less of the total information, but what they do recall is usually the most general statements. The topic sentence and the superordinate statements often occur early in passages or in paragraphs in multi-paragraph texts. Thus, both primacy and/or repetition could be the source for these results. A contrary result was that of Bieger and Dunn (1980). Here, the able sixth grade readers recalled more subordinate than superordinate information. The signalling words described in Meyer (1975) had been deleted, and the number of units at each hierarchical level were not reported. The able and older readers could and did select personally salient ideas. In the follow-up study, after the signals were inserted, all subjects, able and less able, in fourth and sixth grades remembered the most important signalled information. So, as Meyer suggests, the signalling cues do appear to be used to mark the structure of passages.

In a similar study with ninth graders (Meyer, Brandt, & Bluth, 1980), the effects of signaling only appeared for less able readers at immediate recall and not at delayed recall. In fact, most students recalled more in the minus-signals condition at delayed recall. The key word approach to topic importance may only influence immediate recall because the words, such as *but, however, therefore, so that,* etc., are so common in the language that they are not retained as topic indicators over time. Instead, the ideas are assimilated into a content structure for retention. However, the fact that the best readers were not favorably influenced by signal words at any time casts doubts on the use of such terms as indicators of passage structure. The best readers did retain more of the author's top level structure than did the less able readers, but apparently not because of signal words.

A few studies have examined retention of expository information with children in elementary schools. Aulls (1975) found that sixth graders' recall of passage t-units and literal paraphrases of descriptive passages was strongly influenced by meaningfulness of the text. A meaningful text contained likely associations with the children's daily experience, for example, "the housewives' basic tasks" versus "the lens of the eye focuses light." If the child understood the content, then deleting titles and main ideas had little effect, though reordering sentences and dropping connectives did. For the more esoteric topics, all structural changes depressed recall. Again, a similar result appears. When the passage content is within the child's knowledge base and the order of presentation is similar to most prior passages read, titles and main ideas (forms of advance organizers or directed reading activities) are not needed. The children can supply the missing information for themselves. However, when the content is divorced from daily life, whether concrete description of the size of eye pupils or abstract Indian allegories, the students on the average will need both well written material and pre- and postinstruction. Or, as stated by Dooling and Christiansen (1977), "the more abstract the concepts available at the time of the retention test, the greater the role of semantic memory will be in constructive recall" (p. 436).

One of the few studies with young children is that of Danner (1976), who tested second, fourth, and sixth graders and used passages which were topically clustered. His passages were descriptive, rather than narrative, with no change of state, temporal organization, nor an analysis of important versus unimportant ideas. Instead, the passage contained four statements each about appearance, abode, and eating habits of a fox or a polar bear. The children listened to and recalled twice a topically organized passage, the four sentences about the fox's appearance, then the four on abode, and the four on eating; and interwove statements from each of the topics in the other passage. Danner found that all of the second, fourth, and sixth grade children could describe at least four of the topics and 79 percent could describe all six topics, a content effect. Recall increased with age and with organization for all ages. However, the second graders did not remember more on the second trial. Fourth graders did increase recall on the second organized presentation, and sixth graders remembered more under both conditions at the second trial and were the only group to attempt to topically cluster the disorganized presentations in recall.

Neither the Aulls nor the Danner studies examined differences within grades by reading ability, but others have. Good third and sixth grade readers remembered more explicit and more inferred information after reading a description of a dinosaur than did the poorer readers, though inferences were relatively sparse, one-half or less units than the explicit ones for all children (Tierney, Bridge, & Cera, 1978-1979).

Berger and Perfetti (1977) suggest that poor readers may have a general language deficit for all aspects of verbal information processing. Their good fifth grade readers outperformed the less able ones on both literal comprehension questions and free recall for both oral and written expository passages despite equivalence of age, IQ, and prior knowledge of the topics. The good readers' prior knowledge scores were independent of their scores on the questions ($r = .01$); for the poor readers there was a substantial correlation ($r = .52$). Thus, poor readers rely on or need prior knowledge more in selecting answers to questions and/or in comprehending passages than do good readers.

The good readers have had practice with reading; they have learned the more formal structure of writing (Olson, 1977): How the sentences are likely to be organized, common selections for subsequent words in phrases, and myriad other text information. The peripheral knowledged gleaned (though not often taught) about the structure of passages as well as the increased accuracy, automaticity, and fluency obtained through hours of practice reading, give the good readers advantages in learning via print and print based oral presentation that is exceedingly difficult to overcome in any remedial program. It is also likely that instruction and materials suitable for the less able reader are not needed or not sufficient for those who read with ease. The poor readers may or may not have had a general language deficit at the time they began reading instruction, but over the years in which they have *not* practiced reading articles, stories and books, they have likely developed a deficit for any written material, whether it is read to them or they read it themselves.

Task Characteristics

Three general tasks used for measuring comprehension of passages have been selected: recall of passage information, recognition of passage structure, and recognition of inferences. Each shows a somewhat different pattern of development, thereby providing more information on children's understanding.

Recall of Information

Recall of the passage information has been used frequently to measure comprehension. The children either listen to or read a passage, and then re-tell what they remember. Taped oral recall is the most common method, probably because for many young children writing is a laborious task and the results can be illegible. Because of the taping requirement, testing is usually done with one child at a time in a quiet room, a situation quite different from the active environment of an elementary class. But even under ideal conditions, not every idea is restated. Consciously or unconsciously, certain ideas are selected to be retold. By studying both the amount of recall and the qualities of the re-stated ideas by children of various ages, we can learn what children respond to in the passages presented.

Another possible limitation according to Spiro in Meyer (1977) is that requiring information is an unnatural activity and does not generalize to more normal listening and reading behaviors. However, a general belief that pervades the comprehension literatures is that the more prior knowledge the reader possesses on a topic, the more easily readers will accrue new information on that topic. Somewhere the child has to obtain the prior information that facilitates subsequent learning. Major resources for acquiring information are classroom instruction and assigned readings. Children should retain the content presented, an outcome that is quite similar to recall of information. Not everything can be learned by direct, physical experience.

The results of each recall study were tabulated in order to compare the findings. The type and number of stories, the scoring units, the total number of scores where available, the time of recall, and the proportion recalled by grade and the number of subjects in each grade are listed. Table 1 presents the data obtained for eight of the studies using this design. Two problems are apparent. First, the proportions recalled are averaged across treatment variations, such as Aulls' meaningful versus less meaningful expository passages or Mandler's intact versus interleaved episodes. The results for treatments could be included, but there is little similarity in treatments across experimenters. The sizeable differences between .33 recalled in Aulls' study versus the .61 for the sixth graders in Danner's study can likely be explained by the variations in the materials. But this interpretation is questionable because of the difference in scoring units, the second problem. Story nodes, pausal units, T-units, and propositions can be equated, or at least the last three can, but the average ratios have not yet been determined. Whether the variations in recall at particular grade levels are treatment differences, scoring differences, or both cannot be answered. Therefore, the data were examined for general trends, such as the increases by age or by ability, and the interpretations of treatment comparisons are largely speculative.

The first finding that sheer amount of recall increases with age for all types of passages and under all conditions does not appear to be due to capacity by age limitations only (Chi, 1978; Perfetti & Lesgold, 1977). Chi found that ten year old chess experts more accurately remembered more chess positions than college age amateur players, an effect due to greater prior knowledge; the young experts knew many different chess configurations and didn't have to retain piece by piece slots. Also, the chess experiment only required the youngsters to re-place the pieces in the original presentation condition. The task did not require the verbal fluency needed for retelling. Young children may lack an ability to encode or to retrieve verbal information. If the difference between the amount of adult recall versus that of children is a verbal lack, then tasks that require ordering or recognizing the information should not be affected by age. If it is a problem of understanding, then the passage is either partially understood or not understood, and all tasks will be less well performed—not just recall.

In many of these studies, the children listened to the passages that had already been processed by the reader. It is virtually impossible for a fluent reader to abort the suprasegmentals; stress, pitch, and

Table 1. Summary of the Recall Data in Eight Studies

Author and Date	Grade	N	# of Passages	Scoring Unit % Available	Proportion Recalled	Time of Recall
Aulls (1975)	6th	128	2	expository idea units/9	.33	Immediate
Danner (1976)	2nd	24	2	expository	.46	Immediate
	4th	24	2	propositions	.58	Immediate
	6th	24	2	48	.61	Immediate
Berger & Perfetti (1977)	5th	H*20	2	expository	.29	Immediate
	5th	L*20	2	propositions 38	.23	Immediate
Brown & Smiley (1977)	3rd	20	2	stories	.35	Immediate
	5th	20	2	pausal units	.43	Immediate
	7th	20	2	113	.47	Immediate
	adults	20	2		.48	Immediate
Mandler & Johnson (1977)	1st	21	4	basic	.53	Immediate
	4th	21	4	story nodes	.65	&
	adults	21	4	9	.83	24 hours
Mandler (1978)	2nd	24	8	story nodes	.27	24 hours
	4th	24	8	22	.30	24 hours
	6th	24	8		.32	24 hours
	adults	24	8		.35	24 hours
Mandler & DeForest (1979)	3rd	36	12	story	.45	24 hours
	6th	36	12	propositions	.55	24 hours
	adults	36	12	44	.65	24 hours
Waters (1978)	3rd	64	4	subject made	32	14 days
	6th	64	4	passages**	44	14 days
	adults	96	4		55	14 days

* H = good readers; L = poor readers.
** No total scores possible since all passages differed; therefore, raw numbers are reported.

juncture are physical cues as to meaning. The child who listens to the passages receives signals about important words and phrase relationships not available to the child who reads the material. Oral recall mimics the presentation mode, which is an easier task than either comprehension or production (Brown, 1973). Of course, in most cases these children did have less recall than older children and adults, the typical finding, but it may be due to difference in prior knowledge about the topics.

Whatever the source of the quantitative difference in the amount of recall by age and by verbal ability at the same age, the fact that younger and less able readers and listeners remember less should be considered by educators. Amount of information retained is highly correlated with appropriate inferences, problem-solving tasks, and other higher order mental activities. Or, as Brown (1978) states,

"Superior memory seems to be an incidental by-product of fully understanding a text" (p. 212). Superior memory may be more than a by-product; it may be a necessary condition for comprehension.

The educational limitations of the recall findings include at least one situational difference and one experiential difference. The one-to-one of the experimental setting likely induces more attention to the passage than is regularly obtained in classrooms. The retelling instructions resemble the "show and tell" activities and parental questions about daily experiences, more common occurrences in children's lives than answering multiple choice questions, filling in blanks, or other problem-solving tasks. Perhaps, as a result of prior habituation to the task, children's recall is generally quantitatively less but qualitatively similar in ideas stated to that of adults. Thus, recall data may not show the possible developmental increases or changes in verbal information processing capabilities as well as some other tasks, such as sorting out important from less important information, reordering the information into a predetermined "good" order, or recognizing appropriate inferences.

Structural Knowledge

Children are affected by the meaningfulness of the passage as related to their own experiences, remembering more ideas with familiar content. Degraded presentations including random order, deleting titles and main ideas, and list type sentence presentations have only minimal effects in stereotypical passages. Content is apparently a more potent source for problems in understanding than the structure or organization of the passages when the measure taken is recall. However, poor or unusual structure does have a deleterious effect on more difficult content. Structural variables are thus interactive with meaningfulness. The question still remains whether the children are aware of structural patterns, whether they can consciously recognize organization in passages and use this knowledge to aid in learning.

In Danner's study, fourth graders (16 out of 24) and 22 sixth graders could group the individual statements into topics, a task that only five second graders could perform. The older children could also describe relations of sentences in their topic organizations as well as group them. Only two subjects (a fourth grader and a sixth grader) could evaluate passage organization on their own without a concrete task to guide them. Again, there is a seemingly unconscious reaction to good input, even by second graders, but an increase by age in ability to manipulate the input and to provide reasons for their manipulations. In other words, the older children can fix things up; they can't or don't say what was wrong with the material in the first place.

McClure, Mason, and Barnitz (1979) asked children to reorder scrambled, six sentence stories. The best order story was determined by adult ordering. Third graders showed very slight differences in favoring the adult order over question and conclusion forms. Sixth and ninth graders much more strongly favored the adult form.

In a somewhat similar task, third, fifth, seventh, and college students were asked to rate the importance of pausal units within two Japanese children's stories, 390 to 403 words long (Brown & Smiley, 1977). They divided the story in fourths: most important down to least important. They heard the story twice and then rated it by reading the units and rating each one. Their ratings were then matched to a prior set of college ratings. In the recall situation, the children simply listened twice and recalled the story; third graders and half of the fifth grade subjects provided oral recalls and the rest wrote out their recalls. Recall at all ages included the most important units, and amount of recall also increased with age.

But the rating data substantiate the Danner (1976) findings. Here, the young children responded to characteristics of the input, but could not tell why. Third graders did not distinguish between the importance of units; fifth graders could only at the highest level; seventh graders could distinguish the highest and the lowest levels but not the middle groups; and the college students basically replicated all four levels of the original raters. As noted, fifth graders could not identify anything but the most important units, while most of the fourth graders in the Danner study could group by topic. Either grouping by topic (food, home, appearance) is easier than judgments of importance, or the Japanese stories were more difficult because of length or possibly topic for the young children to understand. However, in the Hildyard and Olson study (1978) discussed in the Inference section, with short passages about ordinary events, the children had problems with the tasks. Therefore, it appears that the reasoning/judgmental tasks are the source of difficulty.

It may be that children are not taught how to evaluate the structure of writing, but it may also be that it would be difficult to teach this material until there is sufficient experience with texts. As a rule of thumb, when over half of a group of children at any age can perform a task, those who can't need special instruction. It also might be useful to provide instruction on the task to the next lower grade, in this case third grade, but not to second graders. It is somewhat dangerous to use adult performance as models of desirable outcomes, for young children may not have the minimal skills needed to emulate such models—a frustrating situation for all concerned.

Recognizing Inferences

The previous sections have examined children's recall and understanding of the structure of passages. The ability to make inferences is often considered a higher level task, a sign of greater understanding. But the quality of inferences must be considered. There is an infinite number of ways to make connections between a given text and other ideas, ways which are only limited by human imagination (Cofer, 1941; Frederiksen, 1975). Most studies mention that recall includes some type of inference, such as elaborations, intrusions, additions, and others, and that older readers/listeners make more of them. Of course, they also recall more. Because of the difficulty in determining the appropriateness of produced inferences as a sign of comprehension, this review will be confined to children's ability to recognize inferences. This may be a much easier task; at least, young children seem to believe it is (Speer & Flavell, 1979), but the results can be related to the materials and the conditions.

Under certain conditions, even very young children can recognize unstated but true inferences as contrasted with false inferences. Given the following passage,

The bird is inside the cage, the cage
is under the table, the bird is yellow.

children in grades two and five did not vary in their ability to recognize that *The bird is under the table* is a true inference and that *The bird is on top of the table* is a false inference (Paris and Carter, 1973). Moeser (1976) found that in forced-choice memory (two choices only) for given statements and for true versus false inferences that kindergartners, second grade, sixth grade, and ninth grade children did not differ on either measure. The passages were quite short. "The ants ate the jelly on the table in the kitchen," was the holistic condition. "The ants ate the jelly. The jelly was on the table. The table was in the kitchen." was the ordered-sentence condition, and random order mixed the sentences. The answer choices were simple subject-object or subject-location contrasts: *The ants were in the kitchen* versus *The cat was in the kitchen.* All groups did less well on the ordered and the random condition, but performance was near perfect for kindergartners on the holistic condition. Thus, when the material is presented orally, the passages are concrete statements, and the answer choices a simple match to presentation, there are no problems in coming to the correct decision.

Hildyard and Olson (1978) examined the ability of good and poor readers in fourth and sixth grade to determine whether an inference was true or indefinite (two choices) after having read or listened to 48 two-sentence pairs:

> John has more cake than Mary.
> Mary has less cake than John.

In this case, the second sentence must be true if the first sentence is. However, in the pair,

> John has more cake than Mary.
> John ate more cake than Mary.

the answer should be indefinite. John could have dropped it on the floor, not liked the cake and not eaten it, and so forth. There was no effect for reading versus listening. The good readers did have more correct answers on both true and indefinite. However, both groups were more likely to be incorrect on the indefinite answers, particularly fourth graders, who said that they were true inferences.

In a second study, fifth graders divided by general ability (high or low) either read or listened to a 12-sentence narrative and then were presented with either true or false story inferences, such as 1) the first pair above; 2) true or false statements from the story (memory); and 3) true or false contextual inferences, such as the second pair above. The contextual inferences, type 3, were also divided into those needed for comprehension of the story versus gratuitous inferences. The answer choices were *Right, Wrong,* and *?,* which they answered twice immediately after each of two listening or reading presentations. Able students were more likely to identify gratuitous contextual inferences as uncertain. There was no improvement over trials for the reading group though the listening group did improve. At trial one, the readers were more correct on memory information and the listeners on contextual inferences needed to make the story comprehensive. As the authors state, "it appears that reading tends to bias comprehension toward the verbatim information explicit in the text. Listening, on the other hand, tends to bias comprehension toward the gist or meaning of the story" (p. 116). Grade school children can evaluate inferences as to appropriateness for the given story information, but there is improvement by grade (study 1) and by ability within grade (study 2).

Hildyard and Olson's materials required an evaluation of the implication of the first sentence on the second or on the relation of a statement to more extensive passage information. This is a more demanding task than noting an erroneous subject-location match. Goetz (1979) found that after reading a story, more able and older high school readers were more precise in their ratings of statements as 1) an exact match, 2) a paraphrase, 3) implied by story, and 4) consistent with story, than were the younger or poorer readers. The passages were much longer than any of the previous material, but these effects of age and ability in correctly identifying necessary inferences (implied by story) as different from consistent ones substantiates the grade and ability effects obtained by Hildyard and Olson. When reasoning about the truth value of inferences for a passage is considered, then the more able and older students do better. When the inference judgment is only a match to story information, such as, *the cat, the ants*, and *the kitchen*, there is no change by grade.

Summary

The research does speak to questions of instructional interest. The selection of materials naturally depends on the age and knowledge of the pupils. Most young children in preschool and kindergarten will need some type of external context—pictures, objects, or verbal comparisons with school or home life—to follow stories or descriptions. By first grade, most children have had sufficient practice with listening to and discussing passages that the external aids are not only no longer needed, but can be a detriment to further development of literacy skills (Christina, 1973; Samuels, 1970; Singer, Samuels, & Spiroff, 1974). The numerical qualifiers, *most, many*, and *some*, should be considered in any selection of materials, for the research cited here on the youngest children has not examined individual differences. Some children read quite well at the time they enter school. Others, who do not read yet, still know a lot about texts. Obviously, the external aids are not requisite for their comprehension.

At all ages, introduce difficult content in familiar structures, such as chronologically ordered narratives or exposition with topic sentence first and repetition of important information which is signalled as important in the text. New content, for instance the life history of a gerbil or a description of a tundra, should be presented as simply as possible. Conversely, familiar content should be used for introducing new structures. A spat with a friend at school related by flashback to an early morning home problem is easily understood as a causal sequence, for most children have experienced similar sequences. Stereotypical events are excellent vehicles for teaching new structures.

Poor readers also require more stereotypical content and boiler-plate narratives. The science and social studies texts should point out the important information and the ways in which examples relate to the major points. Prereading activities need to emphasize the expected background knowledge for understanding the information. If some readers do not have this prior knowledge, they are not likely to understand what they read. In other words, they are not able to learn new content through reading alone. The same materials and instruction should not be used with good and poor readers. Either the good readers learn nothing and will be bored, or the poor readers will be so bewildered that they will learn nothing.

Children respond favorably to good organization, but are unable to tell you why. They cannot make evaluative judgments when the tasks require decisions about degrees of importance or appropriate structure. This is not to say that they do not infer. Inferences are present in almost all verbal exchanges, but many youngsters can't or don't provide reasons for their inferences. Perhaps they do not understand the request for a reason; they may have had little exposure to situations where their beliefs needed substantiation. Formal assessment of such abilities is premature in elementary school. But instruction in concrete reasoning, such as directed reading-thinking activities (Stauffer, 1975) or comparisons of text organizations, will help them assimilate necessary background knowledge and encourage the development of evaluative judgments (Vygotsky, 1963).

The language deficit or disability label that is attached to some students in upper elementary school has been attributed to miswirings in the head, illiterate to semiliterate homes, cultural differences, or various other sources. For whatever reason, these children have not learned to read as well as most children in their age group, the defining attribute for ability differences in most experimental studies. Therefore, they likely spend as little time as possible reading, thus avoiding chances to develop knowledge about written structures. As each year in school passes, the gap widens in comprehension of the formal properties of print. It makes little difference whether the material is presented orally or in print. The vocabulary of print, the connectives between sentences, the complex sentence structures, and the organization of paragraphs and longer texts have not been learned. On the other hand, the subtleties of verbal exchanges among peers, the uses of language in asserting leadership, in cajoling others, in obtaining one's personal goals may or may not be part of this general language deficit; these language uses have not been tested. Therefore, it appears more reasonable to aver a reading deficit that appears whenever formal language is used, or perhaps whenever a situation arises that is similar to school, a place where the "language deficit" children have had little success.

A part of the cure, of course, is to provide lots of *enforced* practice time on reading so that the students will develop knowledge of the properties of writing. This practice time has the added benefit of enabling teachers to select advanced materials for the third graders who read at high school levels or any other children who do not fit the norm of the class. Direct instruction on print characteristics, including but not limited to flashbacks, topical clustering, key phrases in comparisons and arguments, and contextual differences in vocabulary meaning, also must be provided. The problem is to ensure that both direct instruction and student practice are allocated time in the classroom schedule. both are needed.

Discourse Analysis as a Guide for Informal Assessment of Comprehension

Nancy Marshall
Montgomery County Public Schools
Rockville, Maryland

In her chapter about formal assessment of reading performance, Drum discusses some of the factors that contribute to performance on standardized tests and the place of these tests in assessing reading abilities. Few people would question the utility of formal tests, for they are designed to produce reliable information about a student's performance when compared to a standard. Norm-referenced tests are designed to show an individual's rank compared to others in the same grade; criterion-referenced tests are designed to show an individual's level of proficiency compared to an absolute standard. Results from both kinds of standardized tests can be used to place students into grade levels, classes, curricula, instructional treatments, instructional groups, and instructional materials with a minimal chance of error.

Standardized tests, however, have serious limitations. They do not measure student performance in the natural context of the classroom; to borrow a term from Cazden (1977), they lack ecological validity. In order to produce objective, reliable instruments, test developers sacrifice the ability to assess the natural context of the classroom, "a context that includes classroom dynamics of noise, interruptions, absences, special dialects, bilingualism, and the like" (Cicourel, 1974, p. 6).

In addition, standardized tests are designed to measure a student's recognition of answers to specific questions rather than student-generated responses. Yet it is the latter that provides the richest source of information about comprehension because it allows us to "examine the structure of the child's accounting practices and reasoning processes in order to draw valid inferences about his competence"

(Cicourel, 1974, p. 5). The key word in the last sentence is *structure*. Student-generated responses are organized in the mind of the student. Analysis of such responses allows us to gain insight into the ways in which an individual organizes information and can be used to help guide instruction designed to promote better ways of organizing information.

Informal assessment can fill both of these gaps. *Informal assessment* is used here to mean a set of guidelines or procedures that enable the teacher to make decisions about student performance based upon informed observation of student behavior in the classroom. Informal assessment relies much less upon paper-and-pencil tests, although the term can be used to include teacher-made tests, and more upon verbal interaction, both among students and between student and teacher. Teachers use informal assessment techniques when evaluating a student's responses to teacher-directed questions, participation in a discussion, or retelling of a story.

In order for a teacher to make informed observations of the various behaviors just listed, specific criteria for determining the appropriateness of the behaviors being observed must be established. This is where research using discourse analysis comes into the picture, for it is with this research that important characteristics of discourse are being identified, the characteristics that are expected to be included in the performance of good students.

Before these criteria are detailed, however, a cautionary note is necessary. No way of objectively measuring natural language has yet been found, and probably never will. As a result, informal assessment is necessarily a less reliable source of information about student performance than is formal assessment. The loss of reliability in informal measures is compensated for by a gain in the range of behaviors being observed. It might be convenient to think of all testing as existing along two continuums: one representing reliability (the consistency of scores) and the other representing ecological validity (the naturalness of the task). As one increases, the other decreases forming a pattern like that shown in Figure 1. To get a complete picture of student performance, instruments that are high on both continuums are necessary (Marshall, 1978).

In the rest of this chapter, I shall describe the current thinking involved in developing informal assessment measures based upon current research into the nature of discourse. I have few references for the development of informal measures since most of the ideas presented here are currently being piloted for the Instructional System in

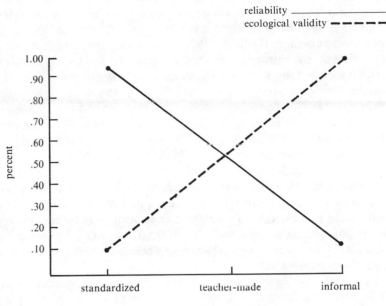

Figure 1. Reliability and Ecological Validity of Assessment Measures

Reading/Language Arts, Montgomery County Public Schools, Rockville, Maryland. There is, of course, a substantial body of theoretical research that will be reviewed in conjunction with the various assessment measures discussed.

Types of Discourse and Comprehension

Students encounter a wide variety of discourse in school, and it is important to assess their comprehension of each type. Before this can be done, however, it is important to understand the nature of discourse in general and of each variety in particular. Discourse, according to Halliday and Hasan (1976), is the basic unit of communication. Discourse can be as brief as a STOP sign or as long as *War and Peace*, but it is discourse because it is a complete unit of meaning requiring no additional linguistic elaboration. Discourse is spoken as well as written. A conversation between friends or a question-answer situation in the classroom are examples of discourse.

Intuitively we know that there are differences among *War and Peace*, a STOP sign, and a conversation. The purpose of this section is to formalize some of these differences in a way that can lead to useful assessment tools. To aid in doing this, a fundamental linguistic distinction must be made clear. Every meaningful utterance has both a form and function (Halliday, 1973). *Form* can be identified as the structure or organization of an utterance. It is the grammatical structure of sentences (Chomsky, 1965) or whole discourse. *Function* can be defined as the speaker/writer's purpose for communicating (Searle, 1975). It includes the relationships between words as defined by case grammar (Fillmore, 1968, 1971) or propositional analysis (Kintsch, 1974). It also includes the way in which information is foregrounded for emphasis (Chafe, 1970; Grimes, 1975).

The form-function dichotomy can aid in clarifying the differences that exist among the varieties of discourse. There seem to be two ways in which information can be organized (form): by temporal sequencing and by topic. There are many reasons for communicating (function), but there seem to be a few primary ones: 1) to affect the reader's emotions; 2) to affect the reader's behavior; and 3) to affect the reader's knowledge.

These categories are not mutually exclusive but, when considered with form, they are a convenient means of formalizing our intuitions about the differences in discourse (outlined in Table 1).

Table 1.   Types of Discourse as Defined by
Language Form and Function

function	form	
	temporal	topical
emotions	narration	lyric
behavior	directions	persuasion
knowledge	temporal exposition	topical exposition

Using Table 1 as a guide, six different types of discourse emerge. Each of these makes different demands on the reader. As a result, each should be taught and assessed differently. Suggestions for both assessment and instruction will appear in the subsequent sections of this chapter.

Assessing Comprehension

Narration

Of the six types of discourse, narration has been the most completely investigated. It can be described by means of "story grammar" which is used to show the relationships among the various parts of the narrative text. A number of story grammars have been developed (Mandler and Johnson, 1977; Rumelhart, 1975; Stein and Glenn, 1979; Thorndyke, 1977) all of which are remarkably similar. All basically divide a story into a series of episodes and the episodes into a series of events. Thorndyke's (1977) grammar follows. Each element is first given as a grammatical rule and is then explained.

1. story → setting + theme + plot + resolution
   All stories have a setting, a plot, a theme, and a resolution.
2. setting → characters + location + theme
   The setting of a story includes information about time and place and description of the character(s).
3. theme → (event) + goal
   The theme (or moral) of a story includes the goal toward which the characters strive as explained in the event sequences of the story.
4. plot → episode 1 (+ episode 2 + ... + episode n)
   The plot of a story is made up of one or more episodes (a series of events which focus upon a specific character, the protagonist).
5. episode → setting + events
   Any episode has both a setting (sometimes unspecified) and a series of events leading toward a goal.
6. Events → instigation (+ reaction 1) + attempts + resolution (+ reaction 2)
   These last two are given using Stein and Glenn's (1979) terms. According to them, the events in any episode form a pattern with some instigating event that states the problem for the protagonist, followed (sometimes) by the protagonist's reactions to the problem, followed by his/her attempts at a solution, followed by a resolution (either positive or negative), followed (sometimes) with the protagonist's reactions to the resolution.

Research into the relationship between story grammar and comprehension for narrative discourse indicates that both children and adults tend to organize stories into a story grammar format, both when creating (Stein & Glenn, 1979) and when recalling (Rumelhart, 1975) narrative discourse. Further, when stories are presented in a form that is a permutation of the typical form (flashback, unfinished ending, etc.), both children (Stein & Glenn, 1979) and adults (Marshall, 1979) tend to retell the story in its more traditional form, even if this means adding information. Even children in first grade make use of the story grammar format when producing or retelling stories.

There is another way to represent the structure of narration. All temporally sequenced events can be shown as a series of causally linked happenings. This causal chaining is used by Schank (1973) and Frederiksen (1975) to represent the organization of narration. However, Marshall (1979) found that readers attend more readily to the elements of narrative structure as an aid in comprehension. In fact, emphasis on causality tended to decrease comprehension somewhat.

It seems, then, that story grammars are a powerful way of representing the structure of narrative discourse. They seem to be descriptive of the way in which narrative information is organized in the mind of both reader and writer. Although the ultimate proof of this statement can never be made, it is a reasonable conclusion based upon the research evidence and one that has direct implications for the development of informal assessment tools.

Story grammars can be used to form the framework for asking questions about a piece of narrative discourse or for scoring a student-generated retelling of the story. In both cases, students are judged on the basis of how complete the information is for each element of the story structure. However, when answering questions, the student focuses upon isolated elements of the story structure while, when retelling a story, the student must use the total structure of the story to organize the elements of the story. Both questions and recalls provide useful information. Questions help the student focus upon the relevant information in the story; retelling forces the student to integrate all the information that he/she thinks is relevant. Since both methods provide useful information about comprehension, both will be discussed here.

Questions. Questions based upon story grammar differ from the traditional comprehension questions because they focus the student's attention upon the exact element of information being questioned. For example, suppose the class has just read "The Ugly Duckling" and one question in the lesson asks students to identify the main idea of the story. What does *main idea* mean in this context? The author's message? The central conflict of the story? The resolution? It could be any of these. By using story grammar, the exact piece of information can be questioned directly, thus helping the student to understand the question and to search for an answer that is relevant.

The use of story grammar to organize questioning also eliminates the questioning of irrelevant details. Just as a main idea question is inappropriately vague when asking about narration, so is the detail question inappropriately focused. Students should be questioned about the various elements in the story grammar. Questions that are not based upon the grammar ask students to recognize or recall elements of the story that are typically forgotten by adults as well as child readers.

Thus, story grammar provides a focus to the questions and, hopefully, the answers about a specific piece of narrative discourse. A basic framework for the questions follows. In each case, the element of story grammar upon which the question is based is also listed.

Setting: Where (or when) did the story happen?
How would the story change if the setting changed?

Character: What is _____ like?
What does _____ do and say that makes him/her like _____?
Why did _____ do _____?

Topic: What is the moral of the story?
What is the author's opinion about _____?

Conflict: What is the problem _____ faces?
How might _____ solve this problem?

Reaction 1: How does _____ feel about the problem?
What does _____ think about the problem?

Attempts: What does _____ do first, second, etc.
Why does _____ fail to solve the problem?
What might _____ do next?

Resolution: What did _____ do to solve the problem?
How was the problem solved?
Who solved _____'s problem?

Reaction 2: How does _____ feel about the solution?
How do you feel about the solution?
How would you solve the problem?

These are some of the questions that might be asked about a piece of narrative discourse. Naturally, they must be modified to fit specific stories. They all focus upon the various elements of the story, however, thus making them useful as an instructional tool and as an evaluation measure. A simple way of keeping track of student performance (informal assessment) is to make a checklist for each student in which successful responses to each category of question can be marked. Such a checklist might look like the one given in Figure 2. If using such a checklist, some record of student performance should be recorded each week. Then a pattern of performance can be detected (as in this sample, where the student is showing problems with the abstraction to the central message of the story) and direct instruction on the kind of thinking necessary to answer this question can be given.

Figure 2. Checklist for Questions about Narration

+ excellent
√ satisfactory
— unsatisfactory

Name _____

story/date	questions							
	setting	character	topic	conflict	reaction	attempts	solution	reaction
XXX	√	√	—	√	—	√	√	√
XXX	√	√	—	√	√	√	√	√
XXX	+	√	—	√	√	√	√	√
XXX	+	√	√	√	+	√	√	√
XXX	√	√	—	—	√	√	√	—

Before leaving this section on questions, one other question must be discussed. So far questions based upon narrative form have been discussed. But all discourse has both form and function. The function of narration, as given in Table 1, is to affect the reader's emotions. You may not like this idea—many seem to find it uncomfortable—but if you stop and think a minute about the stories you like, you will find that each one "grabs" you. A typical response to a story is "I liked it," often without reasons. Stories make us laugh, cry, fear, or feel anger. This is their function—to make us experience life through one or more of the characters.

As a result, it is important to assess a student's reactions to a story. This reaction is another measure of comprehension and can also help us identify other stories for the student. Because of this, an additional column should be added to the checklist given in Figure 2 that indicates student reaction to the story. Again patterns should begin to appear, patterns that show an individual's preference.

Retelling. Story grammar can also be used as the basis of scoring students' retellings or summaries of a story. These can be either written or verbal. In either case, recalls should be scored according to their completeness when compared to the original story. The more elements of story grammar the student can remember, even if in very capsulized form, the better the recall.

This sounds quite reasonable. However, there is an additional factor involved in recalls: memory. Memory is a capacity that develops with age, but exactly the amount of memory to be expected of children of different ages is unknown. Stein and Glenn (1979) have found that most first graders can retell a single-episode story. Research into children's recalls for stories is currently being conducted by a group at Boston University. Berkovich (1979) is studying preschoolers' recalls for parts of stories, while Summers (1979) is studying the recalls of older children in relationship to their comprehension abilities. With these and other such studies, we may soon have enough information to create a developmental scale for scoring children's recalls. Such a scale would indicate the complexity of the discourse to be recalled, the mode of recall (verbal or written), the type of recall (retelling or summary), and the expected completeness of the recall. Until such a scale is developed, our intuitions will have to be used. The suggestions given below are just such intuitions and are currently being piloted in the Montgomery County Public Schools.

Readiness. In addition to using story grammar to shape assessment of student responses to questions and recalls, it can also be used to assess a child's readiness to learn how to read. This is, again, a personal opinion, but it is one based upon observation and upon Stein and Glenn's finding (1979) that first graders could tell stories. Since first graders can create stories and since they learn to read by using stories, they must develop an understanding of story structure before reading. This means reading stories to children and assessing their knowledge of story structure.

To assess reading readiness, give students a picture or a series of pictures in order and ask them to tell you a story about the pictures. A story that identifies the character and specifies the conflict and resolution should be acceptable. Students that just describe the pictures do not yet have a concept of "story." Without such a concept, their comprehension will be limited to the sentence level, and, although they may learn to decode, they will fail to learn that reading is a meaningful activity.

Table 2. Proposed Scoring Criteria for Retelling and Summarizing Narration

Grades	story complexity	mode of recall	form of recall	story grammar elements
K	part of story (heard)	verbal	retelling	events in order character identified
1	single-episode story (heard)	verbal	retelling	events of single episode character identified
2	a) brief multiple-episode story (heard)	verbal	retelling	events in at least 2 episodes theme elements identified
	b) single-episode story (read)	verbal	retelling	events in episode theme elements identified
3	brief multiple-episode story (read)	verbal	retelling	events in all episodes theme elements identified
4	a) complete short story or chapter from book (read)	written/ verbal	retelling	events in all episodes theme elements
	b) whole book	verbal	summary	episodes represented theme elements
5-8	a) complete short story or chapter (read)	written	retelling	events in all episodes theme elements
	b) whole book	written	summary	major episodes theme elements

Research into the utility of story creation as a measure of reading readiness must be done. Of all the contributions of story grammar to the assessment of reading, this may be the greatest since it allows us to observe a child's knowledge of the meaningfulness of discourse. No existing measure of reading readiness can give us this information.

Lyric Discourse

There is, to my knowledge, no research into the nature of lyric discourse, although Ortony's research (1979) into the understanding of metaphor is appropriate. Lyric discourse is used here to refer to prose as well as poetry; it is any description of personal perception. Based upon this definition, one can ask questions about the author's perceptions. Such questions are traditional in literature classes, but they do little to help the reader understand this very difficult type of literature. Research needs to be done before this can be accomplished.

Directions

Once again, there has been little theoretical research into the nature of directions as a form of discourse. However, Jackson (1979) has described the common characteristics of this form. Directions often have:
1. a strong temporal sequence
2. elliptical sentence structure
3. implicit procedures
4. unique abbreviations
5. unidentified referents
6. frequently ambiguous outcomes

The following example demonstrates all of these characteristics.

Aunt Sarah's Delight

    1 cup sugar
    2 eggs
    2 cubes chocolate
1/2 cup butter
1/3 cup sifted flour
1/2 tsp. salt
1/2 tsp. vanilla
    1 cup chopped nuts

Melt chocolate and butter. Beat sugar and eggs. Add flour, salt, and vanilla to batter. Add melted chocolate. Beat. Add nuts. Pour into 8 x 8 greased pan. Bake in 350° oven 30-35 minutes.

First, both the list of ingredients and the directions are given in the order of use. This order is quite rigid. One does not bake before mixing the ingredients or add the chocolate before melting it. At least, if things were done in this order, the results would be most interesting.

Second, the sentences are highly telegraphic. Not only are all the articles removed, but often the object is left unstated. For instance, "Add nuts," can be expanded into its full form: "Add the chopped nuts to the beaten batter." It is up to the reader to flesh out the sentences in the directions.

Third, not all the steps are listed in the directions. "Sifted flour" and "chopped nuts" are terms with implicit processes that must be completed before the step stated in the directions can be followed. In addition, the term "chopped" appears only in the list of ingredients, making it harder to focus upon the implicit step. Thus, readers must constantly recheck themselves as they procede step-by-step through the directions.

Fourth, the reader must become familiar with the unique terms and abbreviations. The reader must know what it means to *beat* the batter and the difference between a *tsp.* and *tbs.* (teaspoon and tablespoon).

Fifth, reference in directions differs from that in other types of discourse. Pronouns are rarely used in directions; instead, confusing lexical substitutions are used. For instance, "batter" is used to stand for a whole list of mixed ingredients. The reader must understand the relationships between terms, and this understanding can be found only in the reader's knowledge.

Last, even if all the steps are followed correctly, the reader may be unsure of the final outcome. Often the only clue as to the outcome is in the title, and titles are often missing or uninformative. In such cases, it is assumed that the reader already knows the end product, but this is not always so, especially with children.

Much research needs to be done in order to understand the significance of the various properties of directions. Which is more important to focus upon, the individual sentences? The final outcome? The words? The abbreviations? Questions like these need to be answered. In the meantime, we should be aware that directions can provide some unique problems and should help students to read this type of discourse.

Questions. One way to do this is to ask questions that can both help the student focus on the unique characteristics of directions and can provide information about student comprehension. Here are some of the questions that might be asked.

order of events:	What should you do first?
	What should you do next?
telegraphic sentences:	What does this tell you to do?
	(Have students paraphrase and elaborate.)
implied procedures:	What are you supposed to do?
	When should you do this?
abbreviations:	What does this mean?

lexical reference: What does this mean?

                       What other words refer to the same thing?

unclear outcome: What are you making?

Recalls. I hesitate to even mention the term "recall" in conjunction with directions because asking a student to recall a set of directions is inappropriate. People usually do not memorize directions in order to follow them. Instead, directions are designed to be used as they are read. So, DO NOT ASK STUDENTS TO RECALL DIRECTIONS. Instead, to assess their understanding of directions, ask them to follow the directions and judge their understanding by the ease with which directions are followed and the appropriateness of the end product.

Readiness. The ability to follow short, verbal directions is often one of the behaviors required of kindergarten children. This is because attention to verbal directions is considered a prerequisite to successful performance in school. Asking students to follow two-or-three step directions is an appropriate task in assessing readiness.

Again, the length of the directions to expect five year olds to follow is established by intuition. Much research needs to be done into the quantity of procedural information a child can process at various ages before we can be sure that a two-or-three step set of directions is appropriate for a five year old.

Persuasion

Persuasive discourse such as advertisements, political speeches, sermons, and editorials makes two demands upon the reader: the topic must be identified and opinion must be separated from fact. Structurally, persuasive discourse looks much like exposition. In fact, Meyer (1979) lists it as one of the kinds of exposition that she has identified. However, the writer's intent when producing persuasive discourse differs greatly from when producing exposition: Persuasive discourse is produced to convince the reader or listener to think and/or act in a specified way. Exposition is written to inform the reader.

To date, no research into the unique characteristics of persuasive discourse has been done. Although rhetoricians may have identified some of the writer's devices, no one knows the effect of these devices upon the reader. Since this type of discourse invades every corner of our lives, it is crucial that we begin to study the ways in which it shapes our thinking.

In the meantime, we can ask students to detect when persuasion exists in discourse, to attend to the words the author uses to persuade the reader, and to abstract the author's attitude toward the topic being discussed. I have no concrete suggestions here and would appreciate hearing from those who do.

Temporal Exposition

The distinction made in this chapter between temporal and topical exposition is a personal one, but it is one that may prove fruitful for both research and curriculum development efforts. Temporal exposition includes all discourse that is written to inform and that contains event sequences. History texts are probably the best example of this type of discourse. Topical or pure exposition includes all discourse that is written to inform and does not contain event sequences. The writing in this chapter is an example of pure exposition. Topical exposition will be discussed in the next section of this chapter; this section will focus upon temporal exposition.

Since no one has, up to this time, discussed the possibility of the existence of temporal exposition, much that is really expository has been labeled *narration*. Thorndyke (1977), for instance, has analyzed the "Circle Island" passage using story grammar. (This passage is a typical social studies text describing the ways the inhabitants of Circle Island solved their problems over the years.) Obviously it is possible to force temporal exposition into a story grammar framework since temporal exposition, like narration, is made up of a series of events. However, there is a difference between these two types of discourse, the difference that exists between history and an historical novel: the difference in function.

The only research into temporal exposition that exists at this time was done by Freedle and Hale (1979). They found that when social studies texts were rewritten as stories, children remembered more of the information. They recommend rewriting social studies into narration for young children. I disagree. I believe that we should be attempting to produce proficient readers, and one characteristic of proficient readers is the ability to read and understand a variety of types of discourse. As a result, I recommend the use of the characteristics of temporal exposition to aid in comprehending this type of discourse.

To do this, it seems reasonable to turn to Schank's (1973) and Frederiksen's (1975) ideas of causal linking. Events in temporal exposition do not always fit into a story grammar framework, but they are always causally and/or temporally linked. In fact, Meyer (1977) focused upon this phenomenon when she found that exposition is often organized in a cause/effect or problem/solution framework. Although focusing upon causality tended to interfere with comprehension of narration (Marshall, 1979), it tends to facilitate comprehension of exposition (Marshall, 1976).

Questions. Based upon what little information is available from research, it seems that it is important to have students identify the events in temporal exposition and to have them understand the relationships among the events. According to Marshall and Glock (1978-1979), fluent readers can understand relationships in exposition while less fluent readers cannot. As a result, two basic types of questions should be asked in order to determine the extent of a student's comprehension of temporal exposition:

> events: What did _____ do?
> How did _____ solve the problem?
> relations: What was _____'s problem?
> What caused _____'s problem?
> What was the result of _____'s actions?

These are only a few of the possible questions to ask. Another set of questions to children make explicit the implied relations in the text. These would have the students supply the missing relational terms between events.

Recall. Students are frequently asked to remember information from temporal exposition. Usually they are asked to remember specific events (e.g., Columbus discovered America in 1492.). Less often they are asked to remember a related set of events. Yet, if we truly wish to assess comprehension of temporal exposition, it is memory for related events that we should measure. Outlines are useful to do this. These outlines need not be formal; in fact, they don't even have to look like a list. Diagrams of the relationships among events are also outlines, and are often more easily produced.

An example might help here. This is one paragraph from a longer passage entitled "Trouble in the Colony" that is currently being used by Kosoff (1979) in her doctoral research.

> The first people to arrive in the new colony settled in the Valley because the Valley land was good for farming. When the good land in the Valley was taken, newly arrived colonists had to settle in the Hills. Life was harder in the Hill Region because the farmland was rocky. Also, the Hill settlers were often attacked by the nearby Sind people. The Sinds did not want the settlers to take over any more of their land.

The relationships among the events in this paragraph are shown graphically in Figure 3. The types of relationships are stated here. They needn't be. The purpose of having students produce displays of this sort is to help them organize information efficiently and to assess their ability to organize. Students working from memory, of course, would not remember all the events. But they should remember the focal ones, the ones toward which the causal arrows point. There are three in this example: The new people settled in the Hills, Hill life was hard, and they were attacked by the Sinds. Students remembering these three pieces of information in isolation are doing well; students who remember these three pieces of information in relationship to each other are doing much better.

Figure 3. Relationships among Events in "Trouble in the Colony"

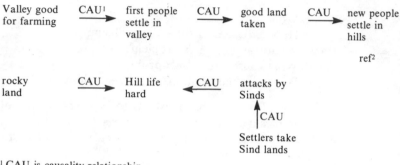

[1] CAU is causality relationship
[2] ref is a referential relationship, in this case the repetition of words

Topical Exposition

Of all the types of written discourse, topical exposition is one of the most difficult to understand (Meyer, 1977; Kintsch, Kozminsky, Sterby, McKoon, and Keenan, 1975). There are several explanations for this. First, topically organized discourse is not based upon the pattern of life experiences; these are temporal. Second, exposition is written less to affect the reader than to present information. Olson (1977) refers to both of these characteristics when he describes the phenomenon of decontextualization in written discourse. For him, written discourse, in its purest form, exists without reference to the world experience of either writer or reader.

In addition to being less dependent upon world knowledge and less appealing to the reader, there is likely to be a third problem with topical exposition. There seems to be no one structure for this type of discourse (Marshall, 1979). This means that there is no framework for the reader to call up to help organize the information. Instead, the reader must recognize the topic and use this to identify information important to remember and less important information (Meyer, 1975). Frequently, the only clues to the organization of information for less proficient readers are the connecting words used by the writer (Marshall & Glock, 1978-1979). These are words like *if, however, for example, nevertheless*, and *therefore*. Without such words in the text, the recalls of less proficient readers are less complete.

Much research into the nature of topical exposition needs to be done. Does it have a specific structure or structures? If so, what is it? How do the traditional ideas of main idea and detail fit with what we know of exposition? These are just a few of the questions that need to be answered.

Assessment. In the meantime, there are a few suggestions that can be made based upon research evidence:

1. People remember superordinate ideas better than subordinate ideas (Kintsch & Keenan, 1973; Meyer, 1975), and they remember subordinate ideas better when these are related with explicit connectors (Marshall & Glock, 1978-1979). As a result, one way to assess understanding of topical exposition is to have the student show the relationships among ideas. This could be done as an illustration, an informal outline, or as a formal outline. The diagram of this paragraph is given in Figure 4. Note that the tree given here represents the super/subordinate relationships among ideas. A tree is a kind of informal outline. Note, in addition, that the superordinate idea here is the one from which all other ideas descend. This is different from the organization of temporal exposition shown in Figure 3. For temporal exposition, the superordinate ideas were those toward which other ideas led. This structural distinction is important to keep in mind.

Figure 4. Relationships among Ideas in Topical Exposition

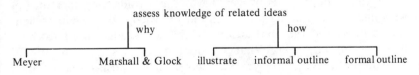

2. Since details are remembered poorly, we should not expect students to remember a plethora of facts. Instead, we should focus both instruction and assessment upon the most important facts, those close to the topic or superordinate but directly related to the topic.
3. Since the presense of logical connectives increases comprehension, these connectors should receive attention both during instruction and during assessment. Students should be asked the meanings of terms like *however* and *therefore*. In addition, students should be asked to supply the appropriate connectors when these are not stated in the text.
4. Concrete information is recalled more readily and more completely than abstract information (Paivio, 1970), and concrete information that is presented with pictorial support is recalled even more completely (Shallert, 1979). Based upon these findings, another instructional and assessment technique would be to have students make illustrations to accompany their texts. The tables and figures given in this chapter are samples of illustrations. They help make ideas more concrete and, therefore, easier to understand. Illustrations would have to be judged for appropriateness and completeness.

Conclusion

Like most reviews of current research, this chapter seems to have uncovered more areas of needed research than areas where research is complete. I do not find this disquieting. On the contrary, I find it exciting. Exciting because research is finally beginning to explain how the comprehension process works. Once we understand the process of comprehension, we can begin to develop instructional and assessment techniques that are appropriate to the process. This is exactly the state of current research and curriculum development.

It is an old Chinese curse to wish upon someone, "May you live in exciting times." It is a curse because of the upheaval that accompanies new developments and the frustration we all feel at the slowness with which things develop. However, I would not trade the experience of watching the continuing growth in our knowledge of the comprehension process and the applications of this knowledge to educational practices for anything. What we do today can shape educational thought and practices for years to come. Such a position has its own rewards, rewards I hope we can all share, now and in the years to come.

Strategies for Controlling Hypothesis Formation in Reading

Bertram Bruce
Andee Rubin
Bolt, Beranek and Newman

Imagine being confronted with the following task: From a limited set of data you are to build an exceedingly complex theory. Every step of the way you will encounter ambiguities. Partial theories will be necessary, but there is no way to be sure until the end that any partial theory can be incorporated into the final theory. Almost all of the possible theories you might consider are wrong, and yet, many of them will have ample supporting evidence. You will be given the data only bits at a time; thus, you may well be sent down what linguists call a "garden path" of misleading theories. You cannot be certain that there is a single theory that best accounts for the data. Even the best theory you find may leave some data unaccounted for. You are to do theory-constructing as you gather the data. The time allotted for the task is vanishingly small, no more than the time it has taken you to read this description of it.

Faced with such a task, a reasonable person might well turn his or her thoughts elsewhere, perhaps to the ballgame outside the window; and that is what many children do when they are given the task of reading. The fact is that reading is a task with all the properties described above: The reader must build a complex theory from limited data in a short time. The data arrive pieces at a time as the eye moves across the page. Reading at a normal pace introduces ambiguity at even the lowest level because the reader can only sample from the text. This ambiguity is magnified at the level of words and sentences. Other ambiguities arise at the higher structural levels. Theories to account for the meaning of parts of the text proliferate because the data are limited and ambiguous, and the theories can become increasingly complex as the reader tries to account for larger portions of the text. Knowledge of the world, the prior text, the author, and the purpose of reading all need to be incorporated into the theories the reader builds, but this knowledge complicates the theories further.

In this paper, we look at the process a reader must use to cope with difficulties of the kinds just described. Essentially, we view reading as a process of forming and evaluating hypotheses to account for the data in the text, and we discuss the central importance in this process of four strategies for controlling the proliferation of hypotheses. The view presented is not unique; what is different is our attempt to draw out the unforeseen implications and consequences of such a view. By taking the notion of "controlling hypothesis formation" seriously, identifying specific strategies and working through an extended example, we describe in more detail the comprehension process when it works—and when it goes awry. Our analysis does not lead to prescriptions of specific instructional methods for reading comprehension. Instead, we hope to provide a concrete reference for teachers of reading to a perspective on the comprehension process which emphasizes: 1) that miscomprehension can be due to good strategies missing the mark; 2) that even a seemingly straightforward text can lead to a large number of varying interpretations when it is read by a group of different readers; and 3) that a choice between two substantially different interpretations can result from a relatively small decision in the comprehension process.

Our analysis includes both a general discussion of the process of answering questions about a reading text passage, and examples from several protocols of students discussing the text. The examples both provide empirical support for the general approach and make the theory more accessible to teachers, students and classrooms.

There is one rather obvious way to cope with a task of the difficulty described above: collect as much knowledge as is possible and apply it at every step of the hypothesis formation process. Such knowledge is of various types. First, readers need knowledge of structures at the levels of letter features, letters, words, sentences, and even whole texts. They also need knowledge of the meaning of these structures, such as the fact that in the passive voice construction the object of an action is in the syntactic subject position. Perhaps most importantly, readers needs pragmatic knowledge—knowledge about the use of language. Included in this last category are knowledge of facts about the world, knowledge of the author, knowledge of the time and place of the writing and reading of the text, knowledge of the task, and knowledge of one's own knowledge and abilities (Brown, 1980). Discussions of the knowledge needed for reading can be found in Adams and Bruce (1980); Rumelhart (1977); and Olson, Duffy, and Mack (in

Bruce and Rubin

press). Coordinating knowledge sources is a complex task, as there is increasing evidence that knowledge sources interact in a *heterarchical* fashion; that is, although they may naturally form a knowledge hierarchy running from orthographic knowledge to expectations about overall text structure, communication is not limited to adjacent members of the hierarchy. Earlier models of reading postulated less complicated mechanisms. The scenario proposed by Gough (1972) and LaBerge and Samuels (1974), for example, involved a visual input being processed sequentially at various knowledge levels, and arriving, finally, at a "meaning." More current models involve each knowledge source putting in its "two cents' worth" at various points in the progression to comprehension of the text (Rumelhart, 1977).

In viewing reading as a *hypothesis-driven* process (Rubin, 1975) we define a hypothesis as a central structure which collects evidence for a particular interpretation of a text. Two general characteristics of hypotheses are important to mention here. First, a hypothesis represents a *possible* interpretation which may later either be proven or disproven. At various points during the reading process it may be in a state of limbo, only partially specified, needing more evidence, or perhaps even uncertain because of conflicting evidence. As a consequence of additional information, the reader may later have to back up and rehypothesize about the meaning of a portion of the text. A second characteristic is that part of the structure of a hypothesis is the specification of those pieces of evidence which support or contradict it. A piece of evidence can even be another hypothesis. Hypotheses are then linked together in a network of "supporting" and "contradicting" relations.

Several existing reading theories share significant properties with the general form described here (although they differ in important details). Goodman (1973) describes receptive language processes in general as hypothesis-based, defining them as "cycles of sampling, predicting, testing, and confirming." He recognizes three levels of cues which readers use: graphemic, syntactic, and semantic; these cue systems are used "simultaneously and interdependently." Productive reading is seen as requiring strategies which facilitate the selection of the most useful cues. Smith (1973) emphasizes the contribution of what he terms "nonvisual" information to reading. This nonvisual knowledge includes what people already know about reading, language, and the world in general. He argues particularly that reading is not decoding to sound, but rather that semantic and other nonvisual processes intercede between visual processes and reading aloud. A different approach, which nevertheless assumes a hypothesis-based process is that of Perfetti (1975). He suggests ways in which the various component processes might interact, basing his overall conclusions on the fact that all the processes which occur during reading comprehension must share a "limited capacity processor."

The limited-capacity processor view suggests a potential problem in the use of knowledge for reading comprehension: Although different types of knowledge are needed to *evaluate* hypotheses, each chunk of knowledge may also aid in the *construction* of new hypotheses. Thus, evaluation and, hence, elimination, of hypotheses vies with new hypothesis formation in determining the size of the hypothesis space. What is needed are strategies for controlling the proliferation of hypotheses. Details of such strategies have been discussed elsewhere (Collins, Brown, & Larkin, 1980; Erman, Hayes-Roth, Lesser, & Reddy, 1980; Rubin, 1975; Woods, 1980). The point we will make here, however, is that strategies that cut down the number of hypotheses for consideration have other, qualitative effects, as well.

We assume that these strategies operate within a process that maintains many hypotheses at once, but actively works on only a few at any one time. New hypotheses are spawned from the ones under active consideration. Thus, a strategy for focusing attention on one hypothesis out of a set of competing hypotheses (or *choice set*, [Rubin, 1975]) would limit the number and type of new hypotheses that are generated. We have identified four such strategies:

1) Jumping to conclusions (choosing one hypothesis out of a choice set and focusing on it despite insufficient evidence).
2) Maintaining inertia (refusing to abandon a hypothesis in spite of contradictory evidence).
3) Relying on background knowledge (using prior knowledge to choose a hypothesis from a set of otherwise equally possible ones).
4) Working backwards from the goal (choosing hypotheses which are clearly and directly related to the goal despite insufficient evidence).

A system using these strategies can begin to cope with a task such as reading. But things do not always go smoothly. The very features that enable the system to handle uncertainties cause it to have somewhat peculiar properties, which may account for both difficulties and successes in reading. In the next section we see how a hypothesis-driven system with these strategies might operate in reading a simple story, and,

Bruce and Rubin

in the following section, how it may also produce misunderstanding. Finally, we discuss a perspective on reading instruction that may be drawn from these examples.

Hypothesis-Driven Comprehension of a Simple Story

If the reading process is in fact hypothesis-driven, we would expect to see evidence of this characteristic in people's reading behavior. In this section, we analyze a short passage and describe how a hypothesis-driven process might answer comprehension questions about it. The passage is taken from the Educational Testing Service's *Cooperative English Tests* (1960). Although we use a test passage and the accompanying test questions in our discussion, our purpose is not to criticize the test, but to explore the processes involved in understanding a passage well enough to answer questions about it.

> "Alice!" called a voice.
>
> The effect on the reader and her listener, both of whom were sitting on the floor, was instantaneous. Each started and sat rigidly intent for a moment; then, as the sound of approaching footsteps was heard, one girl hastily slipped a little volume under the coverlet of the bed, while the other sprang to her feet and in a hurried, flustered way pretended to be getting something out of a tall wardrobe.
>
> Before the one who hid the book had time to rise, a woman of fifty entered the room and, after a glance, cried, "Alice! How often have I told you not to sit on the floor?"
>
> "Very often, Mommy," said Alice, rising meekly, meantime casting a quick glance at the bed to see how far its smoothness had been disturbed.
>
> "And still you continue such unbecoming behavior."
>
> "Oh, Mommy, but it is so nice!" cried the girl. "Didn't you like to sit on the floor when you were fifteen?"

The first question on the comprehension test is:

1. Alice's companion was
   a. a girl
   b. her brother
   c. the family dog
   d. a doll

In order to answer this question, the reader first must identify the characters in the story and decide which one corresponds to each referring expression in the text. This is no simple task, as several different characters are introduced in the first few lines of this story. One coherent hypothesis identifies three separate people: the owner of the voice (later to be identified as "Mommy"), the reader (also described as the "one girl" who "hastily slipped a little volume under the coverlet of the bed"), and the listener (hypothesized to be "the other" who "sprang to her feet"). There are several other only slightly less coherent hypotheses, however, which a reader could easily construct. Certainly the book-hider could be the listener and the wardrobe-looker the reader, rather than vice-versa. Or some readers might postulate that five different people are described, judging the link between "the reader and the listener" and the two girls to be insufficiently clear. In fact, if "another" is substituted for "the other," this link is effectively broken and the number of people in the room becomes unclear. The question itself, which asks about Alice's companion (not companions), actually provides some of the most straightforward evidence that there are only two people in the room when the story opens.

Even if a reader has settled on the interpretation that identifies two girls in the room, further inferences must be made to demonstrate that one of them is Alice. A hint is offered when the "woman of fifty" reprimands one of the girls by name. But interpreting this hint correctly requires postulating that the woman is in fact addressing "the one who hid the book" and, furthermore, that "the reader" described several lines earlier is the same character. If all of these inferences are made and coordinated, the reader of the passage can conclude that Alice's companion was a girl.

The second question is what has been called an "inferential" question and introduces the possibility for even more complex hypotheses:

> 2. When Alice heard the approaching footsteps, she probably was
>   e. angry
>   f. alarmed
>   g. puzzled
>   h. amused

In order to answer this question, the reader must first be able to identify Alice and decide which of the actions described in the story should be attributed to her. As explained above, this in itself involves several plausible hypotheses, and we can add here that it is possible to answer the first question correctly without deciding that Alice is the one who hid the book rather than the one who occupied herself with the wardrobe. Whichever girl is Alice, the description "started and sat rigidly intent" will be relevant to any hypothesis about her reaction, since both girls acted the same. However, this reaction is easily interpretable as either alarm or anger, and the reader must use additional information from the text to decide between the two hypotheses. All the other relevant details occur further on in the text

Bruce and Rubin

than the description of the incident we are interpreting. Alice hides a book "hastily" and later seems concerned that her mother not discover that it is under the coverlet. These actions suggest guilt, but they do not definitively discriminate between alarm and anger, which are both plausible reactions to feeling guilty. In fact, it seems that one of the few phrases which help the reader determine that Alice is *alarmed* is "rising meekly"; if Alice had in fact been angry, she most likely would have acted more aggressively. In this case, an "incorrect" hypothesis has almost as much supporting evidence as the correct one.

The third question is:

3. We may infer that Alice is
   a. stupid and resentful
   b. very much in love
   c. fifteen years of age
   d. a spoiled child

The phrasing of this question alerts us to the fact that inference will be particularly important (although we have just seen that inference is *always* important). In fact, choosing answer c)—that Alice is 15—is risky at best and in no way "provable"; a plausible case could be made for several of the choices. Deciding on c) requires knowledge of a strategy: "if you're being blamed for something, attempt to elicit the sympathy of the blaming authority by getting them to admit they've done the same thing." In order to infer that this strategy is being applied here, the reader must first realize that Alice is being blamed for sitting on the floor, a conclusion which follows fairly directly from the mother's first question, Alice's meek response, and the mother's follow-up question. Then we must note that, in speaking to her mother, Alice has added a piece of information to the description of her action which (under this hypothetical persuasion strategy) indicates she is herself 15. It is worthwhile noting that almost all of these conclusions are based on the reader's understanding of the implications of speech acts (see Cohen & Perrault, 1979). For example, although Alice's final remark is syntactically a question, its real purpose is to *persuade*, not to gain information. Neither is her mother's "How often have I told you not to sit on the floor?" really a question; it is closer to an accusation. The inference of guilt is based on the reader's knowledge of the social conventions surrounding speech acts and of mother/child relationships.

Given that we understand, at least sketchily, how the reader might conclude that Alice is 15, we are still faced with an important problem in understanding how one can answer this question. The problem is one of control structure: How does the reader choose this particular reasoning path out of all the possible ones to follow? Another set of inferences might lead the reader to conclude that Alice's mother is a stern person, but a reader cannot afford to entertain all possible conclusions. In this case, reasoning backward from the question allows the reader to choose the most relevant paths to follow. Good test-takers read over the possible answers to multiple-choice questions and use them to guide their detailed thinking. In this case, in considering answer c, the reader focuses on the final paragraph where there is a reference to age, and attempts to construct a link back to the answer. We can get some feel for the distinction between inferences made while reading the story and those made in response to questions by considering the comparison between a description of Alice given just after reading the story and a description given after answering the questions. Mention of Alice's age would be much more common in the second description; although the information necessary to infer her age is present in the story itself, the actual inference is probably not made (or not remembered) unless explicitly asked for.

There is more evidence of question-directed inference in the fourth question:

> 4. When she heard her name called, Alice was evidently
>   a. reading aloud
>   b. lying in bed
>   c. reading to herself
>   d. making her bed

We know fairly directly that a "reading aloud" is taking place from the phrase "the reader and her listener." By following the chain of references through the next several sentences, we can infer that it was Alice who hid the book. However, we have no reason to believe that Alice was reading rather than listening; the fact that she hid the book supports this hypothesis, but does not confirm it. A "process of elimination" strategy is necessary to answer the question. In this case, two of the other three possible answers are easy to rule out. The only other answer which makes some sense is c.—reading to herself. Alice might have been reading to herself while her companion read out loud, possibly from the same book. Such a hypothesis requires only a little more extrapolation than the "reading aloud" hypothesis.

One implication of these last two examples is that a child may do better on a reading test by using certain strategies which might be termed test-taking skills. These strategies are examples of reading with a goal, and they must be considered part of the knowledge necessary to perform well on such reading tests. The existence of such question-based inference strategies also points out a weakness in determining the difficulty of a text *in vacuo*, i.e., outside of a task definition. It is easier in general to check whether or not a given fact is consistent with a story than it is to answer a more general question.

Finally, the fifth question:

> 5. Alice was worried about the appearance of the bed because
>   a. she had neglected to make it up
>   b. her companion had been sitting on it
>   c. her companion was hiding under it
>   d. she was afraid her mother might find the book

Answering this question is closely related to answering Questions 2 and 3; it requires a global hypothesis about the interaction between Alice and her mother. While the exchange between them demonstrates anger on the mother's part and guilt on Alice's, the topic of their disagreement is *not*, in fact, Alice's real concern. If it were, the answer might be *b*. In fact, it is not too difficult to construct a hypothesis with supporting evidence which would lead the reader to this response. For a reader unfamiliar with the word "coverlet," it may not be clear that the act of hiding the book changed the appearance of the bed. (Consider the difference in effect if the word had been "dust ruffle.") Such a reader might, in reading the fourth paragraph, hypothesize that Alice was concerned that the bed might be rumpled because someone had been sitting on it, since the conversation Alice is having with her mother at this point is about sitting in inappropriate places. This hypothesizing process would lead the reader to choose *b* as the answer.

The hypotheses which lead to the "correct" answer *d* are no less complex. We have already discussed the inference that Alice is the one who hid the book under the coverlet; the final move to comprehending the relationship of that action to her mother requires some pragmatic knowledge about *why* people hide things. In a little more detail, the inferential process might proceed as follows

> *Fact from story:* Alice hid the book under the coverlet.
> *Real-world knowledge:* People hide things so that other people won't find them.
> *Hypothesis:* Alice hid the book when she heard her mother approaching. (From the beginning, Alice knew who it was, although we did not.) When her mother was in the room, Alice was worried about the bed.

Real-world knowledge: Hiding something means you worry about other people finding it when they are around.

Conclusion: Alice was afraid her mother might find the book.

The reader finally arrives at an answer after a long and sometimes tenuous chain of inferences.

In a slightly more rigorous way, we can describe 12 different, reasonably coherent interpretations of this story based on three separate ambiguities. The first ambiguity involves the number of girls in the room. We have already seen how the information given does not clearly answer the question "How many girls were in the room?" and we will describe below how readers made arguments for the answers "One," "Two," and "Three." Two of the protocols below also highlight two possible hypotheses explaining Alice's alarm when she hears her mother's footsteps; readers decide that she is concerned either about being caught with the book or about being caught on the floor. They also differ in their attribution of motives to Alice. Some feel she is sitting on the floor when her mother arrives because she did not have time to get up, but others feel it is a deliberate attempt to distract her mother from the book hidden under the covers of the bed. Taking all possible combinations of options on these three points (3, 2, and 2 options, respectively), we can construct 12 interpretations of the story. With hypotheses proliferating in this way, it's no wonder readers resort to powerful heuristics for limiting the possibilities they entertain.

Strategies for Controlling Hypotheses

The examples in this section illustrate four mechanisms for controlling the proliferation of hypotheses. They are drawn from oral protocols of children or adults answering questions about the above passage after reading it. All four demonstrate ways in which these hypothesis-limiting strategies can go awry, leading the well-intentioned reader to the wrong conclusion.

Jumping to Conclusions

At the beginning of a text passage, the opportunity and necessity of jumping to conclusions with insufficient evidence is greatest. The reader has only a limited amount of information and the number of plausible hypotheses is large. Obviously, the accepted conclusions are sometimes wrong.

Questioner: How many people do you think were in the room before her mother came in?

John (an 11-year-old boy): Including Alice, I think three. Yea, because one's putting up the wardrobe...no, maybe one...two or three, I'm not...I'm sure it's in there.

Q: Why don't you say what you think and then look back and see if you think something different?

J: Sure. I think it was three. Because one of them put the book under the bed and one sprang up to the wardrobe and if Alice was sitting on the floor at the same time and didn't have a chance to get up, then I would pretty much presume that one couldn't have done both those things before Alice could get off the floor. I'll look back now.

Q: Okay...you want to look back now?

J: Sure. Ah...yes..."one girl hastily slipped a little volume"... it could be two...oh, there are only two of them...there's a reader and a listener and it was Alice who put it under the bed.

In this excerpt, we can see that John decided there were three characters in the room because he did not take all the evidence into account. He focused in his inference on figuring out whether or not the same person who was standing at the wardrobe had hidden the book, taking for granted that Alice, who remained on the floor, did neither. John essentially missed the implication of the first line of the third paragraph ("Before the one..."), which clarifies the fact that Alice was the one who hid the book. While his strategy simplified the comprehension process, it led him to the wrong conclusion. Notice that John, who is quite a sophisticated reader for his age, had the ability to analyze and alter his hypothesis in the face of new evidence; this capacity is crucial for remedying the effects of jumping to conclusions.

Maintaining Inertia

A rather surprising example of a reader's tendency to cling to hypotheses even in the face of some conflicting evidence occurred when Karen, a well-educated, literate adult, read the passage and answered the comprehension questions. As it turns out, she answered only 2 out of the 5 questions "correctly." Examining the hypotheses this subject reported in her summary, however, we found that she had carefully and properly articulated a "garden path" hypothesis (that is, one which is plausible except for some easily overlooked piece of refuting evidence).

Karen made only one true mistake: She failed to connect "one girl..., while the other..." with the idea of two girls. Therefore, in her recall, Alice both hid the book and went to the wardrobe; she was also sitting on the floor when her mother entered the room. Like most readers, the subject felt obliged to account for why the book was secret; she assumed that it had to be a diary. Karen paid more attention to Alice and her motives in understanding why she hid the book than do most readers; usually readers think the mother would consider reading the book to be sufficient cause for blame. Her scenario, then, was that Alice was sitting on the floor by herself, reading her diary, when the story opened.

In answering the first question, Karen felt that, given the options, *doll* was the best answer. Little girls do read to their dolls, and a fantasy world is the safest place for a diary's secrets. Since the subject didn't identify "the reader and her listener" with "one girl..., while the other," the usual path to answering this question was blocked. Therefore, she was obliged to rely on a longer chain of more tenuous question-time inferences.

The second question was answered conventionally; as discussed in the last section, Alice hurried to hide the book, so she must have been alarmed.

The third question, beginning "We may *infer* that," suggested to the subject that *further* inferences were called for. Having already concluded that Alice was 15 years old, she regarded that conclusion as explicitly stated, not inferred. Here again, the supposition that Alice was reading her secret diary figures prominently in the sequence of steps Karen took to the conclusion. Alice could most plausibly be "very much in love" because that would be recorded in her diary, and a girl of 15 would especially not want her mother to know that.

The fourth question was answered reasonably given the episodic structure set up to answer the first question. This structure says that when her name was called, Alice was reading to "her listener," the doll. The subject chose to describe it as "reading to herself" rather than "reading aloud" because the doll was only being read to in Alice's imagination. "Alice was *evidently* reading to herself."

At this point, it seems that Karen has really stretched her hypothesis beyond the limits of feasibility. She has had to make the same initial hypothesis. Yet, at each point it is easier for Karen to continue to elaborate her hypothesis than it is for her to abandon it and construct an entirely new one. Her tendency to follow the implications of her initial reaction has led her down the wrong path, even though such a strategy is in general quite effective.

Bruce and Rubin

Relying on Background Knowledge

Carol, a fifth grader, illustrated the third strategy in her interpretation of the text. When a passage is difficult and too many hypotheses suggest themselves, readers may focus on those which are most strongly supported by their own background knowledge.

Carol found the story difficult and had to read it through twice; part of her discussion with the interviewer follows:

Q: Can you remember one specific thing you felt you didn't understand the first time and how it helped you when you read it again?

C: I think about the volume and the coverlet and the tall wardrobe and I didn't really understand that but when I read it over again I said "Oh yeah." I don't know why the mother didn't want her to sit on the floor. I mean I spend half of my life on the floor.

Q: Can you do the summary thing again? Tell us again in a few sentences?

C: Umm, there was two girls and I think this is what happened, she had a friend over or something and that one person who's reading the book to the other person and then they heard the mother come in and then the mother got all upset because she was you know, they were reading on the floor and the - umm, I think it was Alice, the one girl or something said didn't she sit on the floor when you were fifteen and I was a bit sort of flabbergasted at why would someone get so upset about you know sitting on the floor.

Q: Why did Alice slip the book under the covers of the bed do you think?

C: I have no idea, I don't if she (inaudible) trying to put it in her bookcase, I mean if her mother gets so upset that she's sitting on the floor I think she would take a fit that she saw a book on the floor or (inaudible)

Q: You think Alice's mother had ever been angry with her before for sitting on the floor?

C: Yes, because she said how many times have I told you, actually my mother will do that when it's the first time I have ever done it, I think (inaudible) nervous reaction. They sort of want to scare the kids, you know.

We can see from these excerpts that Carol drew heavily from her own interactions with her mother, commenting on both similarities and differences between the story and her experience. The reason she understood the story better the second time was that she had read the part in which Alice's mother gets angry at her for sitting on the floor. This interaction gave her a framework within which to understand the rest of the story, so she returned to the beginning of the story and interpreted Alice's earlier actions in the same light. Based on her hypothesis, Carol decided that Alice's major concern all along had been that her mother would see the book on the floor. In a sense, Carol seized on the one incident in the story that struck a responsive chord for her and used it as her perspective for viewing the whole. In so doing, she misunderstood the beginning of the story—in particular, Alice's motives—but constructed for herself a coherent interpretation. In this way, individual bits of background knowledge may have an inordinate effect on the reader's interpretation, as much of the text is funneled through a narrow interpretive channel.

Working Backwards from the Goal

We return to Karen's protocol for an example of the fourth hypothesis-limiting strategy. We have already seen how Karen constructed the questions; Karen used the important test-taking skill of working backwards from the possible answers. This strategy forced her to integrate the presuppositions of her chosen answers into her hypothesis. Thus, her "wrong" answer for Question 1 strengthened the diary hypothesis, which was therefore trusted again in Question 3. Her answer to Question 4 was based on her answer to Question 1. Indeed, from Karen's point of view all of the questions were based on understanding Alice's diary: its audience, its import, its content, and its secrecy. For Karen, a central strategy for comprehending test passages and limiting hypotheses backfired and in the process of answering the questions, she became more deeply entrenched in her own version of the story.

A Perspective on Reading Instruction

The examples in the previous sections exemplify both the power and potential dangers of hypothesis-limitation strategies. Although meaningful reading could not exist without some such strategies, readers and teachers must also be aware of their potential to lead to misinterpretation. This means that diagnosing reading difficulties may be more difficult than it first appears. Our measures of comprehension invariably freeze the process of comprehending to look at some

Bruce and Rubin

product, which may over- or underestimate the reader's comprehension of the text. The hypothesis-based view we have presented identifies dimensions on which the product may not accurately reflect the reader's comprehension. Getting the right answer may be a result of jumping to a conclusion on the basis of what would ordinarily have been insufficient evidence. A wrong answer may reflect the construction of a hypothesis only distantly connected to the question.

For the task of simple arithmetic problems, it has been shown (Brown & Burton, 1978) that one's first intuitions about the source of a student's difficulties can be far off the mark. Moreover, a simple, underlying misconception about arithmetic procedures may manifest itself in a variety of surface errors. For the much more complex task of reading, we should expect more difficulty in discovering underlying misconceptions which affect the process.

There is one saving grace: The very intricate interconnectedness of the hypothesis network can be turned to advantage. Rather than insisting that an error be traceable to a misreading of one phrase of the text, we should be more inclined to explore the reader's entire structure of reasoning about the text.

"Carelessness" is an attribution that says we do not understand details of the reader's hypothesis instantiation process. The reader (Karen) who missed 3 of 5 questions on the story about Alice was careless, to be sure, but all readers are careless in that sense. It is carelessness with respect to specific parts of the text and a specific hypothesis that leads to difficulties. Successful fast reading occurs when the reader's intentional carelessness causes the reader to miss only the bits of evidence that support incorrect hypotheses or contradict correct ones.

Another characteristic of a hypothesis-driven process derives from the power inherent in having knowledge of the task. By drastically reducing the number of relevant hypotheses, such knowledge increases one's reading effectiveness but, of course, only with respect to the given task. This explains why asking questions before reading is so effective. A question defines the task for the reader, thereby suggesting which hypotheses are most worth developing. Asking questions after reading can similarly focus a reader's interpretation (or reinterpretation) on specific aspects of the story, as was shown in our Alice story protocol. Similar results have been found in research on perspectives-taking (Anderson, Pichert, & Shirley, 1979).

Closely related to the issue of specific questions is that of understanding the general purpose for reading a particular text.

Reading with a different understanding of purpose from that of the author or another reader can lead to radically different interpretations of a text or to comprehension difficulties (Adams & Bruce, 1980). Perhaps some readers' difficulties may be traceable to their failure to read with a purpose, or to their working towards inappropriate goals.

These considerations suggest that it is essential to ensure that the reading task involve a credible purpose and that the text itself not betray that purpose. It is too often the case that the communicative function of a text, e.g., to persuade, to inform, or to entertain, gets obscured in the processes of simplifying and standardizing that are carried out before its inclusion in a school book. When students are trying to master a skill as complex as reading comprehension, they need and deserve texts that provide clear purposes that help control the hypothesis formation process.

Conclusion

One of the great frustrations for a writer is that thoughts can never be completely and accurately encoded into words. It is impossible to draw the line that says, "this thought is not relevant to the present issue." Also, words themselves have histories of personal use which call forth both wanted and unwanted meanings. What a writer can do is to suggest, to point, to indicate, or at most, to draw a blueprint. It is then the reader's task to create anew from that blueprint a meaning that, to the extent that communication succeeds, matches the writer's salient thoughts. Reading is not decoding symbols, but creating meaning from symbols.

As a creator of meaning, the reader draws on many resources, especially various kinds of knowledge and the ability to construct hypotheses. Equally important, the reader has strategies for applying this knowledge, strategies which limit the proliferation of hypotheses. These strategies are necessary and are used to good effect by successful readers, but they also sometimes lead to unexpected difficulties. Understanding this process is an essential part of our understanding of reading. The perspective this viewpoint affords can be an aid to teachers in thinking about the underlying causes of poor reading comprehension.

Bruce and Rubin

Organizational Aspects of Text: Effects on Reading Comprehension and Applications for the Classroom

Bonnie J.F. Meyer
Arizona State University

This chapter reviews research dealing with the effects on reading comprehension of aspects of text structure and coherence.[1] Meyer's approach (1975) to prose analysis, a procedure for identifying text structure, is outlined, and findings from studies utilizing this procedure are discussed. Signaling of text structure, a technique to increase text coherence, has been encouraged traditionally by composition teachers. Studies examining the influence on comprehension of this signaling factor in text also are reviewed. A model is proposed which recognizes signaling to be one factor in a series of interacting reader and text variables which affect recall. The relative effects of signaling on recall are seen to be dependent on such reader attributes as ability to use the "structure strategy" in reading, and adequacy of text organization skills as well as the difficulty level of the text. In addition, the research is examined in terms of its implications for teachers. Applications are made in two areas: guidelines for selecting classroom materials and methods for improving reading comprehension.

Research Approach, Outcomes, and Interpretations

Structure in Text

Through application of Meyer's prose analysis system (1975), all of the information from a text is represented in a detailed outline or tree structure called the content structure. The content structure shows how some ideas in the text are superordinate to other ideas. Some ideas from a text are located at the top levels of the content structure and they correspond to the main ideas, gist, or macropropositions of the text.

Other ideas are located at the middle levels and correspond to supporting details, while others are found at the bottom levels of the content structure and correspond to very specific details. The top level ideas dominate their subordinate ideas. The lower level ideas give further information about the ideas above them in the structure.

The interrelationships among these ideas are classified with labels from case grammar (Fillmore, 1968) and semantic grammar of propositions (Grimes, 1975). Case or role relationships from case grammar specify relationships within clauses and simple sentences, while rhetorical relationships from the semantic grammar of propositions specify the relationships among sentences, paragraphs, and larger text segments. The analysis is a propositional analysis system; certain predicates or relationships dictate moving down a level in the structure and thereby form the hierarchical tree structure.

The rhetorical relationships play a crucial part in the content structure since they interrelate sentences, subordinate certain propositions to other propositions, and give a text its top-level structure. The rhetorical relationships fall into five basic groups: causation (antecedent/consequent), comparison, collection, description, and response (problem/solution) (Meyer, 1975; Meyer, in press).

An *antecedent/consequent* or covariance rhetorical relationship shows a causal relationship between topics. The relationship between the two propositions is antecedent/consequent in the following example taken from an advertisement that appeared in *Better Homes and Gardens* magazine: "If you had two eggs this morning, you're already *over* the daily cholesterol limit." Eating the eggs (antecedent) resulted in boosting you over the cholesterol limit (consequent).

A *comparison* relationship points out differences and similarities between two or more topics. Comparison top-level structures have been found to be particularly memorial (Meyer & Freedle, 1979; Meyer & Rice, 1980). Analogy, alternative, and adversative are three formats of comparison structures. A comparison: analogy relationship is exemplified in the Puppy Chow advertisement: "You should be as careful choosing a puppy food as you are choosing a baby food." A comparison: alternative relationship presents equally weighted, but mutually exclusive, positions as in "Heavy Duty Reynolds Wrap gives you two juicy options (for baking turkey): juicy and wrapped or juicy and tented." A comparison: adversative relationship unequally emphasizes opposing viewpoints or events; an example is found in the advertisement "Our cakes feature delicious almonds, not walnuts."

My colleagues and I have studied students' recall from a number of passages organized with adversative top-level structures (Bartlett, 1978; Brandt, 1978; Haring, 1978; Meyer, 1975; Meyer, Brandt, & Bluth, 1980; Meyer & Freedle, 1979; Meyer, Haring, Brandt, & Walker, 1980; Meyer & Rice, 1980; Swanson, 1979). Most of these passages have been expository text taken from magazines and textbooks; the passages have presented a favored view and an opposing view on topics such as railroad development, loss of water from the human body, whales, and future energy sources. The top-level structures in these passages were often cued or signaled for the reader by such words as "in contrast." An analysis of an Aesop fable (Meyer, Haring, Brandt, & Walker, 1980) showed the fable to be comprised of two sub-stories: one about an honest woodman and the other about a dishonest woodman; the overall top-level structure for the story was comparison: adversative as explicitly signaled by the author in the moral, "Honesty is the best policy."

The *collection* relationship shows how ideas or events are related together into a group on the basis of some commonality, such as a sequence of events organized by time order or space order. The collection: time order sequence is a frequently used top-level structure in social studies textbooks.

Description relationships give more information about a topic by presenting attributes, specifics, explanations, or settings. These descriptive rhetorical relationships subordinate some propositions to others. The superordinate proposition is frequently stated first in a passage followed by supporting propositions which add examples, color, or additional qualities. These descriptive propositions are placed a level lower in the hierarchical structure than the proposition they describe. The who, what, where, when, and why approach of journalists is a further specification of this top-level structure. The who and what refer to the agent, action, patient, and instrument in the major proposition on the topic, while the where, when, and why refer to setting and explanation types of descriptions of the topic.

The *response* rhetorical relationship includes the remark and reply, question and answer, and problem and solution formats; some overlap in content between the propositions interrelated by response relationships is a requirement of this structure. For example, the response: question/answer structure is found in the advertisement "Your shish kabobs look so tantalizing. Should your glasses be spotty? Get the Cascade look...virtually spotless glasses" (note the overlap of spots on glasses). *Better Homes and Gardens* magazine runs a feature entitled, "Tips, Tools, and Techniques," that explicitly signals the response problem/solution top-level structure to its readers; for example, "PROBLEM: After you've waxed the car, dried residue lingers around the grill.... SOLUTION: A flagged-tip nylon paintbrush will remove the polish from crevices without scratching the paint (H.G., Springville, Tenn.)." Scientific articles and fairy tales are often written with response top-level structures. The scientific research report with its problem, method, results, and discussion is a further specification of the response top-level structure. Stories from various cultures appear to differentially specify the response rhetorical relationship (Bartlett, 1932; Colby, 1973; Rice, 1978); story grammars (Mandler & Johnson, 1977; Rumelhart, 1975; Stein, 1979; Thorndyke, 1977; van Dijk, 1976) show how the response relationship has been further specified for stories from Western cultures.

The content structure depicts three important aspects of text: the top-level structure, the macropropositions, and the micropropositions. The top-level structure is the rhetorical relationship that ties all of the propositions in a text together and gives it its overall organization. Top-level structures are typical forms of text that define it as a certain type. They are ways of organizing topics, but are independent of them. For example, the comparison top-level structure is a comparison top-level structure regardless of whether it compares two views on the reading process or two view on nuclear energy. Top-level structures have been referred to in literature as schematic structures (Kintsch & van Dijk, 1978), superstructures (van Dijk, 1979), topoi (Aristotle, trans., 1960), writing paradigms (D'Angelo, 1979), overall writing plans (Meyer, 1979) and patterns (Niles, 1974).

The macropropositions include the top-level structure of a text and the content and relationships in propositions occurring at the top third of the content structure. The macropropositions are the main ideas from passages and are better remembered than the micropropositions found at lower levels in the content structure. Frequently, in well-written texts the macropropositions are explicitly stated. In text of poorer quality, macropropositions must be inferred from the micropropositions by the text analyst and reader by processes on the nature of van Dijk's (1977, 1979) macrorules of deletion, generalization, and construction.

The micropropositions include the propositions at the middle and bottom levels of the content structure. They consist of events, actions, processes, or states often localized in some setting and described in terms of their participants which are identified by case roles, such as agent and instrument. These propositions are found in clauses and sentences and are connected to each other by referential identity and such rhetorical relationships as collections, temporally ordered collections, and antecedent/consequent.

In summary, the text structure specifies the interrelationships among items of information which compose the text, as well as indicating the subordination and coordination of this information (Meyer, 1975, 1977, 1979). Thus, a text structure provides an organizational structure which can be used during reading for understanding information and judging its importance. As an example, Figure 1 depicts the superordinate conceptual structure of an article about supertankers (see Appendix). The macropropositions at the top third of the total content structure correspond to what has commonly been called a text's message; the micropropositions at the middle third corresponds to major details which support the premises of the message, and the bottom third corresponds to minor details (Meyer, 1979; Meyer, Brandt, & Bluth, 1980). The text structure (depicted from the author's perspective) highlights that information which is interrelated by its superordinate structure, while it deemphasizes information interrelated at lower levels (Meyer, 1975).

Five basic research findings have emerged from examining the relationship between the content structure of prose and what people remember after reading it. First, the macropropositions which are located high in the content structure are recalled and retained better than micropropositions which are located at the lower levels (Kintsch & Keenan, 1973; Mandler & Johnson, 1977; Meyer, 1971, 1975, 1977; Meyer & McConkie, 1973; Thorndyke, 1977). Second, the type and structure of relationships among ideas in prose dramatically influence recall when they occur at the top levels of the content structure; however, when the same relationships occur low in the structure, they have little effect on recall (Meyer, 1975). Third, different types of relationships at the top levels of the prose structure differentially affect memory (Meyer & Freedle, 1979). Fourth, students who are able to identify and use these top-level structures in prose remember more from their reading than those who do not (Meyer, 1979; Meyer, Brandt, & Bluth, 1980). Fifth, students can be taught to identify these different top-level structures or writing plans used by authors; this training increases their comprehension of text as measured by free recall (Bartlett, 1978; Meyer, 1979).

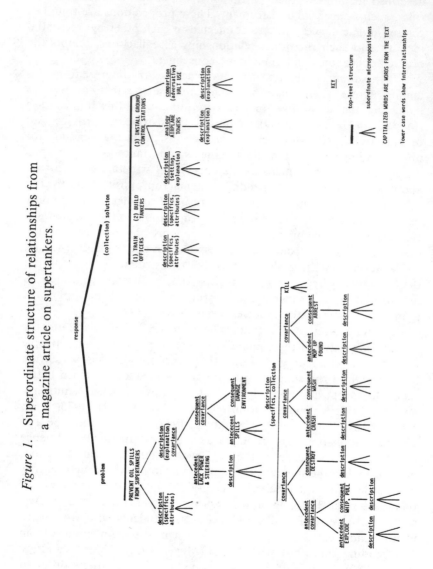

Figure 1. Superordinate structure of relationships from a magazine article on supertankers.

Meyer

Signaling of the Text Structure

Signaling has been defined as information in text which does not add new content about a topic, but which gives emphasis to certain aspects of the semantic content or points out aspects of the structure of the content (Meyer, 1975). The types of signaling which have been identified include explicit statement of the structure of relations in the text structure, preview statements, summary statements, and pointer words or evaluative signaling. The studies to be discussed in this chapter involve only signaling of the first variety, the structure of relationships, and only signaled relationships among major propositions. In some of these studies where recall from passages with- and without-signaling have been compared, signaling words have been deleted in the without-signaling versions, reducing the total number of words. In other of the studies, the signaling words have been deleted, but the number of words in the with- and without-signaling version has been kept constant by adding articles, reducing sentence length, and repeating words.

The signaled relationships at the superordinate level in the structure are the rhetorical relationships of causation, comparison, collection, description, and response. Signaling of these relationships explicitly points them out to readers; examples of signaling for causal relationships include "therefore," "as a result," "so that," "in order to," and "because," and for comparison relationships include "in contrast," "however," "but," and "on the other hand." If signaling is not provided by a writer, then the reader must infer an appropriate logical relationship among propositions. This type of signaling is parallel to Halliday and Hasan's conjunction (1976) cohesion; however, it is examined at the macroproposition level where it interrelates groups of sentences and paragraphs rather than clauses and sentences at the microproposition level of text structure.

Disparate findings have been reported from studies (Britton, Meyer, Glenn, & Penland, in press; Marshall & Glock, 1978-1979; Meyer, 1975, 1977, 1981; Meyer, Brandt, & Bluth, 1980; Meyer & Rice, 1980) which have examined the effects on recall of signaling the rhetorical relationships in text. Figure 2 presents the model which will be used to explain these findings (Meyer & Rice, 1980).

The model is limited to text which presents propositions that are interrelated logically in a hierarchical organization. This includes most expository and narrative text, but not text which primarily presents a collection of descriptions of a topic. In descriptive text (Flower, 1979; see attribution discourse type in Meyer, 1977; Meyer & Freedle, 1979)

Figure 2. Model depicting the interaction of reader text variables
which affect quality and quantity of recall
from hierarchically organized text.

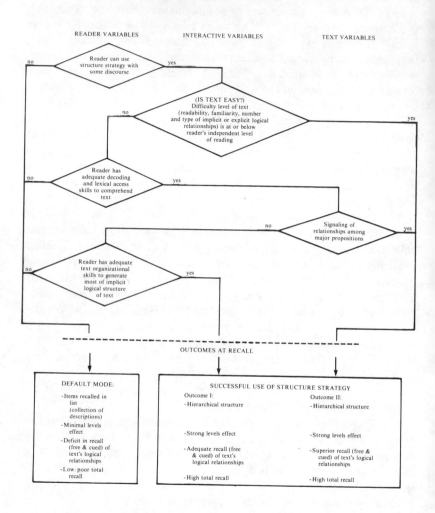

the structure is more linear and list-like than hierarchical.

The model is also limited to adolescents and adults who are attending school. It may generalize to younger children; but the studies have only dealt with ninth graders to graduate students. Data from middle (40-54 years) and older adults (65 and older), who are no longer attending school, suggest that these adults may use strategies for selecting types of information from text to remember (Meyer, 1980; Meyer & Rice, 1979) which differ from the strategy implicitly or explicitly taught in most contemporary schools (i.e., DeBoer & Dallmann, 1960), the *structure strategy*.

The Structure Strategy: Follow the Text's Superordinate Relational Structure; Focus on the Text's Message and How it Relates to Supporting Major Details

The structure strategy has been substantially documented in recent years; it appears to be the dominant strategy employed in prose learning studies by proficient readers at the high school, college, and university levels. Its outcome is superior recall of information high in the content structure as compared to low level information; this has been termed the levels effect (Kintsch & van Dijk, 1978). Also, the superordinate relational structure of the recall protocols produced by deployment of this strategy is similar to that of the text (Meyer, 1979; Meyer & Freedle, 1979). That is, both the protocol and original text have been the same top-level structure (such as problem/solution—see Figure 1) and most of the same major supporting relationships (such as the causal and comparison relationships in Figure 1). This strategy is also related to comparatively high levels of overall recall (Meyer, 1979).

Processing activities hypothesized to be involved in the structure strategy are similar to those in the explanations given for the levels effect by Anderson (1976) and Kintsch and van Dijk (1978), except that primary emphasis is placed on a search for interrelationships among chunks of complex propositions in text. Anderson (1976) explained that high level propositions, i.e., central propositions in the network of this computer simulation model, are more frequently called up to help interpret the more peripheral low level propositions. This constitutes extra rehearsal of high level propositions and results in increasing the probability of their recall. Similarly, Kintsch and van Dijk (1978) explained that high level propositions are processed differently than low level propositions. High level propositions are hypothesized to be more frequently retrieved from long-term memory and kept in the short-term memory buffer as old propositions to be related to incoming new propositions in the reading process. In the Kintsch and van Dijk (1978) model, high level propositions are identified by repetition of arguments or concepts. Their model does not specify how the extreme superordinate proposition is identified; this proposition is crucial since repetition of its arguments dictate moving down in the hierarchy and building the text structure. At present, the superordinate proposition is selected on an intuitive basis in the Kintsch and van Dijk model with the expectation that further work with their macroprocesses component will help to explicate this choice.

The superordinate rhetorical relationships in text in combination with readers' prior knowledge of these forms of relationships appear to play a crucial role in comprehension (Bartlett, 1978; Meyer, 1979) and must be integrated more fully into the macroprocesses component of the Kintsch and van Dijk model. High level propositions need not be identified solely on argument repetition, but they can be identified as the arguments of the most superordinate rhetorical relationship or top-level text structure. The extreme superordinate proposition is then identified as the content bound by the top-level structure. For example in the first paragraph of the passage reproduced in the Appendix, the extreme superordinate proposition is "oil spills." It is explicitly signaled as the "problem" in the first sentence of this passage, and the passage as a whole is written with a problem/solution top-level structure commonly found in scientific articles. Thus, a focus on relationships and top-level structures can be used to specify the superordinate proposition in a structural analysis.

Processing activities used by the structure strategy search for the major text based relationships among propositions. Readers employing the structure strategy are hypothesized to approach text looking for patterns which will tie together the propositions contained in the text; in addition, they search for the author's primary thesis which will provide the content to be bound by these patterns or schemata. Then, they search for relationships among this primary thesis and supporting details. For example, when reading the supertanker text, readers employing this strategy recognize in the first sentence that the propositions may fit what they recognize from their prior knowledge as a "problem" schema. Each new proposition is related back to the "problem," making the problem of oil spills from supertankers continually selected for retention in the short-term memory buffer for interpreting the new propositions. Readers' previous knowledge about problems keeps them searching for causal relationships in descriptive information which is given about the problem, such as why it is a problem and what caused it. Also, prior experience with problems leads readers to anticipate and search for solutions, solutions which must satisfy most of the previously stated causes of the problem. Thus, the problem and its causes are retrieved continually from long-term storage to the short-term memory buffer for relating to the subsequent propositions in the passage. This additional processing of these superordinate propositions and their interrelationships increases the depth with which they are processed (Craik & Lockhart, 1972) and the subsequent ease with which they can be retrieved.

For those readers who use the structure strategy, the top-level structure and major interrelationships are also employed to guide retrieval and production of the recall protocol; it is hypothesized to be a top-down retrieval search guided by the structure of relationships. These readers are assumed to construct memory representations of text propositions which are similar in terms of their hierarchical, logical relationships to the content structure depicted in Figure 1; when recalling the text they begin their retrieval search with the top-level structure and systematically work from the superordinate relationships and content downward. The organization of a protocol written by a student employing the structure strategy matches the top-level structure of the text.

Figure 2 examines the factors contributing to the success of readers employing the structure strategy. The outcome of successfully applying this strategy as it relates to the resultant recall protocol is listed in the figure: 1) a hierarchical, logical structure similar to that of the text; 2) a strong levels effect; 3) sufficient to superior recall of most of the text's logical relationships; and 4) high total recall scores. The model examines both reader and text factors which influence success in employing this strategy. Signaling is one of the text factors.

The first reader variable in the scheme deals with whether or not the reader can employ the structure strategy with some types of discourse. The ability to employ the structure strategy may develop with mental age and schooling. Freedle (Freedle & Hale, 1979; Freedle, 1980) suggests that competence with story structure precedes competence with expository text. However, there is considerable variance in the structural complexity of different types of stories. Use of the structure strategy may progress in the following sequence with different discourse types which are equivalent on other difficulty factors: stories, description, antecedent/consequent, problem/solution, and comparison (argumentative text). If a reader cannot employ the structure strategy with a simple story, then the model shows the other factors are not considered and the reader can be expected to perform in the default mode. The default approach to learning and memory of hierarchical text is devoid of a systematic plan for processing text; the reader has no focus and simply tries to remember something from the text. Recall outcomes from this nonstrategy are listed in the figure: 1) the protocol is organized in a list format, a collection of unrelated descriptions about the passage topic; 2) the levels effect is minimal; 3) recall of the text's logical relationships is poor; and 4) total recall scores are low.

The next factor in the scheme is the difficulty level of the text to-be-read with regard to a particular reader; that is, is the text easy for the reader? Aspects of difficulty level include familiarity with the topic, readability, and the type, order (Irwin, 1980), and number of implicit or explicit logical relationships. If readers can employ the structure strategy with some prose and this particular text easily matches their competencies, then the structure strategy will be successfully employed (see outcome II of the structure strategy in Figure 2).

With this combination of reader and text factors, there would be no expected effects in a study manipulating signaling in text. This may explain the lack of signaling effects with proficient readers in studies by Britton, Meyer, Glynn, and Penland (in press), Marshall and Glock (1978-1979), Meyer (1975, 1979), and Meyer, Brandt, and Bluth (1980). The first three studies utilized college students and found no effects on total recall from manipulating signaling. Meyer (1975) also found no significant signaling effects on the recall of the signaled relationships with college students. In addition, Meyer, Brandt, and Bluth (1980) found no signaling effects with ninth grade expository text for ninth grade students with high reading comprehension test scores (median percentile of 84 on the comprehension test of the Stanford Achievement Test). However, Marshall and Glock, using the same expository passages with junior college students as they used with university students, found superiority in total recall from the signaled passages. None of the extant studies for any samples have reported signaling to affect reading time.

The next variable in the model is adequacy of decoding and lexical access skills (Golinkoff, 1975-1976). If a particular text is above readers' independent reading levels, it may be at their instructional levels or frustration levels. If readers do not have adequate decoding and lexical access skills to comprehend at a single-word level, then the default mode is the outcome. For these students, signaling would be expected to have no effects. In the Meyer, Brandt, and Bluth (1980) study, signaling had no effect on poor comprehenders (median percentile of 32 on the comprehension subtest of the SAT).

The next text variable in the model is signaling of relationships among major propositions. If students with adequate decoding and lexical access skills read text with signaling, then they will successfully employ the structure strategy (outcome II in Figure 2).

However, if signaling is not present, the model shows two possible outcomes depending on the text organization (Golinkoff, 1975-1976) skills of the reader. If these skills are adequate for generating many of the major implicit logical relationships in the structure of the text, then the structure strategy will be employed. The recall outcome will match outcome I of the structure strategy. The protocol will exhibit a hierarchical structure and strong levels effect but will be slightly diminished on the other two outcomes in comparison to outcome II (see Figure 2), due to a failure in generating as many of the text's relationships. On the other hand, if text organization skills are not adequate, then the default mode will result.

Evidence for the first outcome comes from data recently collected on 164 adults who read with and without signaling versions of the Supertanker Passage shown in the Appendix (Meyer & Rice, 1980). Most of these subjects have above average vocabulary test scores, at least some college education, but vary in age and current involvement in school. These data are depicted in Table 1; this is a preliminary look at the data and further analyses require stratification on age, schooling, and vocabulary performance. However, the model would explain these data for over 85 percent of the subjects as following the paths shown on the model in Figure 3.

Table 1. Results from Preliminary Analyses of the Data Collected on 164 Adult Readers Who Read the Supertanker Passage with and without Signaling

Recall Outcomes	Signaling	
	With	Without
% of Subjects Whose Recall Protocols Were Hierarchically Organized with Problem/Solution Top-Level Structures	88%	85%
Levels Effect	High > Low ($p < .00001$)	High > Low ($p < .00001$)
Recall of Logical Relations (N = 14) ($p < .001$)	59%	49%
Total Recall ($p < .07$)	37%	33%

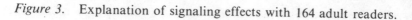

Figure 3. Explanation of signaling effects with 164 adult readers.

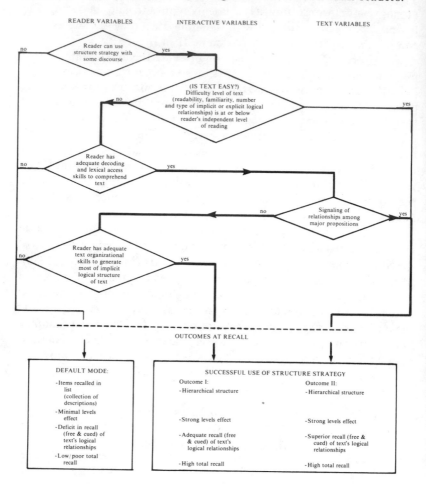

On the other hand, when text organization skills are inadequate, large differences would be expected between students reading text with- and without-signaling (see Figure 4). In the Meyer, Brandt, and Bluth (1980) study, signaling effects were examined with a shorter version of the Supertanker Passage. Signaling was expected to assist students with adequate word knowledge and word attack skills, but poorer reading

Figure 4. Explanation of the data from the Meyer, Brandt, and Bluth (1980) study with underachievers in reading comprehension.

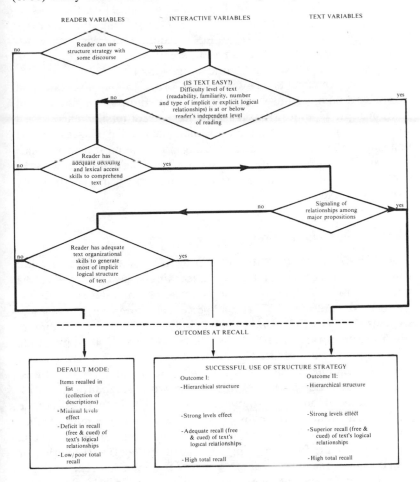

comprehension skills (i.e., underachievers). Twenty-six of these students were identified in one teacher's five classes of ninth grade English. The stanine score of each of these students on the reading comprehension scale of the SAT was at least one stanine below their stanine score on the vocabulary scale. In addition, in order for students to be selected for this subgroup, their stanine scores on the vocabulary scale had to be 4 or greater. The median percentile score on the reading comprehension scale for this group was 43, while their median percentile score on the vocabulary scale was 60. Thus, they were a subgroup of Cromer's difference readers (1970). This study reported statistically significant differences in immediate total recall scores between underachievers who read passages with signaling ($\overline{X}_{mean} = 49$) and those who read passages without signaling ($\overline{X} = 33$).

Thus, the model provides some order to the disparate and surprising findings from studies which have studied signaling of text relationships. Composition teachers have traditionally encouraged writers' use of signaling and have assumed that it aided their readers. At first glance, the lack of dramatic signaling effects for most readers seems surprising. However, the effects of signaling appear to interact with the competency of students in using the structure strategy and the difficulty level of the text.

Application to Education

The research indicates that proficient adolescent and adult readers in the context of the prose learning experiment utilize the structure strategy, while poorer comprehenders employ the default/list strategy. Most of our work with adolescents has been with ninth grade students (Bartlett, 1978; Brandt, 1978; Meyer, 1979; Meyer, Brandt, & Bluth, 1980; Swanson, 1979). We have had over 300 ninth grade students read well-organized passages of expository text written with problem/solution, comparison, and description top-level structures. Slightly less than 50 percent of the students wrote recall protocols with the same type of top-level structure as that found in the text. Most of the ninth grade students rated by standardized reading comprehension texts and their teachers as high in reading comprehension used the same top-level structure for organizing their recall protocols as the author of the passage, while most students with low reading comprehension did not. In addition, students who used the same type of top-level structure as the author remembered much more information from passages than those who did not. The message posited in the passages was particularly well-remembered by these students both immediately and a week after reading. They also remembered substantially more major details and minor details (Meyer, Brandt, & Bluth, 1980). Additionally, in the Meyer, Brandt, and Bluth (1980) study, students who used the same top-level structure as the author performed better on true/false tests of passage content administered a week after reading the passages.

Failure to utilize the top-level structure in text particularly impairs their performance on unfamiliar topics commonly found in school materials, such as railroad development and problems with supertankers. It is less crucial with familiar material where numerous prior knowledge structures or schemata on a topic in memory can increase their likelihood of remembering ideas to list in their recall protocol (Brandt, 1978; Meyer, 1979). Table 2 depicts ranges in the percent of variance in recall accounted for by the degree to which students employ the same type of top-level structure as in the text (scored on a ten point scale, Meyer, Brandt, & Bluth, 1980). The topic of the familiar passage was killer whales; the students had just completed an oceanography unit dealing with this topic and were planning a trip to Sea World the week of the delayed testing.

Table 2. Variance in Recall Accounted for by Using the Top-Level Structure of Text

Recall Task	Standard Text (7 passages for 300 9th graders)	Highly Familiar Text
Immediate	36-52%	22%
Delay	68-80%	30%

A systematic study has not been conducted into the use of the structure strategy by readers of various ages or backgrounds. However, use of the text's top-level structure has been investigated with other than ninth grade samples. Taylor (1980) has looked at use of the text's top-level structure by fourth grade, sixth grade, and college age students with a descriptive passage (general statements followed by specific examples). Use of the top-level structure in recalls written immediately after reading the passage was 82 percent, 47 percent, and 12 percent for adults, good sixth grade comprehenders, and good fourth grade comprehenders, respectively. Elliott (1980) examined the use of two different types of top-level structures (comparison: adversative, and description: attributive) by sixth grade students with average and good comprehension skills. Twenty percent of the sixth graders who read the descriptive passage used that structure to organize their recall; 14 percent of the students who read the comparative passage utilized that top-level structure. In a sample of junior college students (Meyer, Rice, Bartlett, & Woods, 1979) slightly more than 50 percent used the same type of top-level structure as found in problem/solution text when they wrote their recall protocols; those students who employed this strategy remembered more than those who did not. In addition, 80 percent of a sample of 130 Cornell undergraduates used the same top-level structure as that in the problem/solution text (Meyer, 1971, 1975, 1979). In several samples of graduate students and college graduates in young, middle, and old age groups, 85-100 percent used the same type of top-level structure as they read in well-organized passages (Meyer & Rice, 1980). However, they appear to be able to employ alternate top-level structures as evidenced by a group of graduate students who rejected a proposed solution in a passage written with a response structure and employed comparison or antecedent/consequent top-level structures in their recall protocols (Meyer, 1977; Meyer & Freedle, 1979).

To further investigate the value of the top-level structure for readers, we taught ninth grade students to identify four top-level structures frequently found in expository text and to use them in their recall protocols (Bartlett, 1978); these top-level structures were causation, comparison: adversative, description, and response: problem/solution. Students in a week long instruction group and a control group read and recalled passages prior to instruction, 1 day after instruction, and 3 weeks after completion of instruction. The instruction led to significant increased identification of the top-level structure used in text and its use in recall protocols. In addition, the amount of information recalled by the instructed group on each of the posttest sessions was nearly double that of both their preinstruction scores and the scores of the control group for all testing sessions. The study showed that top-level structures can be taught to ninth grade students and this instruction improves their reading comprehension.

Similarly, Armbruster and Anderson (1980) found that instruction in "mapping" improved eighth-grade students' recall of short expository text. The students were instructed to identify relationships which defined the text structure, such as examples, compare-constrast, definitions, property, temporal, and causal. Students learned to represent these relationships with symbols; these symbols were used to form a diagram, or map, of the important ideas in a short text. In addition, instruction in a technique called "networking," similar to mapping, has been shown to improve reading comprehension of adults (Dansereau, et al., 1979).

This research demonstrates that the structure strategy can be taught to students and that this training will result in improved reading comprehension. The research has important implications for both textbook selection and instruction to improve reading comprehension. Textbooks should make their organization highly salient to promote students' use of the structure strategy. In addition, the strategy should be explicitly taught in reading classes and in content area classes with regard to particular texts. However, before fully considering these applications to the classroom another aspect of text structure, discourse type effects, should be reviewed.

It seems reasonable that students who employ the structure strategy will optimize this strategy when reading hierarchically organized text rather than flatter, list-like text which presents collections of descriptions about a topic, but does not interrelate these descriptions conceptually for a reader. However, this list-like text which matches the list-like default strategy of the poorer comprehender may result in better recall for the student who has not mastered or does not utilize the structure strategy. That is, there may be an "aptitude x treatment" interaction between reading strategy and text organization. Unfortunately, at this time there is not sufficient data on this topic to clarify this issue, but the extant studies will be summarized.

Meyer (Meyer & Freedle, 1979; Meyer & Rice, 1980) has developed passages on dehydration and whales where over 90 percent of the text remains constant, but in different versions the content is organized with different top-level structures. Meyer and Freedle (1979) have shown that the hierarchically organized comparison and causal top-level structures result in better recall and retention for graduate students than the list-like description: attribute type structure. As seen in Table 3, this effect appears to hold for high ability older adults (Meyer & Rice, 1980), ninth grade students (Brandt, 1978), and sixth grade students after two readings (Elliott, 1980), but not for low verbal old adults (Meyer & Walker, 1978), poor comprehenders at the ninth grade level (Brandt, 1978), nor above average sixth grade comprehenders with one reading trial (Elliott, 1980).

More research in this area is necessary before stating firm guidelines for text selection, especially since different structures appear to interact with ability level and reading instructions. At this point, it may be well to select texts for proficient readers with a variety of

Table 3. A Composite of Results from Various Studies Examining the Relationship between Discourse Types and Learner Characteristics of Age and Vocabulary and Comprehension Test Performance

Age	Ability	Comparison of Recall of the Same Information from the Dehydration Passages with Comparison; Adversative and Descriptive; Attribution Top-Level Structures
	Learner Characteristics	
	Vocabulary	
Old Adults (62+ yrs.)	High (Md = 77%)	Adversative (53%) > Attribution (34%)
	Low (Md = 20%)	Adversative (27%) < Attribution (48%)
Middle Adults (40-54)	High	Adversative (48%) > Attribution (38%)
	Low	no data
Young Adults (18-32)	High	Adversative (66%) > Attribution (49%)
	Low	no data
	Comprehension	
Adolescents (15)	High	Adversative (55%) > Attribution (46%)
	Low	Adversative (25%) < Attribution (31%)
Sixth graders (11)	Average & Above ($\bar{X}_{\text{grade level}} = 7.3$)	Adversative (40%) > Attribution (20%) —Passages Read Twice
		Adversative (28%) = Attribution (31%) —Passages Read Once

hierarchically organized conceptual structures and to avoid text where topics are discussed primarily by listing attributes with unspecified interrelationships.

In the next sections of this chapter, implications from this research on text structure and signaling will be drawn for establishing guidelines to assist in the selection of textbooks and instruction in reading comprehension. As noted in the previous discussions of the research, the data have been collected primarily with junior high school students through university level students. Further research is necessary before applying these findings directly to students in the elementary school.

Meyer

Textbook Selection

Check match between your goals and the text structure. If information buried at low levels of the text is thought to be particularly important by a teacher, another text should probably be selected or outside materials and aids brought in to emphasize these points. Teachers should be sure that the information contained at the high levels of the text's structure, as indicated by titles, subtitles, italics, abstracts, and summaries, meets their goals for instruction. This information will be primarily what the students remember and it should be supportive of teaching objectives.

Content area texts should emphasize text structure. Textbooks should be selected which assist readers in employing the structure strategy. Use of this strategy will give readers a basis for deciding what is important to remember as well as a conceptual structure for initially interrelating these ideas.

Textbooks in the content areas should be selected with clearly identifiable top-level structures which can assist students in differentiating between macropropositions (main ideas) and micropropositions (details). Textbooks embodying these traits should contain abstracts, preview sections or introductions which explicitly state the macropropositions; these devices tell the reader what is important in the upcoming text. Of course, the top levels of the content structure of this upcoming text must directly correspond to these introductory devices. In addition, the textbooks should provide summary sections which repeat the macropropositions.

Other devices in the text should also focus on the macropropositions. Thematic words and sentences can be emphasized by underlining, italics, and repetition. Macropropositions can also be emphasized by questions, objectives and illustrations directed to them.

Titles and subtitles can be employed to focus on the macropropositions and explicitly signal the top-level structure of the text. For example, a passage explaining how breeder reactors can solve the energy crisis should be titled "Nuclear Breeder Reactors: A Solution to the Energy Crisis" rather than "Fast Breeder Reactor." The first title focuses on the macrostructure and explicitly signals the top-level structure employed. Explicit signaling of top-level structures should be employed in the body of the text as well.

Not only should rhetorical relationships or story grammars comprising the top-level structure of text be explicitly signaled, but so should many of the rhetorical relationships at all levels of the text. This practice will reduce ambiguity and quickly enable the reader to see how propositions are interrelated at high and low levels of the structure. Repetition of referents in the propositions will also increase the reader's speed of comprehending the relationships among propositions (Kintsch & Vipond, 1979).

Textbooks in the content areas, especially textbooks for less able comprehenders, should contain as much explicit signaling of relationships and repetition of concepts as reasonably possible. Their presence in text will reduce the likelihood of students making incorrect inferences or failing to interrelate concepts. On the other hand, textbooks which teach reading comprehension skills should gradually withdraw this signaling and repetition so that readers will be able to apply the structure strategy with any hierarchically structured discourse.

In addition to examining micropropositions of text for signaling of rhetorical relationships and repetition of referents, this level of text should also be examined for inclusion of too much detail, digressions, and complex ordering or propositions. For example, multiple embedded antecedent/consequent relationships among propositions appear to hinder efficient learning (Rice, 1978).

To summarize, explicit signaling of the text structure would seem to be important for content area textbooks in such subjects as science and social studies. As shown in Figure 2, signaling can increase comprehension for certain readers and it doesn't seem to impair learning for those readers who do not benefit from it.

Instruction to Improve Reading Comprehension

Suggestions for instruction to improve reading comprehension deal with teaching students to identify top-level text structures, how to identify and generate macropropositions, and the sequence in teaching these two skills.

Teach use of text organization. In teaching the top-level structures of expository text, students could be asked to identify these relationships of antecedent/consequent, comparison, collection, description, and response in ordinary life situations. Then they could look for these relationships in magazine advertisements. Games could be designed to have students identify these relationships in familiar experiences and advertisements. Next, teachers could explain how these relationships are also used to organize information in textbooks. Students could be taught to look for signal words in text which explicitly cue these relationships as suggested in programs by educators such as Niles (1974) and Sack and Yourman (1972). Next, teachers could provide questions which encourage students to make inferences about how propositions are interrelated when this is not explicitly stated in the text (Trabasso, in press). Then, students should be taught to ask themselves these questions concerning the interrelationships among propositions. Finally, this process should become automatic during their reading.

Further research may show an optimal sequence in which to teach younger children about different types of top-level structures. As skill in utilizing top-level structures increases, the exposure to different forms should increase. Certain content areas typically employ different top-level structures: narrative structures in literature books, letter structures in business writing books, research report structures in science anthologies, and news articles structures in journalism books. These structures and others can be explored with students.

In addition to learning to identify these top-level structures in well-organized textbooks and to use them to retell what they remember from text, students should receive practice in using these skills with less than ideally written textbooks. When text is poorly organized, students should be taught how to use these relationships to reorganize the text into a readily encodable and retrievable structure. An enjoyable first approach to this skill may be identifying the top-level structure of advertisements, evaluating the use of the particular top-level structure for selling the product, and rewriting the advertisement with a better or at least alternative top-level structure. For example, a bold face caption for an advertisement on kitty litter stated "I switched from clay litter to Litter Green when my husband said 'Get rid of the odors, or get rid of the cat!" The relationship between the two propositions is antecedent/consequent, she switched as a result of what her husband said. However, this advertisement could also be written in a problem/solution structure: problem = cat odor, solution = Litter Green, a comparative structure: favored view = Litter Green, other view = clay litter, and a description structure: Litter Green and its extolling qualities.

Students can be taught to diagram portions of the content structure of text. This technique used in the writing and revising of their own compositions should improve their writing skills as well as their reading skills (Meyer, 1979).

Teach identification and generation of main ideas. Students also should be taught to identify the top levels of the content structure of text, the macropropositions, or main ideas. They need to be able to differentiate the important information from the less important information in different discourse types of varying difficulty. The ability to identify a text's top-level structure will facilitate their identification and memory for the macropropositions (Meyer, 1979). Generating summaries, brief outlines, abstracts, and titles for text should increase their ability to identify macropropositions and to construct them when they are not explicitly stated in text.

Use of text structure as the key for finding main ideas. One of the most practical implications from the research presented in this chapter on prose learning may be the recommendation for a switch in the traditional order for sequencing instruction of the above two skills, use of text organization and identification of main ideas. Vacca (1980) summarized the subskill approach to teaching reading comprehension and explained that it has been the primary instructional emphasis of reading programs. He explained that this type of instruction is centered around a set of comprehension subskills arranged in a logical sequence and taught in a prescribed order. After a synthesis of research and opinions of experts on reading comprehension subskills, Fareed (1971) identified a sequence of eight comprehension subskills. The ordering of three of these subskills is relevant to the research findings discussed in this chapter. They are: 1) the reader notes facts and important details; 2) the reader grasps the main ideas; and 3) the reader follows text relationships such as sequences, cause and effect, and compare and contrast. The research indicates that this order of instruction should be reversed if the goal is utilization of the structure strategy and high recall. Instead, readers should be taught different text organization structures and how to identify them and use them as retrieval aids. The information bound by superordinate text structure is the main idea. Thus, utilizing text structure can point readers directly to main ideas. For example, in the Supertanker Passage (see Appendix) the problem/solution structure points the reader to the main idea of the text (environmentally damaging oil spills from supertankers can be prevented by better training of supertanker officers, better building of tankers, and installing ground control stations). The problem/solution structure also helps readers to determine exactly what are the important details. A problem/solution organization requires that some aspects of the solution match some aspects of the antecedents of the problem. Information meeting these requirements would be important details to remember. For example, in the Supertanker Passage, the following details or micropropositions meet these requirements: supertankers currently have only one boiler and one propeller; one aspect of the proposed solution calls for building supertankers with more boilers and propellers.

Teaching students to find the top-level structures of texts provides a way to operationalize the search for the text's main ideas and important details. The research suggests that instruction in identification and utilization of text structure should precede instruction in identification of main ideas.

In summary, research on the structure of prose has implications for educators. Some practical suggestions can be generated from the research findings available at this time. With further investigation in the area, more specific guidelines may be available for practitioners.

Note

1. Some of the research studies reported in this paper were funded in part by Faculty Grants at Arizona State University and Grant MN 31520 from the National Institute of Mental Health.

Appendix

A signaled version of the supertanker passage:
Signaling shown with italics and overall
structure depicted in Figure 1

Some Solutions for the Supertanker Problem

A *problem* is prevention of oil spills from supertankers. *Attributes* of a *typical* supertanker include carrying capacity of a half million tons of oil, size of five football fields, and cargo areas easily accommodating the Empire State Building. *The trouble is that* a wrecked supertanker spills oil in the ocean. *As a result of spillage*, the environment is damaged. *An example* took place in 1970 near Spain when an oil spill from a wrecked tanker exploded into fire. *The fire caused* hurricane-force winds which whipped the oil into a mist and pulled all of it high into the air. Several days later black rain *resulting* from this oil spill destroyed crops and livestock in the neighboring villages. *Another example of damage* occurred in 1967 when the tanker, Torrey Canyon, crashed off the coast of Cornwall and *resulted* in the washing ashore of 200,000 dead seabirds. *An example* which happened nearer to home came to pass in July 1975 when the United States Coast Guard mopped up acres of oil from the beach at Geiger Key, Florida, north of Key West. Guardsmen found chemical clues *which led to* the arrest on November 7, 1975 of a Greek tanker captain, Vasilios K. Psarroulis, *because of* failure to report the loss of an estimated 40,000 gallons of oil. Oil spills *also* kill microscopic plant life *which* provide food for sea life and produce 70 percent of the world's oxygen supply.

Most wrecks result from the lack of power and steering equipment to handle emergency situations, *such as* storms. Supertankers have only one boiler to provide power and one propeller to drive the ship.

The *solution to the problem is not* to halt the use of tankers on the ocean *since* about 80 percent of the world's oil supply is carried by supertankers. *Instead, the solution lies in the following three facts. First*, officers of the supertankers must get top training in how to run and maneuver their ships, such *as that* provided by the tanker simulator at the Maritime Research Center. *Second*, tankers should be built with several propellers for extra control and backup boilers for emergency power. *Third*, ground control stations should be installed at places where supertankers come close to shore *because* they would act like airplane control towers, guiding tankers along busy shipping lanes and through dangerous channels.

Meyer

Classroom Applications of Text Analysis: Toward Improving Text Selection and Use

Robert J. Tierney
University of Illinois
James Mosenthal
University of Chicago
Robert N. Kantor
Ohio State University

The recent plethora of research and interest in the examination of text features has generated a number of new frameworks for assessing texts. These frameworks provide the researcher, disenchanted with sentence-level analysis, new research directions and incentives, and offer the reading educator, previously limited to the use of readability formulae, the promise of a better appreciation of what may contribute to or detract from the comprehensibility of text. Toward providing the educator an introduction to these advances, the present paper discusses some of the perspectives provided by these frameworks. Specifically, the paper addresses the following: 1) the issue of examining the contextual aspects of text; and 2) the use of several frameworks and suggestions for examining the ideas and relationships represented within a text.

Examining the Context of Text

Central to an understanding of the characteristics of text is an appreciation of what a text is. Among many scholars the term *text* has recently come to refer to a unified whole. It can be anything from a riddle to a road sign, from a newspaper article to a whole book. To define a text as a unified whole, however, requires an appreciation of the notion that a text represents language in use. That is, apart from the ideas and relationships which are represented somewhat explicitly within a text, an important aspect of text is the context within which a text functions as a unified whole.

Describing a text's context requires an analysis of the extralinguistic contextual variables involved in the production and comprehension of text. In producing a text, an author goes beyond selecting any assortment of words; rather, an author predicts the reader's context and searches for the words which will create appropriate connotations and denotations in the mind of the reader. In other words, what can be identified as the ideas and relationships between ideas represented within a text are constrained by an author's perception of an audience, an author's perception of the reader's background of experience, an author's perceived goals for a text, and an author's ability to appreciate the effect of a text upon an audience. Likewise, in comprehending a text, a number of factors influence the extent to which a reader's interpretation will vary from an author's intended message. For example, a reader's knowledge, purpose, interest, and attention, as well as the physical and sociocultural conditions of the reading situation, may constrain comprehension strategies in such a way as to influence or even abort the construction of meaning. The point is that external factors influence both the linguistic choices of writers and the possible interpretations developed by readers. It follows that the relationship between author and reader should be viewed as integral to an examination of the context of text; i.e., a consideration of the match or mismatch between author and reader should be regarded as requisite to assessing the extent to which a text fits a particular audience. To this end we propose that an examination of text should include the following complementary analyses: 1) an analysis of the purpose a text is intended to serve; and 2) an examination of the shared experience of author and reader.

Purposes and Shared Experiences of Author and Reader

Examining the purposes and shared experiences of readers and authors involves two tasks. The first task is to determine whether differences exist between the functions a text might serve and the purposes for which a text is read. The second task is to compare the knowledge required to understand a text with the knowledge of the reader with whom it is to be used.

As an illustration of differences existing between the functions a text might serve and those for which it is read, consider the following:

Tierney, Mosenthal, and Kantor

Compare, for the sake of example, the obvious differences between the understandings a reader might be expected to glean from Stephen Crane's *The Red Badge of Courage* (1966), which uses the U.S. Civil War as background, and a chapter in a history textbook which uses the U.S. Civil War as topic. In the former, it is the themes evoked by the experiences of a young man participating in war which are likely to be of direct relevance and importance to the reader. In the latter, it is the facts and concepts that describe the Civil War which are likely to be of direct relevance and importance to the reader. In other words, Crane's text serves primarily a literary function; the history chapter serves primarily an informative function. For Crane's treatment, it might be reasonable to expect a reader to glean an appreciation of the mood of the experience of war; for the textbook chapter, it might be reasonable to expect the reader to develop an appreciation of the causes, progress, and consequences of the Civil War. Obviously, if Crane's novel were not written with the expectation that the reader would be able to identify key events of the Civil War, then it would not seem reasonable to read the text for this purpose. Likewise, if the history chapter were not written for purposes of detailing the mood of the time, maybe it should not or could not be expected to be read for this purpose.

Unfortunately, in our reviews of textbook materials, we have encountered numerous examples where text intended for one purpose is forced to fit other purposes. It is as if some publishers of textbooks often force selections to fit questions. With little regard for the integrity of a selection, some publishers seem to naively presuppose that text well-written for one purpose will be appropriate and well-written for other purposes. For example, in a certain biology textbook, a publisher uses a text describing the changing color of leaves to try to explain the physical process of actual change. Unfortunately, the latter is addressed in the text, and only with considerable "manipulation" or teacher support could the text be expected to extend to this purpose. In the elementary classroom, simple basal narratives are often subtly sabotaged by an excessive use of trivial questioning. In this regard, parents and teachers should be careful that the purpose for which a story is usually read (e.g., enjoyment) is not defeated by poorly fitting questions (e.g., detail questions dealing with trivial information). In our reviews of basal stories, we have encountered numerous examples where stories are manipulated for so-called pedagogical purposes. We are concerned that children may come to believe that the purpose of reading is to be able to answer such questions. We are especially concerned about independent reading of supplementary materials where the children may first look at the questions to be answered and then go on a search to find the answers. Such a tactic is completely contrary to the "text as a unified whole" concept that we discussed earlier.

The point is that there are many situations when a text written for certain purposes cannot and should not be used for other purposes; the teacher's task is to identify as well as avoid these incidences when the text might be so misused.

The second facet of an examination of the purposes and shared experiences of author and reader involves comparing the reader's and author's background of experience. This requires recognizing the differences which exist between the knowledge of the reader and the knowledge which the author assumes the reader possesses. For example, consider the knowledge required to understand the following segment of text based upon an article from a New Zealand publication:

> Our education policy is "back to basics." We will abolish color rods and replace them with old sums and take aways. These have surely stood the test of time. We will back this up with the replacement of compulsory PT for playlunch. Clean sandshoes and uniforms will be our standard.[1]

Or consider the following segment of text submitted for inclusion in a basal reader:

> "The Train Rider" (see Footnote 1)
>
> Carl and Cindy look.
> They listen.
> Then they see the train.
> It has many cars.
> The train stops.
> Carl and Cindy get on the train.
> Their mother gets on too.

It does not take too much effort to identify the readers for whom these texts might be inappropriate or devoid of meaning. The first passage is written for a New Zealand audience, and a reader unfamiliar with the "tongue-in-cheek" writings of Grant and some of the meanings of certain statements would not appreciate the full impact of humor intended. For example, only a reader familiar with the popular sentiments of New Zealanders toward education would recognize the thematic ties which exist between *color rods, sums and take-aways, compulsory PT*, and *clean sandshoes.*

In the second passage, written for a wide audience of school children, the author obviously assumes his or her readers have a certain amount of knowledge regarding the railways—notably, that trains are made up of "cars" and stop at stations. Without these key facts, we would posit that a reader will likely develop an incomplete or unrealistic interpretation. Again our point is that prior to assuming the worth of a text, the shared knowledge between reader and author should be considered. Without this shared knowledge, much of the richness and even simply the cohesiveness of a reader's interpretation will be lacking.

To summarize, defining the context of text (which seems integral to any examination of text) requires extralinguistic analyses. Minimally, such analyses should include an examination of the legitimate purposes for which a text can be used and the audience for whom the text is written.

Ideas, Relationships between Ideas, and Structural Considerations

An important complement to examining the context of text is a description of the ideas, the relations between ideas, and the structural properties within text. Over the past decade numerous systems have been offered for formally representing the information within a text. In this regard, the systems of Dawes (1966), Frederiksen (1975), Grimes (1975), Halliday and Hasan (1976), Kintsch (1974), Meyer (1975a, 1975b), Rumelhart (1975), and Thorndyke (1977) have been seminal. For the purposes of the present paper, several key notions based upon a composite of this work are presented. Although more formal text analysis procedures will be cited, our intent is to offer simplified procedures by which teachers can select and use texts. We begin with suggestions for examining the ideas in a text, move to a discussion of the relation between the ideas of a text, and conclude with a discussion of the structural qualities of text.

Examining Ideas within a Text

Examining the ideas within a text has been central to various methods of text analysis in particular the systems of Frederiksen (1975), Kintsch (1974), and Meyer (1977). To illustrate how the ideas within a text might be formally described, note the following text segment taken from a biology text and an accompanying analysis of the ideas expressed in the text:

"The Garbage Collectors of the Sea" (see Footnote 1)

The garbage collectors of the sea are the decomposers. Day and night, ocean plants and animals that die, and the body wastes of living animals, slowly drift down to the sea floor. There is a steady rain of such material that builds up on the sea bottom. This is especially true on the continental shelves, where life is rich. It is less true in the desert regions of the deep ocean.

As on the land, different kinds of bacteria also live in the sea. They attack the remains of dead plant and animal tissue and break it down into nutrients. These nutrients are then taken up by plant and animal plankton alike. Among such nutrients are nitrate, phosphate, and manganese, silica, and calcium.

As the nutrients are released, they spread around in the water. But they tend to stay near the bottom until some motion of the water stirs them. As you saw earlier, during those seasons when the water is churned up and mixed, the nutrients are brought up to the surface. They may also be brought up by the upwelling action of deep currents. This is especially so along the west coasts of Africa, South America, and North America. Wherever there are regions of upwelling of nutrients, there are rich "fields" of plant plankton, usually during all seasons of the year.

So nutrients are kept circulating endlessly in the oceans, and are used over and over again by plant, plankton and whales alike. When a plant or animal breaks down the sugar-fuel it needs for growth, the energy stored by the sugar is used. Some of it goes into building new body parts and some of it is lost as heat. This is not true of nutrients.

Nutrients are not "used up" in that way. For a while, oxygen, carbon, calcium, and other nutrients that a plant or animal takes in become part of the plant or animal. But when the animal or plant dies, and when it gives off body wastes, the nutrients are returned to the environment and can be used again and again.[2]

A formal representation of this text might entail an analysis similar to that presented in Figure 1.

The system represented in Figure 1 is based on the concept of an idea unit consisting of arguments and relations. In 1.0 of Figure 1, "garbage collectors," "sea," and "decomposers" are arguments, while ISA and QUALIFY are relations. The relations tie the arguments together into a single idea unit. Basically, there are three classes of relations: predication, modification, and connection. Predication is usually defined by a verb in the idea unit: BUILDS UP in 3.0 presupposes, first, the arguments of that which is built up (the remains of plants and animals and body wastes) and, second, a complement which describes what is built up or where something is built up ("on the sea floor" in the present example). Modification is usually realized by words serving an adjectival or adverbial function: QUALITY, "rich" in 5.0 relates the arguments "life" and "rich," with "rich" modifying "life." Connection is usually realized by connectives coordinating arguments within an idea unit or between idea units: LOC (location): ON in 5.0 relates the proposition "life is rich" to the proposition "the continental shelves" via the connective "on."

Teachers would be ill-advised to use analysis methods which are as formal, detailed, or decontextualized as the above-mentioned proposal. Apart from the fact that they would be too time-consuming and cumbersome, such systems disregard the specific uses to which a

Tierney, Mosenthal, and Kantor

Figure 1. Propositional analysis of "Garbage Collectors of the Sea."

The garbage collectors of the sea are the decomposers.

1.0 (ISA, garbage collectors (QUALIFY sea), decomposers)

Day and night, ocean plants and animals that die, and the body wastes of living animals, slowly drift to sea floor.

2.0 (DRIFT, (QUALIFY, slowly) A: $\left(\begin{array}{l}\text{(ocean plants) (QUALIFY, dead)} \\ \text{(animals) (QUALIFY, dead)} \\ \text{(body wastes (QUALIFY, living animals)}\end{array}\right)$ LOC: TO sea floor, TIME: day and night

There is a steady rain of such material that builds up on the sea bottom.

3.0 (BUILDS UP, I: rain $\left(\begin{array}{l}\text{(ISA, rain, material) (REFERENCE, material, 2.0)} \\ \text{(QUALIFY, rain, steady)}\end{array}\right)$ LOC: ON, sea bottom)

This is especially true on continental shelves, where life is rich.

4.0 (BE (QUALITY, true) (QUALIFY, especially), I: THIS (REFERENCE, THIS, 3.0)

5.0 (BE, I: life (QUALITY, rich), LOC: ON, continental shelves)

6.0 (CONJ: WHERE, 4.0, 5.0)

It is less true in the desert regions of the deep ocean.

7.0 (BE (QUALITY, true) (EXTENT, less), I: It (REFERENCE, it 3.0) LOC: IN, desert region (QUALIFY, deep ocean))

teacher or student might put a text. In this regard, a more viable approach would be a simplified form of ideational analysis whereby teachers assess the match between the text and key understandings for which a text is being read. For text with expository tendencies, this might involve assessing the extent to which the idea units within a text support certain informational units. For texts with a more poetic or aesthetic intent, this might entail an examination of the support given setting and theme.

For purposes of illustration, an ideational analysis of the "Garbage Collectors" passage could involve an examination of text similar to that which is depicted in Figure 2. As detailed in Figure 2,

Figure 2. Key concept analysis of decomposition.

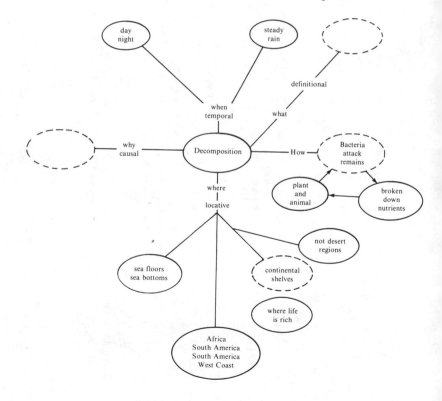

A complete circle suggests definition or clarification
An incomplete circle suggests lack of clarification

Tierney, Mosenthal, and Kantor

consider the support given the concept of decomposition. Units within the text which serve to define, clarify, or modify are circled and their clarity represented by complete or broken lines.

For example, *day and night* and *steady rain* provide ample support for the notion that decomposition is a never-ending process. The locational reference to continental shelves is marked as vague, given the failure of the text to adequately describe or define the continental shelf—a term likely to be unfamiliar to most readers. Also problematic are those unelaborated aspects of the text which intend to specify what decomposers are and how decomposition takes place.

Essentially, our point is that if the purposes for which a text is examined are eventually instructional, then, as a first step, a subjective analysis of text clarity might be initiated informally by the teacher. There are no formal analyses or even much research to date on what constitutes text clarity. The teacher will have to rely on intuition. Intuitive, subjective judgments should be based on the teacher's knowledge of the subject matter *in combination with* the teacher's knowledge of the common experiences of the children. Thus, our evaluation of the reference to continental shelves as vague is based on the fact that the concept of "continental shelf" had not been discussed previously in the text *and* on our subjective hunch that the students for whom this biology text was written would not have been previously introduced to the concept.

Examining Relationships between Ideas

It should be noted that, in an analysis of a text, determining the idea units is only part of the picture. Consider those aspects of text referred to as cohesive ties (Halliday & Hasan, 1976). These aspects of text include features such as pronominalization—the use of *he, her, this, those*, etc.—and conjunctions—the use of *and, but, yet, or*, and also *therefore, however, for example*, and so forth. (Halliday and Hasan's cohesive system also includes the categories of substitution, ellipsis, and lexical cohesion. These categories are omitted from the present discussion because they represent phenomena not as readily identifiable in text as are reference and conjunction.) The referential and conjunctive features of text are termed cohesive because they relate or tie information across a text or with prior knowledge. For example, in "Garbage Collectors of the Sea" the pronoun *they* in *they attack the remains* is related to and resolved by the concept of *bacteria* introduced in the previous sentence. Also, *so* in *so nutrients are kept circulating endlessly* related two idea units as blocks of information. It should be noted that most of these ties cross sentence boundaries.

The worth of a cohesive analysis comes in determining whether or not the use made of certain pronouns and conjunctions is indiscriminate and likely to detract from the acquisition of an integrated interpretation of text. Consider the former—namely, the indiscriminate use of ties such as *it, then, this, there*, as they frequently appear in basal texts. For example, note the author's lack of clear referents for pronouns in the following selection written for a basal reader:

"Be My Friend"

Rabbit was not happy.
He wanted a friend.
"Which animal will be my friend?" he asked.
Rabbit saw an animal in a tree.
It looked like fuzz.

If you reread the last two sentences, you can see that *it* lacks a clear referent. The pronoun has two possible referents—either the *animal* may look like *fuzz* or the *tree* may look like *fuzz*. Similarly, consider the author's use of *this* in the following text:

At the beginning of the school year, be sure to collect your registration materials, pay your fees, and see an advisor. If the library fees are not paid you will be unable to register. Failure to do *this* will require applying for readmission.

In this example, the word *this* is used in a vague or imprecise way. *This* may refer either to the information presented in sentences 1 and 2, or it may refer only to sentence 2.

Now consider the following sentences based on the text "Garbage Collectors of the Sea":

So nutrients are kept circulating in the ocean.
They are used over and over again by plant plankton and whales alike.

So nutrients are kept circulating in the ocean *while* they are used over and over again by plant plankton and whales alike.

So nutrients are kept circulating in the ocean *and* used over and over by plant plankton and whales alike.

This example is especially interesting since a case can be made for the use of three discrete methods for relating the two idea units. A case can be made for: a) the inclusion of *and* (Example 3); b) the omission of the connector *altogether* (Example 1) on the grounds that the relationship has already been established by the reader's interpretation of prior text; or c) establishing an unambiguous relationship with the use of *while* (Example 2). These positions serve to point out some of the problems involved in examining cohesive ties or connectors. It is apparent that the absence of a tie or connector can be as cohesive as the presence of one. The fact is that the presence of a tie does not necessarily establish coherence. That is, there is not necessarily a high correlation between lots of ties and lots of coherence. What this implies for an examination of text is, first, the identification of presupposed idea units and, second, an intuitive evaluation of the extent to which the relationship between ideas is clear.

To reiterate, then, the evaluation of ties and connectors—namely, the presence or absence of clear referents and the conjoining or separation of sentences—is important but cannot be made in isolation. Ties and connectors interact with various other factors, including world knowledge, ideational units, and readers' expectations relative to structure. The important question to ask is, "Does it work?" To determine whether or not a tie works, we suggest it would be reasonable for teachers to examine those ideas within a text which they deem important and then determine the extent to which the ties used render the text obscure, ambiguous, unduly implicit, or just generally indeterminable. A measure of indeterminacy might be the probability that a reader will generate a fragmented interpretation of the text or be unable to resolve presupposing items of text. In some situations this will vary with the complexity of the ideas themselves or the distance between connected ideas. The point is, if a teacher determines that a tie does *not* work, then the teacher has an indication of a possible point of confusion on the part of his or her students.

Examining Structural Qualities

The determination of idea units and ties extends our picture of text, but it does not address how well ideas are structurally related across an entire passage. Consider the structural qualities of expository text and stories.

Structural analyses of expository text. The text analysis system proposed by Meyer (1975a, 1975b) and Anderson (1978) are designed to depict the structural alignment of idea units. These systems attempt to show how an author has organized ideas by means of a tree diagram or flow chart. A general structural representation of "Garbage Collectors of the Sea" based on Meyer's text analysis system is presented in Figure 3. Key arguments and/or idea units appear toward the left margin. Idea units appearing to the right of these key units and connected by a diagonal line are supportive of the key idea unit; for example, Idea Unit

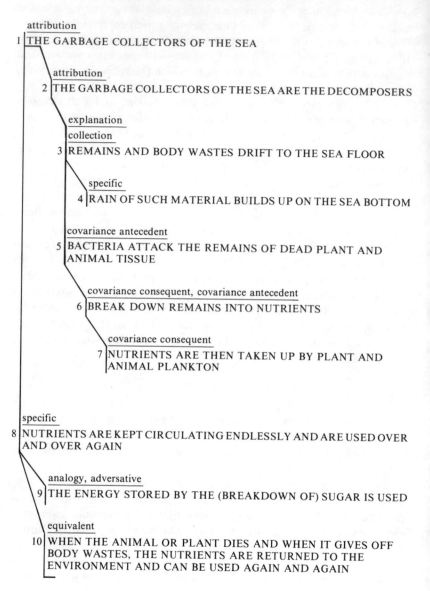

Figure 3. A Meyer analysis of the structural properties of "Garbage Collectors of the Sea."

attribution
1 THE GARBAGE COLLECTORS OF THE SEA

attribution
2 THE GARBAGE COLLECTORS OF THE SEA ARE THE DECOMPOSERS

explanation
collection
3 REMAINS AND BODY WASTES DRIFT TO THE SEA FLOOR

specific
4 RAIN OF SUCH MATERIAL BUILDS UP ON THE SEA BOTTOM

covariance antecedent
5 BACTERIA ATTACK THE REMAINS OF DEAD PLANT AND ANIMAL TISSUE

covariance consequent, covariance antecedent
6 BREAK DOWN REMAINS INTO NUTRIENTS

covariance consequent
7 NUTRIENTS ARE THEN TAKEN UP BY PLANT AND ANIMAL PLANKTON

specific
8 NUTRIENTS ARE KEPT CIRCULATING ENDLESSLY AND ARE USED OVER AND OVER AGAIN

analogy, adversative
9 THE ENERGY STORED BY THE (BREAKDOWN OF) SUGAR IS USED

equivalent
10 WHEN THE ANIMAL OR PLANT DIES AND WHEN IT GIVES OFF BODY WASTES, THE NUTRIENTS ARE RETURNED TO THE ENVIRONMENT AND CAN BE USED AGAIN AND AGAIN

Tierney, Mosenthal, and Kantor

5 is subordinate to Idea Unit 1. Idea units aligned
importance. For example, Idea Unit 8 is equal in
Unit 1 (see Footnote 2). To describe the relation o₁
dominant argument or idea unit, Meyer's structura
series of relations.[3] For example, Idea Unit 2 has th
attribution. This means that the block of information, ₁
through 7, are related via an attributive, descriptive rela
Unit 1.

In a *mapped representation* of the "Garbage Collectors of the
Sea" the mapping technique incorporates the visual-spatial conventions
for diagramming ideas and the relations between ideas. In mapping,
individual idea units are diagrammed as blocks of information via seven
fundamental relationships: concept and example, concept and
properties, concept and definition, temporal succession, cause and
effect, conditions and comparison. An important quality of the map is
that the shape of the map represents the organizational pattern of ideas
within a text.

What utility do these types of text examinations have for a
teacher? Meyer (1977) suggests that a structural examination of text
affords an appreciation of the extent to which key ideas are supported
by a well-structured text. She suggests, for example, that writers would
do well to keep their text tightly structured and place information "to be
remembered" in superordinate positions. Toward assessing text in these
terms, both Meyer's system and Anderson's mapping seem to have the
classroom in mind. Their methods for the visual representation of a text
provide teachers examples of systems which can be easily simplified and
which go a step beyond outlining. Unlike an outline, these procedures
afford an appreciation of the relationships between ideas and sets of
ideas.

But how does one assess whether the structural characteristics of
text will contribute to or detract from meaning? The task of formulating
a map, tree diagram, or flowchart of a text has the potential to yield
several worthwhile indices. For example, assuming a teacher has
isolated the key ideas for which a text is to be read, the salience of these
ideas will likely be related to their level of subordination and "fit" to a
structural alignment. In situations where ideas are difficult to
structurally align and the relationships between ideas are complex, it
seems likely these ideas will be less salient. In all, we would suggest that
the extent to which a teacher has difficulty outlining and describing the
relationships between idea units may be an index of the difficulty the

s will have in dealing with the text for these purposes. To strate, notice that the tie between the two blocks of information in "Garbage Collectors of the Sea" is quite difficult to detail (as indicated on the Meyer analysis by the "?" in Figure 3). The passage seems to make a shift in focus or topic without an adequate transition or preparation for the shift. We would suspect that the problems incurred in mapping these details are similar to problems a reader might have with this same text read for certain purposes.

Although we are hopeful that these structural representation systems will someday be made easy to use and be proven to make quite general predictions about passage difficulty, we hope that the teacher can take more immediate action to evaluate the structural integrity of expository texts used in classrooms. The teacher should examine the text for instances of unmarked topic shifts and for places where important information is rhetorically subordinated or where unimportant information is placed in superordinate position. Care must be employed, however, in evaluating expository structure, for authors may use various kinds of expository structures and rhetorical devices. Some unimportant information, e.g., an interesting anecdote, may precede the main points to be made. Such information is only a problem for children to the extent that they perceive it as being important and understand the rest of the text in light of the initial information. But we have no solid evidence either way. The teacher will have to determine whether an individual student gets off on the wrong track and will have to help the student to recognize that some subparts of a text are interesting digressions. In all of what we say in this paper, we urge the teacher to make a subjective distinction between what may be difficult and what may be deleterious, between challenging and problematic.

Structural analyses of stories. Stories, like expository text, can be subjected to structural analyses. But unlike those for expository text, the intent of most formal structural story analyses is to define the extent to which a story fits a prototypical structure or "grammar"—a structure purported to be based largely on the cultural expectations of individuals (Mandler & Johnson, 1977; Rumelhart, 1975; Stein & Glenn, 1978; Thorndyke, 1977). Typically, a structural account of a story involves defining the relations among idea units in a story in terms of STORY → SETTING + THEME + PLOT + RESOLUTION. Also, categories such as SETTING can be further defined in terms of CHARACTERS, TIME, and LOCATION. The end result is a tree structure which depicts a hierarchy of categories and subcategories. At the lowest level of the hierarchy are the subplots—likely to be episodes embedded within episodes.

Tierney, Mosenthal, and Kantor

Research on these grammars suggests—at least for simple stories—that students internalize these grammars, expect them, and tend to recall information from higher category levels. For example, the structural organization of narratives has been shown to influence what information is recalled or summarized (Kintsch & van Dijk, 1978; Rumelhart, 1977; Thorndyke, 1976, 1977). Stories whose structure violates the prototypical plot structure have been shown to be more difficult to comprehend than stories whose structure is congenial with the prototypical structure. For example, story recall was debilitated by variations from good story form, especially movement of the theme or goal statement to the end of the story (Kintsch, 1977; Mandler & Johnson, 1977; Stein & Nezworski, 1978). Also, the determination of knowledge of a character's goals and plans has been shown to be central to story understanding. Thorndyke (1977), for example, has shown that the deletion of a story character's goal from an otherwise coherent story can reduce the comprehensibility of text. It seems, then, that if simple stories do not fit these expectations, a reader's ability to follow a story line may be hampered.

To analyze stories, then, teachers do not need sophisticated analysis systems. All that is needed is a general framework for analyzing a story—one that follows a basic story structure. Such a framework, mentioned earlier consists of the alignment of story categories and subcategories,[4] shown in Figure 4.

With the general framework for analyzing stories given by the categories of STORY, teachers can gain a more sophisticated understanding of the material the students are being asked to read, and thereby gain greater control over a successful interaction between the reader and the story. For example, a general framework for analyzing stories can enable teachers to determine the extent to which a story deviates from the idealized framework (the deviation is not necessarily good or bad). The teacher can then prepare the students for a deviation if it is extreme, allow for the effect of the deviation on comprehension exercises, make the deviation the point of reading the story, or not read the story at all. Teachers might also assess the extent to which characterization, conflict, and plot progress with the movement of the story. From the teacher's point of view, any extensively negative evaluation of a story's worth may be grounds for not reading the story.

To illustrate, consider the ramifications of these notions for evaluating the following story selections taken from selected basal readers. In the first selection, the author presents a minor conflict, but given the sparseness with which the character's motives are treated, the plot seems hardly worth engaging. The second selection includes

Figure 4. Basic story structure.

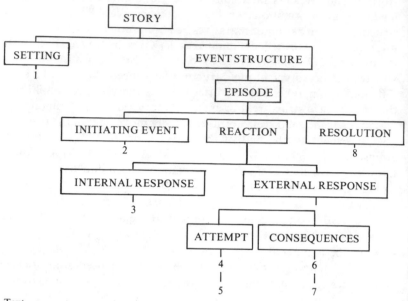

Text

1. Dick lived on a farm in Vermont.
2. One night he heard a fox in the chicken coop.
3. He knew he had to kill it.
4. Dick got his rifle
5. and went to the chicken coop.
6. He surprised the fox with a chicken in its mouth.
7. Dick shot the fox where it stood.
8. Dick buried the fox.

characterization but no real conflict. Again, there does not seem to be a plot worth sharing. The third selection has a similar problem. In this selection there is a conflict, but the events in the story lack continuity and seem unrealistic. Either there are gaps in the plot or the events are poorly aligned. Across selections, then, it would seem that a lack of characterization, conflict, and continuity contributes to an improbable or awkward plot. As Bruce (1978) suggested, good stories 1) display conflicts and continuity, and 2) seem "worth it" when they draw upon the reader's beliefs and expectations.

Selection 1

David's Wagon
Anne Runck

David had a wagon.
He liked to ride in it.

David liked the wagon better
than anything else he had.

One day David wanted to ride in his wagon.
He went to look for it.

He looked in his room
But he could not see the wagon.

David looked under his bed.
But he still could not find the wagon.

He looked in the yard.
The wagon was there.
But there was a robin in the wagon.
There was water in the wagon too.
The robin was taking a bath in it.

Selection 2

A Little Patch of Back Yard

Jonathan Mack's father was going to
paint the back steps.
"I'll go with you," Jonathan said.
They walked outside, and Jonathan
sat down in the back yard.

Ants were marching through the grass
in a long parade. Jonathan lay down
on his stomach to watch.
Pill bugs curled up into little balls,
and beetles crawled under little rocks.
One small brown beetle climbed
up a blade of grass. It fell off
and lay on its back

and kicked its legs in the air.
Jonathan turned it over, and
the beetle hurried away.

Down came a robin. The robin tipped
its head this way and that.
"The robin hears a worm in the ground,"
Jonathan said.
"H'm," said his father.
He stopped to look.
The robin tugged and tugged.

Then—there came Mrs. Fell's cat.
The cat came creeping—creeping—slow—slow.
"Watch that cat!" Jonathan's father said.
"I'll watch," said Jonathan.
"I won't let him get in the paint."

SWISH—
A jay darted down over the cat's head.
The cat jumped back. Away it went—
up and over the fence.
"Cat's gone." Jonathan said.
Away went the robin.
And away went the jay.
The little ants were still marching
in their long parade.

"One patch of back yard is like a
little world," Jonathan said. "You
can see everything here—from an ant
parade to a bird digging for its food.
Most everything's looking for something
to eat."
He thought of the refrigerator.
"I think I'll go inside," he said.
"I'll go the front way. I'll be right
back."
"H'm," said his father. "Get
something for me too."
"Iced tea?" asked Jonathan. "And maybe
some chips?"
"That would be good," his
father said. "Time for a snack."

Tierney, Mosenthal, and Kantor

Jonathan's father had been working
a long time. "Well," he said.
"I've finished my paint job."
He sat down beside Jonathan.
"Time to rest," he said.
A beetle lit on Mr. Mack's hand,
and he watched it a while.

Selection 3

Page 1

What Can I Do?

"I need to get to the airport fast.
What can I do?" said the man.

Pictures

(Man at an office
desk.)

Page 2

"I can ride this to the airport.
But it will not get me to the airport
in time.
I'll miss the jet.
What can I do?"

(Man looks at a
bus.)

Page 3

"Can you get me to the airport
in time for the jet?" said the man.

(Taxi driver stops
to speak to man.)

Page 4

"What you need is a helicopter.
A helicopter will get you to the airport
in time for the jet."

(Man riding in taxi
through city.)

Page 5

"A helicopter!
A helicopter will get me
to the big airport.
With a helicopter ride I'll make
the jet," said the man.

Page 6

"Come with me. Get in.
I'll get you to a helicopter.
And the helicopter will get you
to the big airport in time for the jet."

Page 7
　"What a funny helicopter!
It looks old.
I need to get to the big airport
in time for the jet.
　Can this funny old helicopter get me
to the airport?" said the man.

(Man arrives at
helicopter pad.)

Page 8
　"This helicopter looks old and
it looks funny.
　But it can get you to the big airport
in time for the jet.
　Get in."

　What does this concept of good story form or structure entail for the examination and generation of stories? On the one hand, it can be argued that uniform yardsticks cannot and should not be used to evaluate texts on literary merit. Such yardsticks or frameworks will likely limit variations of aesthetic worth. On the other hand, a general framework used sensibly for analyzing stories—at least simple stories— can provide teachers more systematic and sophisticated procedures for determining the comprehensibility of texts.

Summary and Implications

　One disclaimer needs to be made at this point. That is, we have by no means exhausted the textual features which contribute to the comprehensibility of a text. For example, we have not referenced any kind of syntactic analyses of text. Rather, we have concentrated on ideational and structural properties of text. Furthermore, throughout this paper we have given repeated emphasis to the importance of context. We have suggested that any examination of text features should consider text as language in use. Specifically, our concern has been with the context of text defined by the classroom. To this end, we suggested a framework for examining text in context which involved a consideration of the functions texts are intended to serve in the classroom as well as the purposes and shared experiences of authors and readers.
　Within this framework, we made various suggestions to teachers for examining the ideas, the relationships between ideas, and the structural qualities of text. They include the following suggestions:

Tierney, Mosenthal, and Kantor

1. Ideas might be examined by first isolating the essential understandings students are expected to derive from a text, then examining the extent and nature of support for these understandings provided within the idea units of a text. Where a text has a more poetic or aesthetic intent, this might entail a more thematic analysis of ideas.

2. Relationships between ideas might be evaluated in terms of the probability with which ties are readily understood. A measure of the ambiguity, vagueness, or obscurity of ties and connectors might be the probability with which a reader will generate an inappropriate interpretation for the text. This implies that such factors as context, background knowledge, and reader purpose should be considered when evaluating whether or not a tie works.

3. The structural qualities of expository text might be examined in terms of the ease with which ideas can be mapped hierarchically and relationally. That is, teachers might examine the structural integrity of a text in terms of the extent to which a text and the important ideas therein can be easily fitted to a flow chart, tree diagram, or even an outline.

4. The structural qualities of a narrative might be assessed in terms of the extent to which stories display conflict, incorporate reasonable characterization, and develop a worthwhile plot. It is as if a story should be examined against the reader's expectations relative to whether a story is worth reading.

The potential impact of these suggestions depends on teachers, teacher educators, and publishers recognizing new frameworks for assessing text. In this regard, we would argue that teachers, teacher educators, and publishers have a responsibility to put aside uses of formulae which require sentence length and wordiness to override other text quality considerations. In all, we contend that publishers, teachers, and teacher educators need to give more weight to the beauty and complexity of communication in relation to text selection and use and be less bridled by readability formulae and other restrictive indices. This also implies that new ways of analyzing texts according to cohesive ties or structural "grammars" be looked at for their *conceptual* content, i.e., for the general claims about comprehensibility that they make. Any attempts to use any of the methods of text analysis we have presented as a serious guide to an absolute ranking and selection of texts would lead to a new round of restrictive indices replete with the same problems as the old ones.

We have used the term "frameworks" for assessing texts. Current theoretical work on text analysis should suggest new frameworks or states of consciousness for teachers, teacher educators, and publishers to assess classroom material. This work should not be viewed as a new, improved method for taking the human element off the hook of pedagogical responsibility.

Notes

1. Examples used in this paper are taken from among the following sources: Aaron et al., 1978; Clymer et al., 1976a, 1976b; Gallant, 1975; Grant, 1979.

2. You will note that within this block of information, individual idea units can be several levels removed from the key argument or idea of the block while being immediately subordinate to a key argument or idea unit within the block. Also note that the tie between the two blocks of information is tenuous. (We have identified this by a "?".) In other words, the passage seems to make a shift from decomposers to nutrients without adequate transition or preparation for the shift.

3. Several broad classes of relation are rather self-explanatory and can be identified, e.g., alternative response, descriptive, collection, and causal.

4. Emphasis has been given to characterization, development of conflict, and plot continuity. It must be stressed that these three aspects of a potentially engaging story cannot be isolated within a category of the STORY representation. Characterization progresses within the movement of the story. The development of conflict and plot continuity are part of the same story movement. And the categories of STORY are not absolute entities existing separate one from the other (SETTING can be THEME, THEME can be generalized within PLOT, RESOLUTION can be or is a final EPISODE(S)).

In Search of Structure: Reading and Television

Roselmina Indrisano
Boston University
Joanne M. Gurry
Arlington, Massachusetts, Public Schools

It has been discovered that when adolescents read or view in their leisure time they frequently turn to material which has a narrative structure, such as young adult fiction, episodic television series or TV tie-ins. While these forms diverge in the way the content is structured, coded, and processed, they usually converge in relation to the content they convey. Thus narrative schemata may be used to guide the decoding and comprehension of the message in print or in nonprint media.

Story grammar formulations have isolated some structural dimensions of narrative schemata without restricting those elements to specific content into one medium for communicating stories (Bower, 1978; Glenn & Stein, 1978; Mandler & Johnson, 1977; Rumelhart, 1975; Stein, 1978; Stein & Glenn, 1977, 1978; Stein & Nezworski, 1978; Thorndyke, 1977). Salomon (1979) asserts that it is precisely the conceptual treatment of stories offered by story grammar analysis that renders this form of study useful to comparative media investigations. Research on story structures "may illuminate the ways children learn to cope with different modes of information packagings, beyond what they acquire in terms of knowledge" (p. 54). With regard to differences in content structure, Salomon (1979) suggests the importance of the potential cognitive effects of the way messages are structured within a given medium. He states:

> If media carry any unique significance at all, it must often be in the way events and knowledge are differentially structured. In this way, different experiences are created, suggesting different meanings to be extracted and activating different modes of information processing. For example, the experience gained, meanings construed, knowledge acquired, and processing involved in viewing *The Godfather* on television are unlikely to be identical to those involved in reading the novel. (p. 9)

A comparison of the structures of print and television narratives reveals many contrasts. Novak (1975) suggests three major differences. First, television is a teacher of expectations; it speeds up the rhythm of attention. Characters move briskly and each line of dialogue counts. Any act, such as teaching or speaking, must approach the same pace or appear slow. Second, change of scene and perspective are fast, with the usual verbal transitions (meanwhile, on the other hand, etc.) omitted. Clues are shown, not stated, and the viewer must detect their nonlinear association. Third, the periodization of attention is influenced by the format of segments approximately equal in length. Each segment has its own rhythm, degree of suspense, climax and resolution. Television plots are highly chunked and condensed when compared to most fiction. Thorburn (1976) describes this pheonomenon as localized vividness and elaborates on the idea.

> In its most characteristic and most interesting form, television melodrama will contrive its separate units such that they will have substantial independent weight and interest, usually enacting in miniature the larger patterns and emotional rhythms of the whole drama. Thus, each segment will show us a character, or several characters' behavior and (especially) his emotional responses will intensify, then achieve some sort of climactic or resolving pitch at the commercial break; and this pattern will be repeated incrementally in subsequent segments. (p. 83)

While print and pictorial/aural messages vary with regard to their stimuli or codes, they converge on the level of processing. Two major categories of cognitive operation are suggested by Calfee and Drum (1978). Schema-driven processes are determined by the kinds of information a person can, is required to, or desires to extract, and will influence the type of information sought. Data-driven processing begins with coding elements and proceeds through a number of stages until meaning is constructed.

In comparing the schema-driven processes and the code-driven processes of reading to the operations of viewing, Salomon (1979) makes use of the broad rubrics of "top-down" and "bottom-up" operations eschewed by many reading researchers. Salomon states:

> It is reasonable to expect that, during the time a learner acquires the skills needed to "read" the symbolic forms used in the media, the "bottom-up" direction dominates. With proficiency, however, as skills become automatically employed and organized into larger skill units, the "top-down" direction begins to dominate. (pp. 108-109)

Thus, in viewers who have at least a working or implicit understanding of television's codes in language, schema-driven processes such as those activated by narrative structures, assume priority in extracting knowledge. The parallel drawn from models of the reading process is valuable. Both schematic and textual elements interact to facilitate comprehension, regardless of code.

In summary, studies of comprehension of media, like those of print, are pursuing the nature of the textual-cognitive interaction in the specific domain of code processing and the more broad domains of schema theory.

Research in Narrative Cognitive Development

Although the focus will now shift to cognitive concerns in reading and viewing, issues related to comprehension and processing must not be seen as absolutes but as relative to the growth of the learner. Specifically, attention must be given to cognitive development as scaffolding for the skills and outcomes attributed to media experience. The discussion that follows surveys several studies of students' narrative cognitive development.

Applebee (1978), while not drawing directly from research in cognitive psychology, demonstrates that he is in harmony with this perspective. In approaching "...the plot of children's stories as conceptual structures or modes of organization" (p. 72), he reveals that stories are comprehended differently at different ages and attempts to explore these variations from the perspectives of Piaget and Vygotsky.

In Applebee's studies, young children's concerns with action suggested that for them a story remains primarily a simple patterning of events. Early adolescents' ability to analyze reflected the recognition that a story pattern has purpose and system of ordering. Finally, the generalizations about stories made by older students implied that they saw narratives having broad themes or messages.

Adolescents have arrived at the later developmental stages which makes them suitable for a study of a range of structures in narratives. Applebee states that they are able to analyze and generalize from stories as well as predict what will happen next. Research confirms the developmental nature of story understanding and the ability of adolescents to comprehend and manipulate story categories, to understand stories as wholes, and as modes of expression.

Other researchers have discovered that children's comprehension of television programs increases in predictable age-related stages. Collins (1975) showed that ability to focus on essential information increased with age, while Ward, Wackman, and Wartella (1977) revealed that attention to commercials decreased with age as a result of greater sensitivity to conceptual differences between programs and commercials and among various types of commercials. The effect of format was studied by Huston-Stein and Wright (Salomon 1979, p. 109) with similar results. Young children were most attentive to single, formal formats while for older students formal features (e.g., special visual and auditory effects) were those that best served as syntactic markers for interpreting content. Finally, Leifer et al. (1971) discovered that with increasing age, children remembered better the sequence of events in films and they also understood better the feelings and motives of the characters.

Most researchers conclude that early and midadolescence are critical ages for viewing television. Hendry and Patrick (1977) report that in her 1962 survey, Himmelweit found that 13 to 14 year olds were the peak viewing audiences, while Emmet described 12 through 14 year olds as the heaviest consumers of television in his 1972 study. Below the early teen years, children's schedules are more restricted by their parents, and above this age students had more interest in peer group and social activities.

Even a brief review of the literature on children's and adolescents' viewing reveals broad support for the critical nature of structure. Hendry and Patrick (1977) report several studies of teenagers' viewing preferences. They cite Bogart, stating that family comedy was the type of program most often watched by teenagers in 1953. Adolescents' preferences for television programs seem to have changed little over the years. A more recent study (Avery 1979) revealed that program categories of comedy and comedy-light entertainment were most often chosen as favorites among 12-15 year olds. Westerns, adventure-action and mystery programs were also found high on the list of favorite shows. Most studies of adolescent preference scarcely mention news, information or other contemporary nonfiction categories.

Studies of reading interests of junior and senior high school students reveal consistent trends. Norvell (1973) reports that fiction is the literary type most preferred by both boys and girls and that students preferred titles that fell within stable, general boundaries through the early and middle teen years. His survey also demonstrates that superior, average, and slow students usually enjoyed the same kind of reading materials during this age span. He lists several important interest factors in adolescent reading selections for both boys and girls: action, humor, mystery, and patriotism. Similar preferences were reported by

Indrisano and Gurry

Desjardins (1972) in a mid-Western secondary school. Irsfield's informal survey (1977) of secondary students' outside reading interests tends to confirm Norvell's reports as well as the salience of the movie tie-in. Irsfield identified six interest categories: detective stories, westerns, movie-novel, best sellers, science fiction, and "underground" books about such topics as romance or drugs by anonymous authors.

Despite rapid changes occurring in their lives, adolescents generally maintain stable reading and viewing tastes for typical adolescent fiction genres and serialized dramatic and entertainment programs. Both adolescent leisure fiction reading and serialized television viewing, highly formulaic in structure, are important sources of narrative schemata. Since students usually reach their peak viewing years in early adolescence, this turning point period in media use is critical in their development.

Evidence supports the presence of comparable as well as contrasting structural dimensions in both popular fiction and television programs. Interest in popular narrative forms is not restricted to dimensions of structure in the text, however, concern is also demonstrated for the effect that prolonged or repeated exposure to these forms has on cognition. The reality that some students read or view more frequently than their peers raises the possibility that there are different sets of story schemata for adolescents broadly characterized as readers or viewers.

Although it is now familiar, the statistical evidence confirming the volume of television viewing by all demographic sectors is often overlooked.

> Children under 5 watch an average of 23.5 hours of TV a week.... By his high school graduation today's typical teenager will have logged at least 15,000 hours before the small screen—more time than he will spend on any other activity except sleep. (Waters, 1977, p. 63)

The average 16 year old watches almost 20 hours of TV per week, and the average preteenager watches 23 hours per week (Bantly & Keating, 1978). Heavy television viewing is not a temporary activity of young people. Recent evidence indicates that adults watch even more television than children, an average of about 44 hours per week.

It appears that many young people do not grow out of the viewing habit. On the contrary, they seem to learn it well and continue it into their adult years. The cognitive dynamics facilitating perception and comprehension through television need to be unraveled, if not for the sake of theoretical clarity, then for the urgency of penetrating one of the most powerful mediators of cradle to grave experience.

This review can only suggest broad parallels between adolescent reading and television viewing habits since research methods and studies vary widely. One important general observation, however, is the significance of narrative in print and media experiences of adolescents. A second general point of agreement relates to the phenomenon of an age-related progression of cognitive developments continuing through adolescence. Moreover, in spite of the rapid changes occurring in their lives between the ages of 10 and 15, students seem to maintain fairly stable reading and viewing tastes for traditional adolescent fictional genres and serialized dramatic and entertainment programs.

Through prolonged and repeated exposure to popular narratives, readers and viewers learn their content, but they also internalize the redundant forms in which the narratives are presented. Thus critical structures do not reside exclusively within narratives. Comprehension, enjoyment, or participation in popular literature can only occur to the extent that cognitive paradigms, similar to those in the text, also exist within the reader or the viewer. A repertoire of narrative schemata, the consequence of experience with many stories, facilitates the interaction between the message and the learner, which results in comprehension and ultimately in composition.

Investigating the Interaction between the Message, the Structure of Print, and Television Narratives

Previously cited research in several areas, cognitive development, discourse analysis, and print and media comprehension served as conceptual cornerstones for a study by Indrisano and Gurry (1981), founded on the premise that as a result of prolonged and repeated exposure to popular narratives, readers and viewers not only learn their content, but they also internalize the redundant forms in which the narratives are presented. Thus the critical structures do not reside exclusively within the narratives themselves; they also exist within the reader or viewer. In sum, a repertoire of narrative schemata, the consequence of experience with stories, facilitates interaction between the text and the reader or viewer.

It was hypothesized that students whose leisure time could be broadly described as reading fiction or viewing dramatic programming would have developed narrative schemata as a result of their experience with print or television. If such schemata existed, then they might be demonstrated in students' written narratives.

Subjects

Participants were seventy ninth grade students in four academic levels of a comprehensive high school in a middle class suburb in the northeast. Each student responded to a leisure time questionnaire indicating, among a range of other activities, frequency of narrative reading or dramatic or episodic television viewing. Three subgroups were identified after three separate administrations of the questionnaire over a three month period. One subgroup included students indicating that they read and viewed. The second subgroup included students reporting that they either read or viewed and the third consisted of students reporting that they rarely or never read or viewed narrative material in their leisure time.

Procedures

Following the researcher's protocols, each student wrote a short narrative. The stories were analyzed and categorized by three trained raters on an eleven part continuum, a modified version of the Glenn and Stein (1978) continuum of narrative complexity. The application of story grammar analysis made possible the comparative study of structural variation since story grammar formulations have isolated some structural dimensions of narrative schemata without restricting these elements to a specific content or to one medium. The flexibility of this type of analysis rendered it particularly useful to a study which incorporated aspects of narratives as they are articulated in two different modes, print and television, and in two groups of receivers, readers and viewers.

For the purpose of this study the Stein and Glenn eleven-part continuum was divided into two clusters. The first cluster consisted of sequences, simple structures in which the protagonist did not demonstrate purposeful action, to reach a goal. The second cluster included episodes, more complex stories in which the protagonist did have a goal and a plan for accomplishing the objective.

Findings

Responses to the questionnaire revealed that most students viewed more than they read. Television viewing is a very popular and frequently enjoyed activity of most adolescents in this study. Only a very small number reported rarely or never viewing or reading. The data also indicated that, in general, readers within each of the three major subgroups wrote episodes, stories higher on the continuum, more often than they wrote sequences. Viewers, on the other hand, wrote more sequences, structures lower on the continuum.

Exposure to narratives in print or on television does seem to be related to the development of narrative schemata. Frequency data indicated that narrative structures of readers and of readers and viewers were associated with the generation of structurally complex stories measured by the Glenn and Stein modified continuum. The data do not reveal whether reading, viewing, or their interaction provided the link to internalized narrative structure. It can be noted, however, that in the subgroup of readers or viewers, readers wrote more complex stories than viewers did. Reading with or without viewing in this sample seemed to provide a source of story structure not afforded by viewing alone. Narrative structures in stories written by viewers or by students who rarely or never read or viewed were generally ranked on the lower half of the continuum.

Another finding was that story structure and reading and viewing frequency seemed to be related to academic placement. Students in the upper levels, advanced placement and college groups, tended to write episodes but they were also readers or readers and viewers. Students in the lower groups, general college and noncollege levels, wrote more sequences, but they also indicated that they were viewers or did not read or view. It cannot be asserted, therefore, that students in the lower levels wrote simpler stories only because of factors associated with their placement. Noncollege and general college students in this sample were generally not readers. Those who did read, however, tended to compose stories high on the continuum, as did their college and advanced placement classmates. At all placement levels the general trend revealed by the data was that readers and readers and viewers wrote stories ranked higher on the continuum than did students who did not read or view narrative material. Only associations between students' reading and viewing of narrative material and their academic placement can be made to stories generated. Statements about these factors as causes of students' narrative structures are not warranted.

In the section that follows, the data are presented in summary form and the results of the study are discussed from the perspectives of differences in the learner and differences in the message, or text.

Differences in Learners

Relationship of readers and viewers to types of narratives generated. In general, most students reported viewing or reading in their leisure time. Table 1 presents a summary of the numbers and percentages of students in all subgroups.

Table 1. Numbers and Percentages of Readers and Viewers within Three Major Subcategories

	No.	Percentages of Students Within Subgroups	Percentages of Total Sample
Readers and Viewers			
Read More	5	17.8	
Viewed More	10	35.7	40.0
Both	13	46.4	
Subtotal	28		
Readers or Viewers			
Read	9	26.5	
Viewed	25	73.5	48.5
Subtotal	34		
Neither Read Nor Viewed			
Read More	3	37.5	
Viewed More	2	25.0	11.4
Neither	3	37.5	
Subtotal	8		
Total Students	70		

Table 1 indicates that 88.5 percent of students were either readers or viewers or both. Only 11.4 percent of all students reported that they neither read nor viewed narrative material in their leisure time. This finding is consistent with the research on adolescent media habits, which suggest that when they read or view in their leisure time, they frequently turn to material which has a narrative form whether in print or on television.

Table 2 offers a summary tabulation of sequences and episodes written by readers and viewers. It demonstrates that, in general, readers within each of three major subgroups wrote episodes more often than

Table 2. Numbers and Percentages of Sequences and Episodes Written by Readers and Viewers

	Sequences		Episodes		Within Group Subtotals		Group Totals	
	Number	Percent	Number	Percent	Number	Percent	Number	Percent
Readers and Viewers								
Read More	1	20.0	4	80.0	5	17.8		
Viewed More	5	50.0	5	50.0	10	35.7		
Read and Viewed	2	15.4	11	84.6	13	46.4		
Subtotals	8	28.6	20	71.4			28	40.0
Readers or Viewers								
Read More	3	33.3	6	66.6	9	26.5		
Viewed More	18	72.0	7	28.0	25	73.5		
Subtotals	21	61.8	13	38.2			34	48.5
Neither Readers Nor Viewers								
Read More	1	33.3	2	66.6	3	37.5		
Viewed More	1	50.0	1	50.0	2	25.0		
Neither Read Nor Viewed	3	100.0	0	0	3	37.5		
Subtotals	5	62.5	3	37.5			8	11.4
Totals	34		36		70			

Indrisano and Gurry

they wrote sequences. Viewers, on the other hand, wrote more sequences.

Among the students in the first subgroup (readers and viewers), 71.4 percent wrote episodes. This is not surprising since these students are exposed to a wide variety of narratives in each mode. From the data obtained it is impossible to differentiate which type of narrative, print or visual, had a stronger impact on their narrative sense. But the results do indicate that experience with many narratives is associated with writing a more structurally complex story.

In the second subgroup (readers or viewers), students reporting that they viewed were clearly a majority. Seventy-two percent of the viewers wrote sequences, stories on the lower half of the continuum. Only 26.5 percent of this second subgroup reported that they read in their leisure time. However, of this number 66.6 percent wrote episodes, stories on the upper half of the continuum. These percentages indicate a trend associating the viewing of dramatic or episodic television programming with the generation of less complex narratives, while the frequent reading of narratives is more often associated with the generation of more structurally complex stories.

This finding follows the description of narrative structure reported in the literature. Adolescent fiction has not only been modified in content over the years, there has also been a tendency toward the development of increasingly complex structure. On the other hand, although the content of television programming has become more sophisticated, most serialized or dramatic television programs continue to have structures partitioned at regular intervals by commercials. Unlike print narratives, these breaks continue to segment television narratives into small units, including within their brief span a condensation of the larger patterns and structures of the whole drama.

Relationship between stories generated and academic levels. Table 3 indicates that stories generated seemed to be related to students' placements in four academic levels of their high school English program.

Table 3. Percentages of Stories Generated
by Academic Placement Level

Academic Level	Sequences	Episodes
Advanced Placement	30.0	70.0
College	38.9	61.1
General College	60.0	40.0
Noncollege	70.6	29.4

This relationship seems to be particularly strong for students at either end of the placement spectrum. For example, advanced placement freshmen wrote 30 percent sequences and 70 percent episodes, while noncollege freshmen wrote 70.6 percent sequences and 29.4 episodes. Both middle groups, college and general college levels, tended to write about the same number of sequences as episodes, yet each of these middle groups also tended to divide along lines similar to the group nearest to it at the end of the range. For example, college students wrote slightly more episodes, 61.1 percent, while they wrote only 38.9 percent sequences. General college students wrote more sequences, 60 percent, and fewer episodes, 40 percent. It should be noted, however, that these differences are simply to be viewed as indication of a trend in the data, not as an assertion that students write story structures as a result of factors associated primarily with their academic placement.

A critical point is that reading and viewing patterns also seem to be associated with academic placement levels. Table 4 presents a summary of numbers and percentages of readers and viewers in four academic placement levels. Students in the upper levels tended to read and view or read, while students in the lower levels tended to be viewers or neither readers nor viewers in their leisure time.

Relationship of frequency of reading and viewing to academic placement. Table 5 groups students in different clusters than previously used. Instead of dividing students into three subgroups, they are separated into two groups. The first group consists of students who read and viewed as well as students reporting that they only read in their leisure time. The second category consists of students reporting that they only viewed in their leisure time as well as those reporting that they neither read nor viewed in their leisure time.

This new clustering revealed distinctions in media use at each academic level. Eighteen of twenty advanced placement students, or 90 percent of that level, were among the readers and viewers or the readers. However, fourteen of seventeen noncollege students, or 82 percent of that level, either viewed or neither read nor viewed in their leisure time. The middle levels, college and general college, reflect the patterns of the groups at either end of the academic range represented here. For example, 55.5 percent of the college students read and viewed or read. Among the general college students, however, 73.3 percent reported viewing or not reading or viewing in their leisure time.

Table 4. Readers and Viewers in Academic Placement Levels

	Advanced Placement		College		General College		Noncollege	
	No. of Students	Percent of Level	No. of Students	Percent of Level	No. of Students	Percent of Level	No. of Students	Percent of Level
Readers and Viewers	12	60.0	9	50.0	4	26.6	3	17.6
Readers or Viewers								
Readers	6	30.0	1	5.5	2	13.3	0	0
Viewers	1	5.0	7	38.8	6	40.0	11	64.7
Neither Readers Nor Viewers	1	5.0	1	5.5	3	20.0	3	17.6

Table 5. Number and Percentages of Students Who Both Read and Viewed and Students Who Read Compared to Students Who Viewed or Who Neither Read Nor Viewed

	Advanced Placement		College		General College		Noncollege	
	No. of Students	Percent of Level	No. of Students	Percent of Level	No. of Students	Percent of Level	No. of Students	Percent of Level
Readers and Viewers and Students Who Read and Not Viewed	18	90.0	10	55.6	6	40.0	3	17.6
Viewers and Students Who Neither Read Nor Viewed	2	10.0	8	44.4	9	60.0	14	82.4

The authors can only report observed trends in the media viewing habits of this population of ninth grade students and cannot assert any reasons or causative factors influencing these patterns. The indicators are that reading and viewing of narrative material seem to be associated with students' academic placement levels. It cannot be asserted that students in lower levels wrote stories less structured on the continuum only because of factors associated with their placement, however. Noncollege and general college students in this sample were generally not readers. Those who did read, however, tended to generate stories high on the continuum as their college and advanced placement peers did. At all placement levels the general trend revealed by the data is that readers and viewers or readers wrote stories ranked higher on the continuum than did students who viewed or who did not read or view narrative material. While an association between students' reading and viewing of narrative material and their academic placement can be made to stories generated, no statements about these factors as causes of student narrative writings can be made from the data obtained.

The combined influences of academic placement level, leisure time reading and viewing preferences, and the cumulative narrative experiences of adolescents are complex. Advanced placement and college students' English programs included more fiction reading and more sustained reading than those of their general college and noncollege classmates. Additionally, the upper division courses provided students with more direct study in the forms of the genres read than the lower division courses. Furthermore, students' preferences for reading and viewing and the frequency and quality of their interaction with books or with television are products of home, school, and personal influences. Finally, by the time they reach adolescence, students have had multiple experiences with narratives from a variety of sources. Thus, while it is possible to discuss a relationship between reading and viewing frequency and narrative structures at a given point in their lives, the factors influencing narrative schemata are intricately interwoven and cumulatively developed.

Differences in Messages or Text

Relationship of reading and viewing frequency and rankings of stories. A positive, significant, yet low, correlation ($R = 0.3396$) was obtained between students' self-reports of frequency of reading fiction and rankings of stories. However, there was no correlation ($R = 0.0186$) between stories generated and reports of frequency of viewing.

Although this correlation is very low, it does provide encouragement for the trend revealed in the percentages. Reading fiction seems to be associated with complexity of narratives generated.

Summary of Findings

The following conclusions on the relationship of adolescents' narrative reading and viewing and the development of narrative schemata revealed through a story grammar analysis of written stories are suggested by the data.

Both reading and viewing narrative material were very popular leisure pursuits of most ninth grade students in the sample. Students reported that they viewed television more frequently than they read, however.

The use of both narrative print and television media was more frequently reported among upper division academic levels, students in advanced placement and college sections. Students in lower division groups, general college and noncollege sections, tended to be viewers or to be neither readers nor viewers in their leisure time.

In many instances, exposure to narratives was related to the development of story structure. Students who read and viewed, or those who read, tended to generate stories which were structurally different from those who viewed or who neither read nor viewed. The group composed of readers and the group composed of both readers and viewers employed complex story schemata in a story generation task.

Students who read and viewed generally wrote structurally complex stories measured on the modified Glenn and Stein continuum. The data from this study cannot reveal whether reading, viewing, or their interaction provided the link to internalized narrative structure. However, in the group of either readers or viewers, readers wrote more complex stories than did viewers. For this sample, reading with or without viewing seemed to provide a source of story structure not afforded by viewing alone.

There is a constellation of factors associating reading, but not viewing, with complex story generation. Correlational data revealed positive, significant, but low relationships between self-reports of reading frequency and ranks of stories.

Statistical analysis was limited by the restricted numbers of students in the study. Frequency data and percentages, however, indicated clear trends linking reading with complexity of story structure in this exploratory study. They also indicated that viewing or little reading or viewing was not associated with the generation of structurally complex stories.

With regard to the use of grammar, it was discovered that student narratives can be clustered and ranked using the modified Glenn and Stein continuum. The category descriptions were identified in the narratives generated by adolescent subjects, and they did discriminate most simple from complex narratives.

Application

The theory and research presented in the first part of this chapter, and the findings of the study reported in the second part, provide the basis for the final section, reflections on possible application to classroom practice.

Impact of Structure and Medium

From the literature it was discovered that the type of message which most frequently engages the adolescent is the narrative, and the medium which is most often selected is television. It would also appear that while the essence of narrative comprehension, the story schema, is similar in print and in television, the structure of the forms varies, particularly with regard to time, space, and code. Thus, while story grammar theory is amenable to both forms, the differences in structure impact on the reader or viewer's interaction with the medium and may affect comprehension.

From the study it was observed that exposure to a particular type of structure, print and/or television is coincidental to the type of narrative produced. Adolescents who frequently interact with print or print and television seem to write more complex structures than those who interact only with television or who are limited in the use of print or media.

In planning developmental, remedial and/or leisure reading programs, narrative reading should be encouraged and the use of television viewing without related reading activities should be avoided. Viewing alone seems to discourage the development of structural complexity. Reading and viewing, however, seem to be rich sources for the development of narrative schemata. Television-related reading should not be confined to read-along script programs or to television tie-ins but should lead to the development of reading interests in a variety of genres and content areas.

As a formulation of structural elements universally identified in simple stories, story grammar can be applied in several ways. First, it can be used by teachers and students in comparative study of television and print texts. Application of the grammar to familiar texts can allow students to discover structural properties of texts and to draw conclusions about the relative complexity of the reading and viewing material they enjoy. Second, the grammar can be employed by teachers, parents, curriculum planners, and textbook authors in formulating questions to guide student reading and viewing before, during, and after experiences with narrative texts. The grammar provides a focus for identifying the critical parts of stories and the junctures of their interrelationships. Third, the schema can be used by teachers and planners as a developmental hierarchy for leading students from levels of simple to complex structures in reading, viewing and writing. Elements of the grammar can be studied and discussed following reading or viewing and before writing. Elements of plot and characterization are particularly amenable to this type of analysis.

Finally, if the grammar has psychological validity and does correspond to cognitive narrative schemata, then tests of reading comprehension should account for this phenomenon. If readers and viewers do not use cognitive schemata for guiding reading of a text, or for storing and retrieving narrative data, then instruments for reading comprehension should account for these recent formulations of reader-text interaction.

Reading and Viewing Habits

With regard to the learner, the literature suggests that cognition develops in an age-related progression and that this development is basic to, and is influential upon, the process of comprehension, whether of print or media. This theory is reminiscent of Piaget's concept (1972) of adaptation wherein learners assimilate increasingly complex structures and, in turn, accommodate structures of greater complexity.

It was further suggested that cognitive development guides thematic and structural preferences and thus impacts upon reading and viewing habits. Apparently, early adolescence is a peak time for television viewing, with narrative the type most frequently selected, a preference also reflected in comparable reading habits.

The findings of the study indicated that in addition to the influence of familiar structure as composing patterns, academic placement is also related to these phenomena. Thus, it is possible to suggest that a profile of the adolescent writer who employs complex structures is that of a student in a higher academic placement who is a frequent reader or reader and viewer.

In contrast to what is sometimes provided in remedial programs, students in the lower academic divisions should not necessarily be restricted to structurally simple narratives. While these students may have difficulty with syntactic and semantic components of some texts, evidence indicates that these students can and do learn structurally complex forms from reading and viewing and can use them in a story generation task.

Perhaps the most important task for the teacher of each level of learners is to help them to raise to conscious awareness their understanding of the structure of narratives. The availability of such knowledge at the metacognitive level renders structure as an accessible guide for comprehension and composition. The reader or viewer can use the structure as a map for comparing print to media or two narratives in the same medium. The knowledge of structure can also facilitate the student's ability to answer and to ask questions, the latter a particularly useful skill for adolescents as they seek to become independent learners. Finally, such knowledge can be used to guide the writing of narratives in the form of scripts for media and narratives for print publication, and to perfect these products through analysis, and comparison, joining the processes of writing, reading and rewriting.

It is perhaps appropriate that these reflections end with the thought of a philosopher. In the dawn of the age of television when language found its permanence largely in the form of print, Langer (1971) wrote

> Language is much more than a set of symbols.... Its forms do not stand alone, like so many monoliths, each marking its one isolated grave; but instead, they tend to integrate, to make complex patterns, and thus point out equally complex relationships in the world, the realm of their meanings. (p. 135)

Indrisano and Gurry

PART THREE   The Reader and the Teacher

Learning Social Context Characteristics in Prereading Lessons[1]

Jana M. Mason
University of Illinois
Kathryn Hu-pei Au
Kamehameha Early Education Program

An area of reading research in which interest is fast growing is the study of actual classroom instruction. Perhaps the main reason for this trend is that we have begun to recognize how little we know about the conditions in which children must learn to read, in real classrooms (Cazden, in press). Until very recently, we had little information even at a basic descriptive level. For example, we did not have data on the amount of time generally allocated for reading instruction, and, of this time, how much children spent academically engaged in reading. Fortunately, these gaps in our knowledge are fast being filled (Fisher, et al., 1978). The conviction that we should try to find out more about what actually transpires during classroom reading instruction is further reinforced by the growing body of evidence that cognitive tasks cannot be interpreted accurately apart from social setting characteristics (Cole, Hood, & McDermott, 1978). The idea is that research results are misleading unless cognitive processes, such as those involved in reading, are studied in conjunction with the social circumstances in which skills are learned and practiced. However, if we study the ways in which cognitive and social processes are interrelated in classroom reading instruction, we might then be able to improve the quality of instruction. Cazden (in press) states the argument in the following way:

> Learning to read, like mature reading later on, is certainly a cognitive process; but it is also a very social activity, deeply embedded in interactions with teachers and peers. Hopefully, as we understand those interactions more fully, we will be able to design more effective environments for helping children learn.

In one set of studies which rely on ethnographic techniques, analyses of teacher-pupil interactions have begun to show how the nature of the social structure in a classroom can affect learning. Children may need to understand the rules governing participation in classroom lessons, that is, rules for speaking and listening during group activities, in order to benefit from instruction. Analyses of social participation structures in instructional settings (which have shown that the predominant structure is a teacher question followed by a student response and then a teacher evaluation) have obtained evidence of communication mismatches between students and teachers. Au (1980); Boggs (1972); Cole, Hood, and McDermott (1978); Collins and Michaels (1980); Erickson and Mohatt (1977); Kochman (1972); Michaels (1980); Philips (1972); and Shultz, Erickson, and Florio (in press) found discontinuities between turntaking structures used in school and at home. They found, principally, that minority culture children did not adjust easily to the prevailing social interaction patterns. Au further demonstrated that, when children were allowed to use a turntaking structure that was more familiar to them, their rate of topically relevant verbal interchange, interest in the lesson, and attentiveness to reading increased. McDermott and Aron (1978) showed that turntaking structures for children in the bottom reading groups were different from and, moreover, more disruptive to learning than were the structures utilized for the top groups. Collins and Michaels (1980) reported differences in the way a lesson is structured and in correction procedures provided for good and poor readers, differences which favor good readers. These studies suggest that school achievement is in part a function of the means by which children are allowed to participate in a classroom lesson. That is, how a lesson is socially structured can influence children's willingness or ability to attend to a cognitive task. None of these studies, however, has centered on the development of young children's ability to participate within a well-defined context nor on teachers' responses to improvements in children's interactive skills. We hoped, by analyzing children's social interactions with a teacher but in an academic setting, that we would find changes over time in children's ability to interact with a teacher. We also hoped, by grouping together for instruction children whom we knew from our tests differed somewhat in their understanding of reading, that it would enable us to propose a model indicating how children might use social interactions to signal their knowledge to others and how teachers use interactions to foster learning.

In the study to be described here, we focused on the relationships between cognitive tasks and social skills that would be relevant to prereading or beginning reading instruction, studying lessons given to small groups of children. We analyzed four children's interactions with a teacher, comparing an early lesson with one that occurred later and looking for differences in the social interaction patterns of a high

Mason and Hu-pei Au

knowledge child (one who had many prereading skills) in comparison with three other lower knowledge children. Because we wanted to study the early use of social skills in an instructional setting, we arranged to work with preschool children who had not already learned to work in group settings. Some of the methods we used are termed "microethnographic" because our aim was the fine-grained analysis of a relatively small sample of behavior, in this case two videotaped lessons. We think that microethnography makes it possible for researchers to sort out many of the complexities of lessons in order to reveal relationships previously unseen. In addition, we applied methods of discourse analysis. Specifically, we looked at the relationships among academic tasks, social interaction (turntaking) structures, and participants' speech acts.

Methods

Subjects and Setting

Fifteen children, aged 3.7 to 5 years, were given ten 15-minute prereading lessons. Four of the children, whose lessons we analyzed for this report, were selected from among the 15 because, based on parent interviews and a test we gave, these four were representative of children just beginning to understand what it might mean to read. Three of the children knew a few letter names but were not able to read any words. The fourth, although also not reading words, knew half or more of the letters, showed more interest than the others in letters and words, and was beginning to figure out how to spell short words. The teacher who conducted the lessons was experienced, with a sound background in reading instruction, and was not the children's regular classroom teacher. The lessons were conducted in a small room at the church sponsored daycare center where the children were enrolled. The church was located in a mid-sized town in Southern Illinois. The children were middle class in socioeconomic status and their mothers had fulltime jobs or were attending college.

Procedures

The lessons consisted of letter, word, picture, and story tasks that had been tried out in earlier work with preschool children (Mason, 1980). For all the tasks, the children sat around a small table with the teacher. The teacher was instructed that for most tasks children were to be called on one by one, in the same order each time, so that they would learn how to take turns during the lessons. Instruction took place daily, in the morning, with lessons planned to last about 15 minutes. Four of the sessions were videotaped, the second and fifth being transcribed for purposes of this analysis. The remaining seven videotapes, including those made of the three other groups, were more briefly studied to verify the patterns of change over time and of signaling used by the more knowledgeable child in each group.

Identification of tasks and turntaking structures. The teacher followed closely the tasks set for the lessons by the researcher, enabling the tasks seen in the videotapes to be easily identified and categorized. Also, because at least one turntaking structure had been specified for her, this area of the analysis was made somewhat easier.

Following the procedure outlined by Erickson and Shultz (in press), transcripts were made of the second and fifth lessons. Both the transcripts and the videotapes were studied until we could determine when the teacher shifted to a new task or to another way of managing turntaking structures (in those transcripts, this consisted of 1) teacher talks, children listen; 2) teacher directs, children take turns responding; and 3) children talk, teacher answers). Both were discerned from proxemic cues of the teacher (shift in body position or change in focus of attention), intonation and use of key words signaling the introduction of something new (e.g., "Now" with rising tone), and a return to speaking to the group as a whole, rather than to individuals. After marking off task and turntaking structures, each remark by teacher and children and nonverbal response of children to task demands that signified a new intent or message were coded. Each lesson was considered to have begun when the teacher, after having seated the children, verbally introduced the initial reading task. It was considered to have ended when, in the first case the teacher announced, "Okay, I think that's all we have to do today," and in the second when she said, "Okay" after the children agreed that they had read enough stories.

Identification of speech acts. Work by Dore (1976, 1977, 1978), Lieven (1976), and Shields (1976) provided the basis for a modified classification of verbal utterances and nonverbal responses, adjusted to focus on the intent of a classroom lesson. All were classified according to their explicit or implied intent and tagged with a minus sign if the remark was out of place with regard to the turntaking structure then in force. Since most of the interactions were dominated by the teacher around academic tasks and required information about degree of compliance or correctness, we separated assertive remarks into two

Mason and Hu-pei Au

categories (*statements* which were related to the topic and *comments* which dealt with other child-inserted topics) and separated responsives into *correct* or *incorrect* categories. *Performatives* were chosen to capture children's attempts to express their ability or interest in carrying out an academic task. *Requestives* coded the few occasions that children asked for something. Regulatives and expressives were separated into *repetitives* (when a child repeated immediately afterward someone else's remark) and *conversational devices* (a catch-all category for an assortment of miscellaneous remarks). Since nearly all of the children's remarks were made to the teacher, coding of intended listener was not necessary. The teacher's remarks were classified into requestives (*prompts, directives*, and genuine *questions*), assertives (*statements*), regulatives (*conversational devices* to order, maintain, or extend an interaction), responsives that attempt to change behavior (*admonish, correct, aid*), and responsives that do not attempt change (*accept, praise, repeat, answer*). Her remarks were also coded with respect to the intended listener. More complete definitions of each type of speech act are presented in the Appendix.

Results

Tasks

Seven different tasks were identified, four of which appeared in both lessons. The tasks are listed below, in the order in which they occurred in Lesson 2. Times given are accurate to about ± 3 seconds.

1. Identifying a child's name on a card (.6 minutes, Lesson 2 only). The teacher asked the children, "Who knows whose name is on this card?"

2. Finding the letter-of-the-day from a box of letters (3.4 minutes in Lesson 2, 2.3 minutes in Lesson 5, 5.7 minutes total). The teacher held out a box containing letter cards and children attempted to pick out a *t* in Lesson 2 and an *m* in Lesson 5.

3. Thinking of a word that begins with the letter of-the-day (1.15 minutes in Lesson 2, 1.8 minutes in Lesson 5, 2.95 minutes total). Children were asked to say words that began with a *t* in Lesson 2 and with an *m* in Lesson 5.

4. Drawing the letter-of-the-day and pictures of objects beginning with the letter (4.2 minutes in Lesson 2, 4.4 minutes in Lesson 5, 8.6 minutes total). Children were asked to draw a *t* or *m* then, with the teacher's help, to think of and draw pictures of objects that began with the letter.

5. Reading stories (4.55 minutes in Lesson 2, 5.8 minutes in Lesson 5, 10.35 minutes total). After the teacher read a brief story, she asked each child to read one or two pages of it. The stories were in small booklets, and each was designed to incorporate many words beginning with the same letter. The *t* story was learned in Lesson 2 and the *m* story in Lesson 5. Also, other stories already learned were reread.

6. Reading and pointing to the letter-of-the-day (1.3 minutes, Lesson 2 only). In Lesson 2 she introduced this task with, "Now this time I'm gonna read it (one of the stories described in Task 5) but I want you to show me all the words that start with 'tuh'." In Lesson 5 she briefly attempted to introduce this task again, but the children continued to read without pointing, so no additional time in it was recorded.

7. Handing a letter card to the teacher (.3 minutes, Lesson 5 only). The teacher inserted this task before Task 3 by asking the children to hand her a card as she named a word that began with the letter, e.g., "Could you give me an *m* for marshmallow, please?"

The four tasks which occurred in both lessons (tasks 2, 3, 4, and 5) accounted for 27.6 of the 29.8 minutes. The other three tasks (1, 6, and 7), which appeared in only one lesson, encompassed little lesson time (only 2.2 minutes).

Turntaking

Based on earlier work by Au (1980), Mehan (1980) and Sinclair and Coulthard (1975), three turntaking structures were identified in the two lessons: 1) child-initiated remarks (CIR), 4.4 minutes in Lesson 2, 4.7 minutes in Lesson 5, 9.1 minutes total; 2) teacher question-child response-teacher evaluation (QRE), 7.6 minutes in Lesson 2, 7.4 minutes in Lesson 5, 15.0 minutes total; and 3) teacher direction-child listen (TDL), 3.2 minutes in Lesson 2, 2.5 minutes in Lesson 5, 5.7 minutes total.

The CIR structure is evident when a teacher responds to a child-initiated remark. It occurred for the longest duration when the teacher set up a drawing and printing task (Task 4) for the children to carry out and briefly otherwise when another turntaking structure was supposedly in force. In the drawing task during the CIR structure, the teacher either responded to requests, talked to individuals, or occasionally addressed comments to the whole group. For example, in Lesson 5, both KR and TO had initiated requests for help in drawing letter Ms. She finished helping TO saying:

T: There you did it, TO. (Moves to KR.) Oh that's a—Do you want a little one, KR, or a big one?

KR: Uhh.

JE: Here's a picture of mud.

T: You're right. That does look like mud. Put an M by it. (Moves to AN.) Okay, AN.

JE: I'm goin' to make a big M. Make a monster.

T: A monster: Okay. You put an M by it.

KR: I'm goin' make my mud.

T: Mud? ⌈What is that?⌉ (Starts to move to KR but stops by
   TO).
KR: ⌊ Inaudible ⌋

As is evident from this portion of the transcript, children are free to comment whenever they please without regard for the teacher's activity or attention, although the teacher attempts to respond to each child's request or remark.

The QRE structure, which prevailed here as it does also in most primary grade classrooms, occurring for half the lesson time, is one in which a series of short dialogues transpire between the teacher and a single child. In these lessons the teacher gave each child a turn in a counterclockwise direction around the small table, usually by mentioning the child's name and/or directing her gaze to the child. Occasionally she also added, "It's your turn." Following her directive or prompt and a response by the child, she typically acknowledged or evaluated the response. Each three part interaction generally took only 5-10 seconds. Usually the other children remained attentive while one child was receiving a turn. Here are examples from two different tasks.

(Teacher has children reread a story from the S booklet, Lesson 2.)

⌈ T: What was this one, TO? A—
│ TO: Snail.
│ T: A smiling snail. Very good. What was this one, AN?
│ AN: A sneeze—a sneezing snake.
│ T: Right. A sneezing snake.
│ ALL: ⌈Laugh
│ T: ⌊Now JE hasn't seen this one before.⌋ I'll go. A splashing—
│ JE: Spider.
│ T: Yeah. What're they doin', sitting—
│ KR: in a
⌊ T: at supper

(Teacher has asked children to find M's in a box.)

T: JE, you find an M.
   (JE picks letter card.)
T: Oh he got one. A—oh AN. Can you find an M, our letter for today? (AN picks letter card.)
T: Huh, you did. Let's let TO get one.
   (TO picks letter card.)
T: Huh, good.

The TDL structure was used by this teacher principally to introduce the procedures for working or responding. During this time the children were supposed to listen but not speak. Duration of this structure never exceeded 36 seconds and more often occurred for 6-12 seconds. Here are two examples from the second lesson.

(Children are about to read a story.)

T: Now. Let's look at our Tuh story. Remember from yesterday? I read it first and then you read it (after an interruption by TO and JE, she continues). This is a story about Teeny Tiny (continues by reading the story).
(After she reads the story she says)
T: Okay, let's see. TO, can you tell me what's this page?

Mapping of turntaking structures over tasks. The four tasks which occurred in both lessons were conducted almost entirely in either the CIR or the QRE turntaking structure, apart from some time in the TDL structure, when the teacher explained the task to the children. Thus, Tasks 1, 2, 3, 5, 6 and 7 were conducted principally in the QRE turntaking structure, while Task 4 was associated with the CIR structure. The occurrence of turntaking structures within tasks across the two lessons is shown in Figure 1. It was apparent, as others have demonstrated (e.g., Sinclair & Coulthard, 1975), that changes in lesson content were usually marked by the teacher taking control of the floor, using the TDL structure to speak to the group. As seen in Figure 1, the later lesson showed fewer shifts in task and turntaking structure. There were 6 tasks and 30 turntaking structure shifts in Lesson 2 but 4 tasks and 23 turntaking structure shifts in Lesson 5.

Violations of turntaking rules. Each turntaking structure carries with it particular rules for social interaction. It is readily apparent, for example, that the QRE structure requires children to take turns responding. Not only does the teacher point to, turn toward, look at, or name the child who has the turn, but children who speak out of turn are admonished while those who remain silent are often helped or prodded

Mason and Hu-pei Au

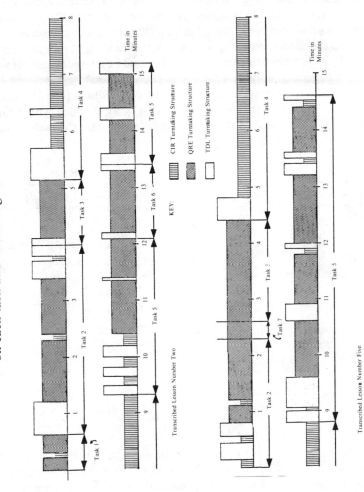

Figure 1. Transcription of lessons 2 and 5 in terms of time spent on each task and turntaking structure.

KEY:

▨ CIR Turntaking Structure

▧ QRE Turntaking Structure

☐ TDL Turntaking Structure

Transcribed Lesson Number Two

Transcribed Lesson Number Five

Time in Minutes

until they do respond. That the TDL structure allows only the teacher to have a turn is evident by the response to an interruption—the teacher either ignores it or gives a very brief answer but returns immediately to the topic. The CIR structure, by contrast, allows anyone to talk, but since communication is the purpose, speakers should not interrupt each other. Ideally, children should vie for the floor but then be quiet when another person is speaking. Children, then, have a complex set of school social interaction patterns to figure out: When ought they remain silent, when is it sharing-turns time, and when can they speak out? How does the teacher signal these changes to the children?

To study whether children learned to follow the rules that were evident in these transcripts, their remarks were coded with a minus if they violated a rule of the turntaking structure that was then in force. Violations were then categorized as shown in Table 1.

Table 1. Violations of Turntaking Rules

Structure	Lesson 2	Lesson 5	Total
TDL			
Interrupts teacher	5	2	7
QRE			
Inserts statement or comment out of turn	3	1	4
Inserts answer out of turn	11	11	22
CIR			
Overlaps teacher's utterance with statement of a request	15	3	18
Overlaps other child's utterance	1	0	1
Total	35	17	52
Percent of children's total remarks	25%	8%	15%

In every category there were no more violations in Lesson 5 than in Lesson 2, and altogether a reduction by three times in the proportion of violations. However, two borderline types of remarks which occurred only in Lesson Five were not included here: 1) There were six insertions of statements by children during the TDL structure, but these occurred when the teacher had paused because she was at the end of a statement or directive. Since the children may have believed she was at a juncture between turntaking structures and since they did not in these

Mason and Hu-pei Au

cases overlap her speech, these were not counted as violations. 2) There were nine occasions when, during the QRE structures as a child hesitated in answering, another child whispered the answer to him/her. Since the child spoke directly to the turntaker, without usurping the other's turn, these remarks also were not counted as violations. Both of these borderline cases seemed to us attempts to "bend the rules," and are based on an understanding of the rules, rather than a lack of knowledge of them.

Speech Acts

The four children produced a total of 140 speech acts (verbal utterances and nonverbal messages) in Lesson 2, and a total of 215 in Lesson 5, as shown in Table 2. There were substantial changes over the two lessons in the type of speech acts children used. They more than doubled their self-initiated remarks (requestives, assertives, and performatives) and remarks that could extend an interaction with the teacher (regulatives and expressives), but they had fewer responsives.

The teacher produced a total of 637 remarks (Table 3) which were nearly evenly divided between the two lessons. The only noticeable change for the teacher was in the incidence of the two types of responsives. There was a decrease over time in change-initiating responsives (help, correct, or admonish) and an increase in other responsives (praise, accept or repeat). These changes probably occurred because the teacher adjusted the tasks to children's knowledge.

Table 2. Children's Speech Acts

Speech Act	Lesson 2		Lesson 5		Total	
	N	Rate per Minute	N	Rate per Minute	N	Rate per Minute
Requestives	1	.07	9	.62	10	.34
Assertives	14	.92	31	2.12	45	1.51
Performatives	5	.33	17	1.20	22	.74
Responsives	79	5.20	69	4.86	148	4.97
Regulatives and Expressives	34	2.24	84	5.92	118	3.96
Inaudible	7	.46	5	.32	12	.40
Total	140		215		355	

Table 3. Teachers' Speech Acts

Speech Act	Lesson 2		Lesson 5		Total	
	N	Rate per Minute	N	Rate per Minute	N	Rate per Minute
Requestives	108	7.11	99	6.78	207	6.95
Assertives	39	2.57	27	1.85	66	2.21
Regulatives	65	4.28	57	3.90	122	4.09
Change-initiating Responsives	65	4.28	40	2.74	105	3.52
Other Responsives	60	3.95	77	5.27	137	4.60
Total	337		300		637	

Table 4 shows a breakdown of the children's speech acts according to the turntaking structure. A comparison over the two lessons of the child-initiated remarks (summing requestives, assertives, and performatives) indicates that these remarks increased principally during the CIR structure (14 such remarks in Lesson 2 but 44 in Lesson 5). However, increases in use of regulatives and expressives occurred almost entirely during the QRE structure (24 remarks in Lesson 2 but 67 in Lesson 5). This suggests that the children adapted their verbal interactions with the teacher to fit better the turntaking structure imposed by the teacher. However, to guard against the possibility that the effects attributed to learning of turntaking rules were actually the results of particular tasks, children's speech acts were tabulated according to lesson and task. As shown in Table 5, speech acts increased in all four tasks which occurred in both lessons. Thus, there is little evidence to suggest that task differences affected speech rate changes (for example, it was not true that easier tasks generated a greater response rate).

Table 4. Frequency of Children's Speech Acts as a Function of Lesson and Participation Structure

	Lesson 2			Lesson 5		
	TDL	QRE	CIR	TDL	QRE	CIR
Requestives, assertives, and performatives	2	5	14	5	8	44
Responsives	0	71	8	0	69	0
Regulatives & Expressives	0	24	10	3	67	14

Mason and Hu-pei Au

Table 5. Change in Children's Speech Acts as a Function of Task

	Lesson 2		Lesson 5	
Task	*n*	Speech Acts/min.	*n*	Speech Acts/min.
2	20	5.9	27	11.7
3	11	9.6	25	13.9
4	30	7.1	49	11.1
5	64	14.1	107	18.4

The following examples from the transcripts show how much more smoothly Lesson 5 occurred as the result of the children's greater social and cognitive understanding. Children interpreted a greater number of task-appropriate remarks at appropriate junctures in the turntaking contexts.

Lesson 2, CIR Structure, Task 4

> T: Let's make a *t* for - um - a toaster.
> Can you make another T for Toas⌈ter?⌉
> KR: ⌊Look!⌋
> T: Okay. Now let's think of a picture you could draw and make a t to go with it. (Leans toward TO). What has - what has a t sound?
> KR: ⌈Toooo   ⌉
> JE: ⌊inaudible⌋
> T: A toad or a turtle or a turnip.
> ⌈Who could make -⌉
> AN: ⌊What is that -   ⌋

Lesson 5, CIR Structure, Task 4

> T: Okay, which one are you goin to make? (Speaking to TO)
> ⌈Shall we make the big one?   ⌉
> AN: ⌊I can't make an - any either.⌋
> T: That's very good, AN. Try again.
> That's really very good.
> JE: I made a m, a small m.
> T: Oh, very nice.
> KR: I can't make one.
> JE: I'm goin to make a picture of mud.
> T: There, you did it, TO. (Moves to KR.) Do you want a big one K - Yes? A big one?
> KR: Uh uh.
> JE: Here's a picture of mud.

Lesson 2, QRE Structure, Task 2

T: Get a T outa here.	T places box in front of AN.
Huh. Good gir.	AN picks letter.
JE: (inaudible)	T places box in front of JE.
T: There's some big ones	JE picks letter.
and some little ones.	
Good JE.	
Okay KR.	
Huh, Good boy.	

Lesson 5, QRE Structure, Task 2

T: KR. Let KR go	T places box before KR.
next.	
JE: I got a big one.	
TO: I got a big one too.	
T: Did you get one?	KR picks letter.
Everybody got a big	
one this time.	
TO: But not AN.	
T: Didn't ya, oh, you're	
right TO. She got a	
little *m*.	
There you go JE.	T puts box before JE.
JE: Big *m*.	
T: Another big one.	

Reduction of speech acts while giving directions. Another aspect of social learning is evident as the teacher realizes the children understand the task, reducing task descriptions. Among all four tasks that were repeated, she used fewer words and phrases and often made fewer directives or descriptive statements. There were 17 separate remarks over the four tasks in Lesson 2 and 13 in Lesson 5. All the teacher's TDL remarks for the four tasks are reported below. The number of remarks made are noted after each task.

Lesson 2, Task 2 (after drawing for children a printed upper and lower case T).

T: Now, let's see if you find the T. All right? This is first time for JE but TO did this yesterday. TO, you want to pick the first one? (4)

Lesson 5, Task 2 (after drawing M's)

T: Let's see how many m's you can find in this box. Let's take them one at a time. JE, you find an m. (3)

Mason and Hu-pei Au

Lesson 2, Task 3

    T: Now let's think of some words that begin with T. Like let's start with TO. Who else—what else w—starts with tuh? (3)

Lesson 5, Task 3

    T: Now you tell me—You give me an m for—you give me a word that starts with m. (1)

Lesson 2, Task 4

    T: I have some paper here and what I would like you to do is to make a couple of T's for me. I'll give you a word that has a tuh sound and I'd like you to make a T to go with that word. Okay? I'm gonna give you a nice black pen and you can make your T just like this one up on the top. (7)

Lesson 5, Task 4

    T: Could you make me—print a couple of m's? We'll print an m for monster and milk and then we'll draw a picture of a monster or a milk carton or a marshmallow. Let's all make an m just like at the top of your paper. Make an m right up there just like it. (5)

Lesson 2, Task 5

    T: Now let's look at our tuh story. Remember from yesterday. I read it first and then you get to read it. (3)

Lesson 5, Task 5 (after a child interjects the comment that he's going outside to play)

    T: Huh, do you know what? You guys (inaudible) you didn't hear our m story. Know what it's about? A monster. (4)

    Truncation of teacher's QRE directives. A change was observed in the patterning of interaction during QRE structured tasks, both within and across lessons. The teacher usually shortened her directives to individual children as task performance and responding began to operate smoothly. Here are the directives given during the letter selection task in the two lessons. We omit the first, because it appeared directly after the general directions for the task, and some in the middle because they are similar to the middle ones that are reported.

Lesson 2

    Directive 2: Okay, AN. Let's let AN go and then JE. Get a T outa there.

    Directive 3: There's some big ones and some little ones.

    Directive 4: Okay KR.

    Directive 6: Okay TO. Look again. See what you can find.

    Directive 8: JE picks letter before teacher verbally directs him.

Directive 10: Okay TO.
Directive 11: Okay AN. They're getting very hard to find now. There's just a couple left.
Directive 12: JE. There's one real silly-looking T. See if you can find that one. You have to be very good to be able to find it.
(last)

Lesson 5

Directive 2: Oh, AN. Can you find an *m*, our letter for today?
Directive 3: Let's let TO get one.
Directive 4: KR. Let KR go next.
Directive 6: AN. Let's let AN go next then you can go TO.
Directive 8: Okay KR.
Directive 10: Okay AN.
Directive 11: Okay TO. Look closely. You may have to move em around a little bit.
Directive 12: Okay. Let's see, KR. I see it. This is a tricky one. Can you see it?
(last)

Directives changed within each lesson. At first, the teacher reminded the children of the task, in the middle she usually reminded them only of their turn, with an okay and their name, and at the end, because of the scarcity of letters, she added comments, offering hints so that they would be successful. Over the two lessons, there was a decrease principally in her initial description of the task. However, she continued to issue regulatives to maintain a rapid response rate and again provided additional comments at the end.

Effects of Competency Differences Among Children

When we study lessons as social contexts, we should expect to find interactive effects: not only does the teacher influence students, but students in turn affect the teacher. To identify these effects, we needed to have children in a group who differed from one another. We chose a contrast in knowledge about reading, placing one higher-knowledge child in each group of four children. That allowed us to measure both differences in children's displays of competence as well as differences in the teacher's responses. That is, the first step in the analysis was to confirm that the one high-knowledge child either used more speech acts altogether or used them in different proportions than the other three.

The second step was to determine whether or not the teacher responded differently to this child than to the others.

Differences in children's display of competence. Differences among the children were expected, based on a notion that competence is evident by the use of clear and accurate statements and a larger number of correct responses. Thus, we tabulated for each child the number of performative statements (e.g., "I can do...") in conjunction with statements made about the task (e.g., "this is a picture of mud"), requests to do the activity first, alone, or without help (e.g., "I wanna read it by myself"), and correct responsives. It is important to note, while children were given an equal number of opportunities to respond and did not differ in the incidence of requestives, regulatives, or expressives, that they varied as expected in their use of assertives, performatives, and responsives.

Differences among children on the quantitative characteristics (presented in Table 6) show clearly that JE, the child with the most knowledge of prereading, made a larger number of descriptive statements to the teacher about the tasks, more often issued remarks about task-related activities and, despite receiving no more directives than others to answer, found more opportunities to express his knowledge. Here are some of his remarks, nearly all of which drew a teacher response. In comparison to other children's remarks, also presented below, JE's statements show his greater ability to describe accurately the tasks.

Table 6. Differences among Children in Their Displays of Competence in Performing Tasks in Lessons 2 and 5

	High Knowledge		Low Knowledge	
	JE	AN	TO	KR
Requestives	3	3	2	2
Assertives	12	5	8	11
Performatives	12	2	3	5
Legal responsives	39	20	24	30
Illegal responsives	15	0	6	1
Whispered responses to turntaker	9	0	0	0
Total correct responses	43	17	20	19

JE: (1) I made a gigantic T.
(2) Look at my gigantic T.
(3) Want me make a smaller m?
(4) I'm goin to make both m's.
(5) Here's a mouse.
(6) I'm goin to color in the pictures.
(7) I wanna read that all by myself.

JE's first five remarks were made during the letter-picture drawing task. All were appropriate to the task and secured a teacher response. In remark (7) he asked to read the m story.

KR: (1) Look at the tree I made.
(2) Look at those pears on there.
(3) Look at this. A person's splashin in it.
(4) I wanna do that.
(5) I can make a little - (gestures to complete thought).

All of KR's remarks were made during the letter-picture drawing task. Remark (2) occurred when he was supposed to be drawing t pictures, No. 3 referred to his picture of mud, in No. 4 he wanted to draw a letter, and in No. 5 he was talking about the letter m.

AN: (1) And this is gonna be - this is a monster.
(2) I wanna make a flower.

AN's second response occurred after the teacher tried to interest her in drawing something that began with m.

TO: (1) I made mud.
(2) I'm - I'm doing it.

TO's second response occurred during story-reading. He wanted his turn to read.

Even before the end of the second lesson (which was JE's first lesson since he had been absent the day before), JE had begun in several ways to demonstrate his greater competence. On the easy, letter-picking task (Task 2), JE found letters before the teacher could issue a directive. Then, following the task of pointing to letters in the story (Task 6), the teacher commented to all the children, "All those words have a T at the beginning, don't they?" JE, apparently noticing T's at other locations in words, added, "And at - in the middle and in the last." After one reading of the new story by the teacher, JE began to insert the correct word or phrase both during his own turn and when others had been nominated. In the fifth lesson he was even more confident. Twice he reached for the book, thrice requested to read it, and on several occasions told other

Mason and Hu-pei Au

children the word if they hesitated. In addition, when drawing, he was able to ask the astute question, "What else starts with M?" and was the only one to be able to say, "I don't know that word."

Differences in the teacher's verbal response to children. Relying on our intuitions that teachers try to foster correct responses and also are more apt to notice clear and accurate statements, we expected that the high competence child's statements and responses would be somehow highlighted by the teacher. We tabulated separately the remarks made by the teacher to each child. Differences in her use of speech acts are shown in Table 7.

Table 7. Teacher Directives, Responses and Comments to a High Competency Child in Comparison to Low Competency Children

| | High | | Low | | |
	JE	AN	TO	KR	Total
Requestives (directive, question, prompt)	44	49	38	38	169
Responses that attempt to change behavior (correct, admonish, aid)	21	19	14	17	71
Responses that have a neutral effect (accept, repeat, answer)	31	13	18	15	77
Responses that favorably evaluate (praise)	15	6	7	7	35
Assertives or regulatives that extend interaction with child (statements, conversational devices)	30	15	24	26	95
Total number of remarks	141	102	101	103	447

While the teacher made similar numbers of requestive remarks and change-influencing responses to all children and gave them about the same number of opportunities to respond, she did not distribute her other remarks equally. She more often verbally noted JE's responses or remarks (by repeating, praising, or acknowledging) and also carried out longer or more frequent interchanges with him. As a result, nearly a third of all her remarks were directed to him while the other children each received a little less than their quarter share.

Additionally, two unusual remarks by the teacher occurred in Lesson 2 (letter picking) which set JE apart from the other children.

Noticing how quickly he found letters, she exclaimed, "Oh, JE knows right away." To AN, however, she said, "Can you find one? There's a couple more left. Let's look through um. C'n you find one? See a T?" KR was also helped: "Let's look. There's some big ones and some little ones." TO was nearly helped: "Now there's just a—that's a good pick." Further, to JE on his last turn, she challenged with, "There's one real silly looking T. See if you can find that one. You have to be very good to be able to find—there you did it." By contrast, when KR got the last turn for the same task in the fifth lesson, she implied a readiness to help saying, "Can you see it?" Thus, even with a task that all of these children were able to accomplish, the teacher made remarks that in subtle ways differentiated JE from the others. JE's greater competency was acknowledged through special comments to him and a greater readiness to help the others.

Another revealing incident occurred in Lesson 2 during letter drawing (Task 4). The teacher had been telling the children what they could draw that began with T, because none had yet thought of any words by themselves. Turning to JE, she said "How 'bout a turtle. Can you do a turtle?" JE shook his head, looked down at his paper. "Whatchado?," she asked. JE answered, "Teetertotter." She was apparently surprised that his competency extended this far, for her praise was loud with a strong emphasis on his answer, "Teetertotter, that's great. That's just exactly right."

Differences in selection of turntaker. Another way to highlight a response is to give a child the first turn for a task. To look at this we compared the teacher's selection of the first turntaker. In Lesson 2, TO was asked to begin letter-picking, letter-word matching, and on three occasions to start rereading a story (where the orderly sequence was broken in order to begin with TO). JE and AN were each asked to begin one of the story rereadings, and JE was asked to begin the name-card task. In Lesson 5, JE was asked to initiate letter picking, word repetition (Task 7), letter-word matching, and two of the four story-reading occasions. The other two story readings were begun in the regular sequence by KR. Thus even though the teacher had agreed beforehand to assign turns in the same sequence from child to child, she most often started Lesson 2 tasks with TO (perhaps she did not yet realize JE's greater competency) and nearly always chose JE to begin Lesson 5 tasks.

Discussion

Did the children know better by the fifth lesson how to interact with the teacher? Evidence from several sources indicates that the answer is yes. The first piece of evidence comes from incidence of violations of turntaking rules (Table 1). In all categories of violations children made fewer inappropriate remarks in Lesson 5 than they did in Lesson 2 (17 versus 35). Taking into account the fact that children made half again as many remarks in the fifth lesson, the disparity becomes even larger (8 percent of all Lesson 5 remarks and 25 percent of Lesson 2 remarks). Our interpretation that the reduction of violations is due to social learning is compelling because reductions occurred for all tasks (Table 5).

The decrease over the two lessons in inappropriate remarks which was accompanied by an increase in children's speech acts is the second piece of evidence that children were learning the social interaction patterns. While there was little change in children's responsives, incidence of requestives, assertives and performatives increased from 20 remarks in Lesson 2 to 57 remarks in Lesson 5. Regulatives and expressives increased from 34 to 84. When these were broken down according to the participation structure in which they had occurred (Table 4), it was apparent that most of the increase in self-initiated remarks occurred during the CIR structure while the principal increase in responsives occurred in the QRE structure. This indicates that the children adapted to the particular turntaking structures, utilizing both structures more effectively in order to increase their participation in the lessons.

Finding that the children did learn to make more accurate and more extensive use of social patterns to participate in the lesson permitted us to ask a question about effects on the teacher. Were the changes in children's social knowledge noticed by the teacher and if so, what were her responses? An analysis of task directions, given for the same tasks in Lessons 2 and 5, suggests that the teacher did perceive these changes. In Lesson 5, she gave a briefer description of each of the four tasks that had also occurred in Lesson 2. An analysis of her directives in the QRE structure also supports this interpretation. She made fewer controlling statements in the Lesson 5 task than the Lesson 2 task. Further, there was an orderly truncation of directives within each task, so that "Okay" or the child's name often became sufficient to cue the right child to answer a question or carry out a task.

Next, we looked at the effect on the teacher of children who differed in their knowledge about reading. The teacher's responses to the children indicated without doubt that she was affected by JE's displays of competence. While giving the children an equal opportunity to respond, she repeated, acknowledged, or praised JE's answers far more frequently than those of the other children (Table 6). This seemed to be an appropriate action in this context because it made the other children better aware of good or correct answers. Interestingly, in a later interview, the teacher reported that until reading this chapter she had not realized the extent of JE's influence.

The final effect of JE's competence that we analyzed was teacher selection of the first responder. While in Lesson 2 (JE's first lesson), JE was twice chosen to be first, and in Lesson 5 he was chosen to begin five of the seven tasks. This was also an appropriate response, because it helped to minimize children's errors. That is, a high knowledge child is more likely to model the task accurately, making the task somewhat easier for the other children. The teacher's choosing JE most often in Lesson 5 indicates that she was reacting to his greater competency and adapting her lesson structure accordingly.

A Social Interaction Model

While the patterning of social interactions revealed by this analysis of two lessons given to young children may not prevail in public school classrooms among older children, it ought to provide a model for teachers of the social strategies to be aware of, particularly when introducing young children to formal lessons. It is apparent that teachers often play a role not unlike that suggested by Bruner (1976), Cazden (1979), and Snow (1976), who studied how young children learn through interaction with their mothers. They showed that a predominant pattern is a routinized game between mother and young child in which the child is given an increasingly larger role to play until the game can be carried out successfully with mother as onlooker. In similarity to the QRE structure, the mother asks questions to which she knows the answer, and the child's principal role is to perform without error. However, there the similarity ends because in a school setting, a teacher must interact with a group of children rather than a single child, and must somehow figure out how to provide opportunities for several children to perform flawlessly, yet gain increasing expertise. Evidence from this study suggests that the problem of how to interact with a group of children rather than one child can be resolved by routinized use of a familiar participation structure, that is, by making frequent use of exactly the same interaction pattern with repeated use of the same set of tasks. With its repetition, the teacher can gradually diminish his or her role until a word or nod is sufficient to initiate the next round of student participation. Our teacher used the QRE structure to achieve this effect. However, to keep children from feeling that they had no interactional rights (Au, 1980), she occasionally allowed the CIR structure, that is, she relinquished her control of the setting so that children could initiate requests or statements to her. Flawless performance, or minimizing errors, is addressed by 1) coupling a familiar participation structure with a task so that children can focus on the cognitive rather than social demands, 2) revising tasks or giving more clues about the answer when errors are high, 3) giving the hard questions to more competent students and easy questions to less able students, and 4) highlighting and prolonging interactions with high competence children in order that their display of knowledge can serve as a model for other children. In this study, these were achieved in the following ways. First, coupling of the QRE or CIR participation structure with particular tasks occurred throughout the lessons. Thus, the children quickly learned to expect a certain way to interact with the teacher as soon as a task was announced. Second, when errors were high, the teacher eliminated the task in later lessons or preceded the task with more information and gave more clues during its occurrence. That meant a decrease over the set of lessons in wrong responses. Third, dispensation of hard items to more able children meant, here, turning to JE. Although the teacher was committed to circling round the group for turns so she could not pick out hard items for him to answer, she was able to give him the first turn of most tasks. The fourth point, of highlighting responses of more able children was very apparent. JE was praised and his answers accepted or repeated by the teacher far more frequently than the other children.

The model proposed of social interaction in the primary grades is characterized by establishment of routinized macrostructure (task and turntaking procedures) but also by frequent modification of microstructures (type of speech act, particularly incidence of teacher responsives to children's answers) and ordering of turntaker. Macro-structures are established by the teacher and based on their familiarity to the children, are gradually or rapidly learned. As they are put into place (become routinized), the social interaction between teacher and students proceeds more smoothly, making it more likely that messages from a teacher about the nature of the task or messages from children about their need for help, preferences, or understanding of the task become easier to communicate and easier to interpret. The microstructures, manipulated by the teacher to improve children's opportunities to learn, serve as fine-tuned adjustments on the lesson as a whole.

Note

1. Research reported herein was supported in part by the National Institute of Education under Contract No. HEW NIE C-400-76-0116 and was prepared principally during the first author's sabbatical leave in 1979 at Stanford University. The authors wish to thank Christine McCormick, Larry Shirey, and children, teachers, and parents of the day care center for their help.

Appendix A

Speech Act Classification System

Student speech acts

Requestives. Asks for information, help, or permission: "I can't make *m*'s." "What is that thing up there for?"

Assertives

Statement. On-task remarks which describe or report information about the lesson: "I got a big one"; "A person's splashin in mud."

Comment. Off-task remarks which describe or report information that are not related to the current task: (T introducing lesson) "I don't like mayonaise"; (T starting to read story) "I don't have my picture in yet."

Performatives. Claims of action carried out or about to be carried out: "I'm goin to make both *m*'s"; "I make mud."

Responsives

Correct. Satisfactory verbal or nonverbal response to teacher's prompt or directive: JE picks letter from box; T: "What's your *m* for?" TO: "Marshmallow."

Incorrect. Unsatisfactory verbal or nonverbal response to teacher's prompt or directive: TO picks a card. T: "Oh is that a *t*?"

Ignore or avoid. No response to teacher or rejection of teacher's answer: T: "OK, what's your last *m* for? Mud?" JE shakes head; T: "AN, could you make a little mommy?" AN does not respond.

Regulatives and expressives

Repetition or acceptance. Repetition of teacher's remark or acknowledgement of teacher's remark: T: "Say mud." KR: "Mud;" T: "What's on your car? A tire?" JE nods.

Miscellaneous conversational devices. Attention getters, politeness markers, fillers, exclamations: "Yuk"; "Umm"; "Aak"; "Look!"

Mason and Hu-pei Au

Teacher speech acts

Requestives

Prompt. Examination-type question or request to student when answer is known by teacher: "Who knows whose name this is?"; "What are they doin?"; "Can you give me an m word?"

Directive. Action request: "Put it right here." "Okay KR," (placing letter box before child). "Can you make a *t* for a toad? Make a *t* for a toad."

Question. Question when answer is not known by teacher or when clarification is needed: "You got both monster and a mud or is that a mommy?"; "Shall I help you make an *m*? Is that what you need, AN?"

Assertives

Statement. Expression of information, rules, explanations or descriptions of lesson content, or of students' role: "Okay, this is called teeny tiny"; "I see it. This is a tricky one"; "It's the letter *m* and it's our special letter for today."

Responsives that do not attempt to change student behavior

Answer. Responses to student questions: JE asks, "Want me to make a smaller *m*?" T: "Yes"; JE asks, "What else starts with *m*?" T: "Mouse."

Acceptance. Acceptance of student's response with a neutral marker: "Okay"; "Right"; "Thank you"; "Yes."

Praise. Marks student's response with a positive statement: "Good"; "Super"; "Wonderful"; "Very nice."

Repetition or expansion. Repetition or expansion of student's response or remark: AN: "Mouse." T: "Mouse."

Responsives that attempt to change behavior

Admonishment. Criticizes, rejects, or otherwise attempts to change behavior: JE gives answer out of turn. T: "Shh. Let AN do it now."

Correction. Completion or correction of student's answer or statement: Child misreads word saying, "Frog." T: "Toad"; KR has made a picture, saying, "Hey but that's a -." T: "A picture of a T word." KR: "But that's a -." T: "A turnip."

Aid. Giving partial information to student which makes task easier or supplies answer if child hesitates. T helps by exposing a *t* card in a box saying, "Let's look through um"; T gives one of the words in a sentence saying, "What kinda table? A teeny -"; T repeats what child read, hesitating at point where he made an error, saying, "A teeny tiny -."

Regulatives

Conversational devices. Rhetorical questions, speaker selections, boundary markers, etc.: "Okay"; "Now"; "All right"; "Ya know what?"

Reading Books with Children: The Mechanics of Parental Influence on Children's Reading Achievement[1]

Beverly A. Goldfield
Catherine E. Snow
Harvard University

Advice to Parents: Help Your Children Learn to Read

Teachers and educational practitioners generally believe that literacy experiences in the home can contribute to children's reading achievement. They tell parents that what happens between parents and their children at home may be an important factor in the children's school success. They emphasize that many kinds of shared family activities can stimulate and sustain a child's early interest in and positive attitude toward reading. For example, parents are encouraged to provide reading materials and to set aside a time and place for reading activities (see Table 1). Other suggestions relate less directly to book reading, but emphasize the importance of varied background experiences and a rich verbal environment for reading success. The underlying message to parents, in both cases, is that the home environment can exert a powerful influence on children's reading achievement. Typical examples of the advice to parents on improving children's reading can be found in Larrick (1958), Siders (1977), and Truby (1979).

Table 1. Ten Commandments for Parents
(From the brochure, "Parents: Help Your Child to Read Better,"
published by the Parent Committee of the Michigan Reading Association,
cited in News for Parents from IRA, Vol. 2, #3, January 1981)

1. I will read to my child daily.
2. I will help my child start a word collection of at least one unknown word daily.
3. I will listen to my child read daily.
4. I will take dictation (talk written down) of the stories, poems and sayings my child creates.
5. I will help my child pursue an interest and find five books to read on this topic.

6. I will praise my child for at least one success daily.
7. I will arrange for my child to use the library and visit bookstores or counters to select his or her own books.
8. I will help my child find a listener to read to (another child, grandparent, or friend).
9. I will allow my child to buy books and educational games.
10. I will listen to my child daily about his or her school reading of stories and progress in learning to read.

What is the evidence that home variables do affect academic success? Is there research to substantiate the claim that parents influence school learning? In this paper we will examine the advice offered to parents in handbooks and home literacy guides with respect to the relevant research findings on home variables and reading achievement. We will also take a closer look at one home reading-related activity to detail the literacy skills that can be acquired in this kind of parent-child interaction.

Research on Home Factors in Reading Achievement

Access to Reading Materials

One suggestion frequently offered to parents is to allow children access to reading materials. Parents are encouraged to purchase books and magazines of interest to children, or to make them available through regular trips to the local public library. Educational research has corroborated the correctness of this advice for promoting children's reading success. For the most part, such studies have identified good and poor achievers in elementary school classrooms, then interviewed parents of both groups of children about their home activities. Access to books was one factor found to be correlated with school achievement in such studies. The availability of appropriate reading materials in the home was related to higher reading scores in fifth and sixth graders (Van Zandt, 1963), high verbal performance in fifth grade children (Biny, 1963), and high scores on language factors in reading readiness tests administered to first grade students (Milner, 1951). As Clark (1976) points out, however, access to books does not necessarily imply a wealth of personally owned materials. Books were frequently borrowed from the local library by children in her sample of early fluent readers, and these children continued to use library books throughout the early school years:

> The local library was a crucial source of reading material for these children even at this early stage, but particularly when they were re-interviewed several years later. Few obtained sufficiently exciting or stimulating reading material through the school or in great enough quantities. (p. 50)

Similarly, Sullivan (1965) found that SES did not predict the amount of reading material in the homes of first grade children, suggesting that money to buy books is a less important variable than parental beliefs about the importance of books.

Parental Support for Reading

It cannot be concluded from such studies, however, that access to books is in itself a determining factor in reading achievement. Both the availability of reading material and success in learning to read may be mediated by a third factor: parental interest in and support for reading. Parental support, in turn, is made explicit by what parents actually do to promote reading at home. Several studies using home interviews have found that parental behavior differs for groups of good and poor readers. In general, good readers had parents who themselves took the time to read at home, and also encouraged their children to read (Cousert, 1978; Paul, 1976; Van Zandt, 1963).

The Dave Scale (1963) has been widely used to help identify the home variables which influence academic success. The scale was originally constructed to isolate characteristics of the home environment which would correlate with school achievement better than previously used social status factors. Six groups of "environmental process characteristics" were hypothesized to determine the home's influence on education: 1) achievement press, including parents' aspirations for the child, and interest in and rewards for educational achievement; 2) language models, i.e., the quality of the parents' language and the standards parents expect in the child's language, 3) the availability and quality of academic guidance, e.g., help with homework, in the home; 4) activeness of the family, as reflected in the extent and content of indoor and outdoor activities; 5) intellectuality of the home, including the nature and quality of toys and opportunities for thinking in daily activities; and 6) work habits in the family, including preference for educational activities. Responses from a parent interview designed to elicit information about these home factors were found to correlate highly (+.80) with fourth grade achievement test scores (Dave, 1963). In interviews with black, low SES parents of high and low reading children in grades 1-3, Baumer-Mulloy (1977) also found a significant relation between achievement and all six factors of the Dave scale.

The research findings reported above are reflected in advice to parents. Parents are urged to set an example by their own use of print, both in routine activities and during quiet moments set aside to read newspapers, magazines, or books. The verbal environment of the home, reported above as one of the 6 home factors to correlate with achievement in the Dave (1963) study, has also been demonstrated to be important in experimental studies. For example, Levenstein and Sunley (1968) trained mothers of 2 year olds in verbally-oriented play with toys and books during a four month intervention program. When compared with a matched control group who received no intervention, children in the experimental group obtained significantly higher posttest IQ scores.

Reading Aloud

One literacy activity which is universally recommended is that parents read aloud to their children. Reading together is described as an enjoyable, shared experience which may form the child's earliest notions of what reading is all about. Books looked at and read with caregivers introduce the child to print, to the narrative structure of story-events, and to the variety of information that can be obtained from a text. Even toddlers in the earliest stages of language development can begin their literacy-learning through moments spent looking at and talking about the simple objects and events displayed in picture books.

The efficacy of advice given to parents to read aloud to their children is also confirmed by research findings. Children who scored high on language factors in first grade reading readiness tests had more books read to them by personally important adults (Milner, 1951). Reading achievement in third grade was also reported to be highly related to being read to in the preschool years (Cousert, 1978). Durkin (1966) regards being read to at home as an especially important source of children's preschool interest in reading. She compared 30 early readers (children who could read prior to beginning school) to 30 matched, nonearly readers, and found that more mothers of early readers read to their children, pointed out words, and discussed the pictures. Clark (1976) also observed that one-third of the parents in her sample of young fluent readers still read to their children when they started school—that is, after the children themselves knew how to read.

The effects of home reading experiences on academic readiness and IQ scores have also been examined in several experimental programs. In a study by Hoskins (1976), the parents of 64 children participated in a three-month summer program just prior to their entry into kindergarten. Parents in this experimental group read aloud to their children at least sixty minutes per week. When compared to a control group, the experimental children scored significantly higher on the Stanford Early Achievement Test administered in the first few weeks of school. Swift (1970) also reports a successful parent training program which centered on verbal interaction around book reading sessions. Parents in this study were taught to help their children relate personal experiences to a story, and to extend children's ability to use their own words to retell parts of the story.

Microprocess Research on Reading Books

Although the findings from parent interview studies and a few intervention studies suggest positive educational effects from reading to children at home, these data give us little insight into the specific benefits to be gained from this kind of parent-child interaction or the process by which reading aloud produces such benefits. Relatively little research has involved direct observation of the literacy training which takes place when parent and child read and enjoy a book together. This kind of "microprocess" research examines the actual event of reading aloud and attempts to determine what the child actually derives from the experience.

The First Stage: Labelling

A few studies have focused on parents and toddlers looking at picture-books. For these very young children, "reading aloud" consists mostly of locating and labelling simple objects, animals, and other familiar items on a page. In a longitudinal study (child's age 8 to 18 months) of joint picture book reading in one mother-child pair, Ninio and Bruner (1978) observed that the book reading sessions took on the structure of a dialogue, with parent and child alternating their turns in the conversation. The sessions were also highly routinized, with predictable cycles of initiation and responses. For example, the mother in this dyad used four utterance types which were strictly ordered within the conversation. A book reading cycle might begin with a maternal attentional vocative such as "look," a query such as "What's that?" or a label "It's an X." Maternal feedback utterances such as "Yes, that's X," or "No, that's not X" always followed a child's response (see Table 2). Thus the book reading sessions became a familiar routine well-suited to the teaching of labels.

Table 2. The Dialogue Associated with Picture Book Reading with Young Children (adapted from Ninio & Bruner, 1978)

	Mother	Child
Attentional sequence	Look!	(touches or looks at picture)
Query sequence	What's that?	(vocalizes, smiles)
Labelling sequence	It's a (label)!	(smiles, looks at mother)
Feedback sequence	Yes, a (label).	

At a slightly later age, different book reading formats may represent specific vocabulary acquisition routines. Ninio (1979) observed 20 mother-child dyads during book reading sessions, with infants ranging in age from 17 to 22 months. Three repetitive formats were noted, each of which was associated with a different measure of vocabulary in the infant. An interaction cycle initiated by a maternal "What's that?" question was related to the size of the infant's productive vocabulary, and was used most often with active, well-developed infants. Mothers who used the question "Where is X?" frequently had children with a relatively large comprehension vocabulary. This question was used mostly by mothers with relatively nonverbal infants. Frequency was used mostly by mothers with relatively nonverbal infants. Frequency of maternal labelling statements was correlated with the child's imitative vocabulary, and characterized book reading with relatively passive infants.

Building Event Structures

In addition to stimulating vocabulary acquisition, picture book "reading" may provide a specific, recurrent context in which previous conversations can be remembered and used by children to extend and elaborate their own conversational repertoire. The book reading context is unique in that the attention of the participants is jointly focused on an illustration of an object or event which remains exactly the same from one time to the next. This makes each page or picture a fixed and bound stimulus amenable to predictable comments over time. In an analysis of book reading in one mother-child pair over a one-year period, we found that that child, N (2.6 years to 3.6 years of age) acquired lexical items, syntactic forms, and general knowledge about the world from repeated conversations around pictures in a storybook dictionary (Snow & Goldfield, 1980). Information from previous conversations about a given picture, especially if it had been introduced by mother and imitated by N, was likely to be spontaneously introduced by N at later discussions of the same illustration.

During this same one-year period, we observed that the structure as well as the content of the storybook dictionary conversations became much more complex, with N elaborating more and more upon information from previous discussions (Snow & Goldfield, 1981). In the first set of transcripts, when the child was 2 years, 5 months old, we find that much of the conversation centered around establishing labels for the objects and characters in the pictures—as Ninio and Bruner (1978) described for their subject. A few weeks later, conversation was more focused on understanding the event that was pictured. N's questions were now more likely to be "What's happening?" whereas previously they had been mostly "What is that?". Several months later, when N was 3 years, 4 months old, he had started asking "Why?" about the same pictures. Having collected information about the basic event structure from the previous conversations, he was now interested in understanding the causes and motives that were antecedent to the events pictured.

There was enormous development in the complexity of information dealt with during the successive conversations between N and his mother about the same set of pictures. This development was possible because the same book was available to be read again and again, and because N was sufficiently enthralled by that particular book to want to read it many times. Parents are often puzzled by and, understandably, impatient with their children's insistence on frequent rereading of the same set of books. We think the development observed in N's conversations may help explain children's preference for repeated exposure to a few books; if the story or pictures are complex enough, the child needs repeated exposure to develop a full understanding of the event presented. Although it may be the same story for the parent every time it is read, it becomes a richer and more interesting story to the child with each successive reading.

Relation Between Books and the Real World

Real world experiences were often introduced by N's mother to support his understanding of events in the book. During an early book reading session, when N was 2 years of age, he was initially confused by a picture which showed Grover in the bath with soap bubbles on his head. The event was clarified when N's mother related the pictorial event to personal experience by initiating a play episode in which she "pretends" to wash N's hair. The book reading dialogue evolved into a play session which re-created the familiar experience of taking a bath.

The efficacy of relating real-life experiences to events in books has also been demonstrated for children learning to read. The success of the ETR (*E*xperience, *T*ext, and *R*elationship) reading method used in the Kamehameha Early Education Program is based on the close relation of this instructional method to the "talk story" popular in the children's native Hawaiian culture. In another experimental study of classroom reading comprehension, Hansen (in press) found that when teachers introduced a reading lesson by telling children what the story was about, and later asked them to tell about related experiences, comprehension of story material by second graders and poor readers in fourth grade was significantly improved, when compared to using either technique separately or to simply previewing new vocabulary items.

Learning the Mechanics of Reading

In addition to contributing significantly to a child's language learning and acquisition of knowledge about the world, book reading also introduces some of the more "technical" prerequisites to learning to read. The relationship of print to sound and meaning, and the left to right sequence of words on a page and pages in a book, are conventions which may be made explicit when reading aloud. In a study of preschool literacy experiences of children from low-income families and communities, Anderson, Teale, and Estrada (1980) observed a book reading session between a 3:9 year old boy and his father which shows much of this kind of informal instruction going on. The format is a typical book reading routine, with the father calling for, and the child providing a label for the pictures of household objects displayed in the book. The father is careful to point out and follow the appropriate order in the text:

> F: We have to start reading here
>   What's this say? (pointing to words of the title moving from left to right direction)
>   Things in...? (waits approximately 3 seconds)
>   Things in My House (turns to first page of text)
> C: Shoe (pointing to picture on the bottom of the page)
> F: No, we have to start up here at the top (points to the first word of sentence at top of page)

Notice that here and in the following sequence, Father is making the connection between word, print, and picture by asking for the object label while pointing to the text beneath the picture.

F: So what's this? (pointing to the word "hammer" and partially obscuring the picture)
    A....
C: Hammer
F: A...(pointing to the word "shoe")
C: Shoe

When the correct label is not forthcoming, Father introduces real-world knowledge and then proceeds to "sound out" the word, giving this child a preview of behavior which teachers use extensively in the early years of teaching reading.

F: A...
C: ...(looking at book)
F: It's what you measure things with
    A...
C: ...
F: /ru.../
    (begins to sound out word/
    /ru: lir/
    (C mimics this sounding out)

Acquiring grapheme-phoneme correspondences may have a long history in book reading interactions. In several recordings of N and his mother looking at an alphabet book, there is a noticeable development in the kind of information which N is able to supply. In the earliest transcripts (N is 2 years, 6 months old), N knows the appropriate response category, that is, letter names, but he does not always correctly match letter names and symbol:

	M: what's this?
N: that's a B	
	That's a B.
	What's this?
'nother B	
	Where's another B?
this	
	That's an E.
E	

	What's this?
That's an X...K	
	K, that's right.
S	
	S
K	
	K

Three months later, N is collaborating much more in the alphabet routine by elaborating his response to include a word which identifies the picture that illustrates the letter's initial sound:

	M: This is an ABC book.
eh eh dis eh banana	
	That's right
	And what's this?
das da dat's a banana	
	That's the B for...
dat's a banana	
	B for banana.
B for banana	
	A for apple.
A for apple	
	C for cup
C for cup	
	What's that say?
C for plate	
	(laughing) No, it's P for plate.
P for plate	

Although his grapheme-phoneme knowledge is still a bit shaky, N is participating in and becoming familiar with a special kind of literacy experience which will become quite important when he is ready for school.

Conclusion

We have reviewed the evidence from correlational and experimental studies that literacy experiences such as being read to at home may enhance reading achievement in school. Further research in which the "microprocess" of a book reading session is observed demonstrates just what can be learned from and about reading books, and how important the collaboration of the adult is in enabling that learning to take place. The child who participates in early book reading activities may be well on the way to acquiring skill with the kind of oral and written discourse which will be required in the classroom. It has been pointed out (Scollon & Scollon, 1979, 1980) that technical reading skills are just one part of the ability to function as a literate member of a literate society. In many ways, preschool children who have had extensive experiences of the type described in this paper are highly literate, even though they are unable to read. They are well-skilled in the mechanics of dealing with books, of orienting to print, and of extracting information from pictures. Even more important though, they have acquired a set of expectations about the way in which material is presented and information is exchanged in literary (and schoolroom) settings.

The point that literacy modes can be distinguished from simple written material is very important in understanding why some children may have problems in dealing with many classroom activities including reading. Teachers often expect children to understand and to present information in modes for which the rules are drawn more from literacy than from oral discourse.

Michaels (1981) for example, found that in the first grade classroom she observed, the teacher had an underlying schema of what constituted appropriate discourse during oral "sharing time." Her questions and comments to students during this activity reflected her requirement that a "sharing time" be centered on a single, elaborated topic and that each child 'tell only one thing' but tell it completely. These are precisely the rules for writing a good paragraph. McNamee (1979) also observed kindergarten teachers developing children's narrative skills by asking questions which organized the child's recall of events in a story and directed attention to the kinds of information it was necessary to encode. She was modelling for the child the structure of "a good story" and then collaborating with the child to produce a rendition close to that model, just as N's mother was doing with the much simpler stories in the Richard Scarry *Storybook Dictionary*.

These kinds of classroom activities and literacy skills may appear far removed from the toddler's pointing to and labelling objects in a picture book. Yet these early book reading activities and classroom narratives share basic features. In each case a topic is established as a

Goldfield and Snow

focus of interest and interaction. From here, development proceeds in learning how to comment upon and elaborate information to create a story. The goal of this process is the literate child, able to read complex texts and to understand their structure well enough to write them too.

Note

1. This paper has benefited from our discussions about the relationship between family factors and literacy achievement with Jeanne Chall and the members of the Harvard "Families and Literacy Project" (funded by NIE, Grant #NIE-G-80-0086), and especially from the availability of the annotated bibliography on Families and Literacy prepared by the project by Vicki Jacobs.

A Comparison of Successful and Less Successful Learners: Can We Enhance Comprehension and Mastery Skills?[1]

John D. Bransford
Nancy J. Vye
Vanderbilt University

Barry S. Stein
Tennessee Technological University

In this chapter, we explore the issue of why some children are better able to learn from written documents than others. We also discuss some procedures designed to help children learn how to learn. The research to be reported involved fifth graders. All could decode relatively effectively, but the students differed in their abilities to understand and remember information that they read. We asked classroom teachers to help us identify successful and less successful learners who were relatively proficient at decoding; we also used achievement test scores to define our groups. In general, our "successful" learners had stanine scores of 7 or 8 on the reading comprehension subtest of the Comprehensive Test of Basic Skills; the corresponding stanine scores for the less successful learners were usually 3 and sometimes 4. It is important to note that our successful and less successful learners also differed in other areas, including achievement in mathematics, language, and so forth. Our successful learners consistently scored above the national average for their grade while less successful learners scored below the average. We also expected (and confirmed this when test scores were available) that our two groups of students would differ on standardized measures of "intelligence." In our opinion, however, scores on intelligence tests generally reflect the amount of previous learning but do not necessarily indicate potential to learn how to learn (see Feuerstein, 1980).

This paper is divided into three sections. In the first, we discuss some cognitive activities that seem to underlie effective comprehension and mastery. We then describe several studies designed to assess differences in the way that successful and less successful learners approach the problem of learning new information. In the final section we focus on the issue of helping less successful students learn how to learn.

Some Cognitive Activities that Facilitate Learning

The purpose of this section is to discuss briefly some cognitive activities that seem necessary to understand and remember the types of materials that we have been presenting our students. The passage presented below provides one illustration of these materials; it describes two types of robots, each of which has a particular type of head, arms, body, feet, and so forth. The instructions are simply to try to learn about the robots and to be able to remember each robot's parts.

> Billy's father works for a company that makes robots. His company made robots for a business that washed outside windows. They needed two kinds of robots. One kind of robot was needed to wash the outside windows in two-story houses. These windows were small. The other kind of robot was needed to wash the outside windows of very tall, high-rise office buildings. These windows were big.
>
> Billy went to visit his father at work. He saw the new robots that his father had made. The robot used for houses was called an extendible robot. It could extend itself so it would be almost as tall as a two-story house. Billy saw that this robot had spikes instead of feet. It had legs that did not bend. Its stomach could extend in length to make it taller. The arms on the robot were short. Instead of hands, it had small sponges. In its head was a nozzle attached to a hose. Billy also saw that the extendible robot was made of heavy steel. It had an electric cord that could be plugged in. The robot also had a ladder on its back.
>
> Billy then saw another robot called a nonextendible robot. This robot could not extend in length. Billy saw that this robot had suction cups instead of feet. It had legs that could bend. Its stomach was padded. The arms on the robot were long. Instead of hands, it had large sponges. In its head was a bucket. Billy also saw that the nonextendible robot was made of light aluminum. There was a battery inside the robot. The robot also had a parachute on its back.

When college students were read this passage they were able to remember most of the properties of each robot; they were also able to explain why each robot had particular properties. For example, they remembered that the nonextendible robot, the one designed to wash outside windows in high-rise buildings, had suction cup feet (to help it climb); that it ran on a battery rather than on an electric motor with an extension cord (high rise buildings would require too long a cord); that it was made of light aluminum (so it wouldn't be too heavy); that a parachute was attached to its back (in case it fell) and so forth. Similarly, the students remembered that the extendible robot, the one that washed outside windows in two-story houses, had spiked feet (to help it gain stability by sticking them into the ground); that it ran on an electric motor with an extension cord (the cord need not be too long); that it was made of heavy steel (for stability), and so forth. Note that the preceding passage did not explicitly state why each robot had the properties that it did. The students spontaneously activated knowledge that enabled them to understand how the properties of each robot permitted it to perform its particular function. We assume that the act of using information about each robot's function to understand why it had particular properties is an important aspect of the comprehension process, and that it also facilitates retention. If students could not understand why each robot had particular properties they should have a difficult time answering questions such as "What kind of feet did the extendible robot have"?

The latter hypothesis was supported by data from an additional condition in the study. A second group of college students heard the robot passage *without* the first paragraph; they therefore received no information about the function of each robot. These students were much poorer at remembering each robot's parts. Students in the second group (the one that did not receive the first paragraph) reported that they tried to invent a particular function for each robot but most were unsuccessful. They were therefore unable to understand why each robot had the properties that it did.

The results of the robot study are hardly earthshaking, of course, but there are several aspects of the data that will become significant when we discuss our work with successful and less successful fifth graders. First, all the college students spontaneously attempted to understand why each robot had particular properties. Second, the students who did not receive information about the functions of each robot (who did not hear the first paragraph) found it difficult to remember which robot had which properties. Overall, our college students realized the difficulty of remembering a set of seemingly arbitrary facts, and they attempted to remedy this situation as best they could, either by using information about the functions of each robot, or by attempting to invent functions to fit the facts. The college students in the first group (the group that was provided with information about appropriate functions) also revealed a sensitivity to the dimensions of "precision" (e.g., Stein & Bransford, 1979); their elaborations (explanations) of each robot's properties were precise in the sense that they helped differentiate one robot from the other. For example, when asked to explain why each robot had particular properties, the students never said "The spiked feet on the extendible robot could help it crush

Bransford, Vye, and Stein

ice" or "The nonextendible robot had bendable legs because most robots have bendable legs." These elaborations are not precise in the context of the robot passage; they would not help one remember which robot had which features because they are not specific to each robot's functions. Our work with academically successful and less successful fifth graders emphasizes the importance of *evaluation* (e.g., of arbitrariness) and of *precision*. Examples of this work are presented below.

Some Comparisons of Successful and Less Successful Learners

Our previous discussion emphasized the importance of evaluating materials and of activating knowledge (e.g., about the functions of each robot) that can help to clarify the significance of factual content (e.g., that can help one understand the reasons for each robot's properties). In the present section we emphasize the importance of evaluation and precision when discussing differences in the way that academically successful and less successful fifth graders approach the problem of learning new information. We begin by describing their attempts to learn the robot passage that was presented above.

The robot passage was presented to groups of academically successful and less successful fifth graders. Students first read the passage aloud. We helped them decode any words they found difficult and explained the meaning of any words they did not know. We explained that we wanted them to try to *remember* which kind of hands, feet, arms and so forth that each robot had, and to understand *why* each robot had these parts. We also gave the students the opportunity to study the passage for as long as they wished before taking a test.

The results indicated that the academically successful fifth graders performed in a manner similar to the college students. They seemed to use the information about each robot's function to understand why it had particular properties because they were able to remember most of each robot's properties and to provide a precise explanation (elaboration) of these properties. An additional group of successful fifth graders received an *explicit* version of the robot passage which explained the reasons for various properties in the text. Students in the explicit group remembered the same number of properties, and provided the same number of precise explanations (elaborations), as did those in the implicit group (those who received the passage printed earlier). Both groups remembered and explained approximately 14 properties out of a total of 18.

The academically less successful fifth graders exhibited a very different pattern of performance. Those who received the implicit version of the robot passage remembered an average of only five properties (recall that we had helped with any difficult words and permitted unlimited study time). Those who received the explicit version of the robot passage did much better, they remembered an average of nine properties and were able to give explanations of these as well. The performance of the less successful students who received the explicit version of the robot passage was still significantly inferior to that of the successful students who received the implicit version. For present purposes, however, the important point is that the less successful students who received the implicit version exhibited very little tendency to attempt to understand why each robot had particular properties (even the explicit version requires active attempts to understand; no passage is ever totally explicit). All the less successful students appeared to be motivated to do well, and all studied the passage after reading it. However, their primary mode of study was simply to reread the passage without asking themselves why each robot had particular properties.

The data from the robot study are consistent with the results from other studies that we have conducted with academically successful and less successful fifth graders. In another study, for example, students received a passage about two different types of boomerangs. Each boomerang had particular properties and particular functions; the passage was therefore analogous to the robot passage described above. Once again, academically successful students spontaneously used information about the function of each type of boomerang to understand its structural features, and vice versa. The less successful students took a much more passive approach to the problem of learning the information. Their primary mode of study was simply to reread the passage. After rereading, they would invariably declare themselves ready for the test.

The most striking result from these studies is that the less successful learners exhibited only a superficial knowledge of each topic despite their apparent motivation to learn, and despite the fact that they seemed to feel ready to take the test. The less successful students therefore appeared to have difficulty assessing their current level of mastery; they had little idea of how to judge their readiness for a test and how to make information easier to understand and retain. From our perspective, the ability to assess one's current level of comprehension and mastery is extremely important. Without such assessments, one has no information about the need to study selectively, ask questions, and so forth (e.g., Bransford, 1979; Bransford, Stein, Shelton, & Owings, in press; Brown & DeLoache, 1978). Our less successful students seemed to take a mechanical approach to studying, they simply reread the materials. They did not appear to evaluate whether they had understood and mastered the information, and they did not attempt to make the information less arbitrary by asking themselves about the reasons for various facts.

It is important to note, however, that the robot and boomerang passages contained some potentially difficult concepts. Since our less successful students have acquired less knowledge than their more successful peers, it is possible that all the performance differences between our groups stem from knowledge-base differences. The fact that we helped students with any difficult words provides no guarantee that the less successful students had the potential knowledge necessary to understand the passages. Students may have been reluctant to ask the meaning of various words, for example, or may have failed to understand our explanations. Furthermore, one can be familiar with all the words in a passage yet still lack concepts or schemata necessary to understand and learn (Bransford & Johnson, 1972; Dooling & Lachman, 1971). If one lacks the knowledge necessary to understand, perhaps the best strategy is simply to reread a passage and hope for the best on a subsequent test.

Because of potential knowledge base problems, it seemed important to conduct some studies that used relatively simple sets of materials. We wanted to get a clearer idea of whether less successful learners are indeed less likely to use potential knowledge to make information more meaningful because this might be one of the primary reasons why they have acquired less knowledge than their more academically successful peers. In short, lack of content knowledge may indeed be a *cause* of poor performance (see Anderson & Freebody, 1979), but it can be viewed as a *symptom* of inefficient learning activities as well (Bransford, Stein, Shelton, & Owings, in press).

One of our studies (Owings, Peterson, Bransford, Morris, & Stein, 1980) was designed to investigate the issue of problem recognition. In order to deal with the problem of learning difficult factual content, for example, one must first realize that it is indeed difficult. To what extent would our academically successful and less successful fifth graders realize that some materials were more difficult to master than others, and how would this affect their attempts to adapt to the task?

Based on previous interview data, it seemed clear that even the less successful fifth graders could use some sources of information to assess learning difficulty. They knew that difficulty of vocabulary affected learning; the length of a passage was another cue that they used. However, suppose we used very simple vocabulary, kept passage length constant, and varied the arbitrariness of comprehensible factual content. Would the less successful student realize that comprehensible but arbitrary facts are harder to learn than non-arbitrary facts?

To explore this question we created a set of simple stories that each had two versions. In one version each statement was non-arbitrary or well-motivated. In a story about boys discussing their activities, for example, *The sleepy boy had taken a nap, The hungry boy had eaten a hamburger*, and so forth. To create the arbitrary version we re-paired subjects and predicates with the constraint that each sentence still be comprehensible. For example, *The sleepy boy had eaten a hamburger*, and *The hungry boy had taken a nap*. Similar versions were created for other topics. All students read one version of a story (either arbitrary or non-arbitrary), studied as long as they wished, read the opposite version of a second story about a different topic and studied it. They were then shown both stories and asked to state which one was harder to learn and why. Students then received a memory test (e.g., which boy had eaten a hamburger?). It is noteworthy that all the students in this study had participated in practice sessions and hence knew the type of test to expect.

The results indicated that the successful students were nearly perfect in their judgments of learning difficulty. They could also explain why the arbitrary stories were harder to learn. This knowledge seemed to guide their efforts to adapt to task difficulty; they studied longer for stories that were hard to learn than for those that were easy to learn. The academically less successful fifth graders exhibited a very different pattern of performance. They were less accurate in their judgments of learning difficulty and studied no longer for the arbitrary stories than for the non-arbitrary stories. These children were able to use other cues to assess learning difficulty, such as passage length and difficulty of vocabulary, but failed to use arbitrariness of relationships as a cue. Nevertheless, their memory for the easier, non-arbitrary stories was much better than for the arbitrary ones, which suggests that the easier stories were indeed more congruent with their knowledge. Furthermore, at the end of the experimental session, we were eventually able to get the less successful children to notice the difference among the stories, and they also became able to tell us how the arbitrary stories could be revised to make them easier. They therefore seemed to have the potential to differentiate the two types of stories yet failed to do so until explicitly prompted by us.

We recently completed an additional study that was designed to assess students' assumptions about learning difficulty. Academically successful and less successful learners were presented with pairs of sentences such as the following:

The strong man wrote a letter to his friend.
The strong man helped the woman move the heavy piano.

The rich man walked home for dinner.
The rich man lost the key to his safe.

The task was to choose the member of each pair that would best enable one to remember which man did what, and to explain the reasons for one's choice. The answer "both are equally easy or difficult" was also allowed, although students were asked to explain this answer as well.

Note that the second member of each of the preceding pairs provides information that helps one understand why a particular type of man (*strong, rich*) might perform a particular type of activity. We refer to these as "precise" sentences. Note further that the presentation of information that helps one understand why it might be appropriate for each particular man to engage in a particular activity (e.g., The strong man helped the woman *move the heavy piano*) is analogous to providing (or generating) information that can help one understand why a robot, boomerang and so forth has particular properties. For example, the non-extendible robot discussed earlier had suction cup feet *in order to help it climb.*

College students who received 10 pairs of sentences such as those presented above almost always chose the precise member of each pair and could explain why. The majority of the successful fifth graders performed in the same manner. In contrast, only one of the less successful fifth graders consistently chose the precise sentences. The rest chose sentences on the basis of hypotheses such as "This one is shorter so it will be easier to remember." This is a reasonable hypotheses, of course, but it doesn't work for the types of sentences included in our list.

After rating the 10 pairs of sentences, students received a memory test (e.g., Which man *wrote a letter*? Which man *lost the key*?). The memory test presumably provides a basis for evaluating one's previous hypotheses about learning difficulty, because one can ask why some sentences are easier to remember than others (students' memory for precise sentences was always better than their memory for imprecise sentences). We were therefore interested in the degree to which students would learn from the memory test. Following this test, students received a set of 10 new sentences and were asked to continue the rating task (plus explain their answers). Those successful students who had failed to notice the precision dimension during the first set of trials switched to precision during the second set. In contrast, the less successful students showed no improvement following the memory test. These students were therefore less sensitive to the problem of learning arbitrary facts during the first phase of the experiment, and they were less likely to use their own performance on the memory test to evaluate the initial hypotheses about learning difficulty that they had espoused.

It seems useful to consider one additional study that was designed to assess differences in students' approaches to learning. The purpose of this study was to prompt students to generate their own elaborations and to assess whether these elaborations were precise or imprecise. The students were presented with a list of sentences such as *The tall man used the paintbrush, The hungry man got into the car*, and were asked to generate phrases that would help them remember which man did what. The children were also shown that each statement dealt with a different type of man (e.g., hungry man, tall man, strong man). Children were divided into three groups on the basis of teacher ratings and test scores: academically less successful, average, and successful. All were in regular classes in the fifth grade.

Five measures were used to assess performance. The first was the precision of student-generated elaborations (as judged by three independent raters). There were large differences among the groups, with the successful, middle, and less successful students receiving precision scores of approximately 70 percent, 50 percent, and 30 percent respectively. Successful students generated continuations such as *The tall man used the paintbrush to paint the ceiling*; less successful students' continuations were more similar to *The tall man used the paintbrush to paint a chair or a picture*. The second measure was cued recall (questions were of the form *Which man got into the car?*). Again there were large differences among the groups, with successful students performing best. The third measure was a conditional memory score: memory given that initial elaborations had been precise or imprecise. Precision had powerful effects on all three groups with precisely elaborated statements being recalled best. The fourth measure assessed students' confidence in their answers during testing. We looked only at cases where students had produced the correct answer and measured

Bransford, Vye, and Stein

confidence as a function of whether the initial elaboration had been precise or imprecise. All groups were more confident given that their initial elaborations had been precise. The final measure assessed students' awareness of the relationship between their initial elaborations and subsequent retention. Did they seem to understand why they remembered the ones that they did? The majority of the successful students could explain this relationship, approximately 30 percent of the middle students could do so, and only one less successful student did so.

Overall, the results suggest that the successful students approached the task in a different manner from the less successful students. The successful students seemed to attend to the details of each statement and to activate knowledge that could make the facts less arbitrary. In contrast, the less successful students produced continuations that could be true of any type of man but were not uniquely related to the particular type of man. These students seemed to have the potential to clarify the significance of the information (we document this later) yet failed to utilize their potential. If less successful students take this approach in a wide variety of situations, it could have pervasive effects on their abilities to learn.

To summarize, the studies discussed above suggest that academically less successful students experience learning difficulties even in situations where the content knowledge necessary to perform adequately is potentially available. One reason for these problems may be that the students don't spontaneously assess the difficulty of the information they are trying to learn; in part, because they don't realize that factors such as arbitrariness lead to learning difficulty. Less successful learners also exhibit much less of a tendency to use potentially available information to make facts less arbitrary and hence easier to design training exercises that result in improvements in less successful students' learning performance. The purpose of the next section is to discuss some of our attempts to help less successful students learn how to learn.

Learning to Learn

In our attempts to help academically less successful fifth graders learn to learn, we have found it useful to begin by creating special sets of materials that enable the students to experience the effects of their own learning activities. For example, imagine reading 10 sentences such as the following:

The kind man bought the milk.
The short man used the broom.
The funny man liked the ring.
The hungry man purchased the tie.
The bald man read the newspaper.
The tall man used the paintbrush.

People who simply read each of these sentences have a very difficult time remembering which man did what. As noted earlier, these sentences are difficult to remember because the relationships between the type of man and the action performed are arbitrary. We also noted that these relationships become less arbitrary if one activates knowledge that clarifies why each type of man performs each activity; for example, the kind man might buy some milk and give it to a hungry child, the short man may use the broom to reach the lightswitch, and so forth.

When academically less successful fifth graders are asked to read and remember a list of 10 sentences such as those presented above (without any instructions to elaborate), they usually remember from one to three sentences. (The memory test involves questions such as "Which man did X?") We want them to realize that these sentences are extremely difficult to remember because we eventually want to help them learn how to make the sentences easy to retain. However, the students would undoubtedly feel very badly about their performance if we simply gave them a memory test with no explanation. We therefore preface our training sessions by emphasizing that the goal is to understand why some things are harder to learn than others. The students are told that even college students have a difficult time remembering the sentences they will read (which is true, if college students simply read each sentence), and we remind the fifth graders of this fact while they are taking the memory test. The purpose of this exercise is to set the stage for: 1) analyzing why the materials are so difficult to retain; 2) getting the children to activate relevant knowledge that can make the sentences less arbitrary and hence easier to retain (i.e., getting the children to precisely elaborate each sentence); and 3) allowing the children to experience the dramatic improvements in memory that occur when precise elaborations are produced.

After the memory test, we return to the sentences from the original list. Given a statement such as *The kind man bought the milk*, for example, we first prompt students to ask themselves questions that will enable them to realize that the relationship is arbitrary. We might therefore ask, "Is there any more reason to mention that a kind man

Bransford, Vye, and Stein

bought the milk than a tall man, or a mean man?" This sets the stage for the next step which is to prompt students to activate knowledge that can make the relationship between "kindness" and "milk-buying" less arbitrary (e.g., "Why might a kind man be buying milk?"). The third purpose of our intervention is to prompt students to evaluate their own continuations. For example, less successful students might say or write, *The kind man bought the milk because he was thirsty.* We would then ask, "What does this have to do with being kind? Wouldn't a mean man be just as likely to do the same thing?" Given these explicit queries, the children are eventually able to write continuations that clarify the significance of kindness; for example, *The kind man bought the milk to give to the hungry child.*

During the first few trials of the intervention the students frequently need to be reminded to ask themselves relevant questions. For example, they may eventually activate information that clarifies the significance of the first sentence yet fail to do this spontaneously for the second sentence. After a few trials, however, most children begin to internalize the process of question asking and to evaluate whether their elaborations clarify the significance of the facts. For example, given the base sentence *The rich man walked to the store*, one student said, *to buy some candy.* She then remarked, "Wait, candy doesn't cost that much; I need something different," and after a brief pause said, smiling, *and bought the whole store.* Many of the children's responses were quite creative, and they seemed to thoroughly enjoy the task.

After the children have precisely elaborated the set of 10 sentences, we administered the same memory test that, earlier, had been so difficult. Nearly all of the children do perfectly. The most interesting data involve their excitement and pleasure; a task that had initially been extremely difficult has become very easy to perform. We believe that the two most important aspects of these initial training exercises are: 1) that students begin to understand why some materials are harder to learn and remember than others; and 2) that they begin to realize that they have some control over their own comprehension and memory processes. For many students, these insights seem to be very important; this affects their attitudes toward subsequent learning tasks.

What can students who have received this initial phase of precision training now do that they could not do previously? For example, will they now recognize that new sets of arbitrary facts are difficult to learn? Will they create elaborations that are precise? Will they be able to understand and master the information about the robots and so forth? We consider each of these questions in turn.

Consider first the paired-comparison task described earlier: Children were asked to choose the member of each pair of sentences that would enable them to remember which man did what (e.g., *The rich walked home for dinner* versus *The rich man lost the key to his safe*). Less successful learners who had not received precision training almost never focused on the precision dimension. Those who received precision training always focused on precision and were able to explain their choices. Note that the sentences used during precision training were always different from those used on the paired-comparison task.

In another study discussed previously, we presented students with arbitrary sentences (e.g., *The tall man used the paintbrush*) and asked them to generate continuations that would facilitate memory. Untrained less successful learners always generated continuations that were sensible or "semantically congruous." However, they rarely generated continuations that clarified why it might be appropriate for a particular type of man to perform a particular action (i.e., their elaborations were generally imprecise). After precision training (using sentences that differed from the ones in the original study), we presented students with the sentences used in the original study and asked them to generate their own continuations. Over 90 percent of these were precise. It is also encouraging to note that the memory performance of the less successful students who received precision training was excellent. These data suggest that there are some universal principles of learning (e.g., precision) that affect successful and less successful students in the same way.

What happens if less successful learners who have received the initial phase of precision training are now asked to learn the information in the robot passage? We had suspected that the initial phase of precision training would be insufficient to allow students to transfer to passages such as the one about the robots. After working with a few children, we have concluded that our suspicions were correct. These attempts at training and transfer have been very illuminating, however, because they provide information about important components of the learning process and hence about ways in which the precision training must be extended. Some examples of the problems our children have encountered are discussed below.

One of the most obvious sources of difficulty for the children was the fact that the initial precision training task involved sets of unrelated sentences whereas the robot passage involved an interrelated set of relationships. For example, consider the task of precisely elaborating a statement such as "...this robot had suction cups instead of feet."

Students must first realize that "this" refers to the nonextendible robot, and that the latter washes outside windows in high-rise buildings and hence needs to have some way of reaching them. The robot task is therefore relatively complex; it is difficult for the children to transfer from the sentence task to the more complex robot passage without additional help. One might argue that the initial precision training task is potentially misleading because of its focus on sets of unrelated sentences, but we find that it provides an excellent starting point for training. The task is challenging without being overwhelming, and it permits a relatively dramatic improvement in memory once precise elaborations are produced.

A related difficulty for our students seemed to stem from their failure to develop a precise understanding of the first paragraph of the robot passage. This paragraph provides the context which must guide all subsequent elaborations. Many of our students understood only that the robots wash windows; they therefore lacked information necessary to understand why one robot had one set of properties and the other had different properties. For example, students who failed to realize that one robot rests on the ground whereas the other climbs had a difficult time understanding the reasons for spiked feet versus suction cup feet.

When we have helped our students understand the first paragraph of the robot passage and then explicitly prompted them to elaborate, we find that they are able to provide precise elaborations for most of the robots' properties. Their memory scores are excellent as well. These results are encouraging but they are far from a demonstration of spontaneous transfer. We had to provide considerable guidance in order to help the students complete the task.

In our most recent work, we are extending our precision training in order to prepare students to learn more complex sets of materials. Students are first trained on the sentence task and are then helped to see how this exercise relates to the problem of learning from passages. Our new training passages have a structure analogous to the robot passage but differ in content. Our initial attempts at this extended precision training are very encouraging. Students begin to understand that they have considerable control over their own learning processes. They show marked improvements and become motivated to continue to learn how to learn.

Perhaps the most important aspect of precision training involves its emphasis on evaluation. Children seem to enjoy evaluating whether passages seem arbitrary. They also accept the challenge of evaluating reasons for their own memory performance and seem to enjoy activities that encourage them to revise passages in order to make them easier to understand and remember. This emphasis on evaluation and revision seems especially important because many of the passages that children are asked to read in school seem to be quite arbitrary. For example, one passage designed for elementary school students discussed the topic of "American Indian Houses." It consisted of statements such as "The Indians of the Northwest Coast lived in slant-roofed houses made of cedar plank...Some California Indian tribes lived in simple, earth-covered or brush shelters...The Plains Indians lived mainly in tepees," etc. The story provided no information about why certain Indians chose certain houses. For example, it said nothing about the relationship between the type of house and the climate of the geographical area, nor about the ease of finding raw materials to build houses depending on the geographical area. Furthermore, the story said nothing about how the style of house was related to the life-style of the Indians (e.g., tepees are relatively portable). If students either do not know, or fail to activate this extra information, the passage is essentially a list of seemingly arbitrary facts.

Lessons that involve passages such as the one just described (we have found numerous passages that are quite arbitrary) may not help students develop the ability to evaluate the degree to which they have understood and mastered information. For example, if students are instructed to "learn the information in the passage" they may assume that the passages are optimally written and hence may simply try to re-read the information while studying. If they then do poorly on subsequent comprehension and memory tests, the invited inference is that "they can't learn." Our assumption is that *no one* can learn if the information seems arbitrary and is not precisely elaborated. In short, we assume that there are some universal principles that affect human comprehension and memory; our goal is to help students become aware of these universals. The "precision training" we have described is one approach to helping students understand some of these universal principles. If students are helped to use these principles to evaluate and revise materials, they should learn something about their roles as learners, and should develop the ability to learn on their own.

Summary and Tentative Conclusions

Our goal was to discuss some learning activities that seem necessary for effective comprehension and mastery and to ask whether academically successful and less successful fifth graders differ in the degree to which they employ these activities. The discussion focused on the importance of evaluating whether information seems arbitrary and on the importance of activating information that enables one to clarify the significance of factual content. Unlike academically successful learners, our less successful fifth graders seem not to understand the relationship between arbitrariness and learning difficulty, and they fail to spontaneously activate information that can make facts less arbitrary (i.e., they fail to produce precise elaborations). Not surprisingly, their memory performance is therefore poor.

The discussion of our initial attempts to help less successful learners learn how to learn was designed to serve several functions. First, the training studies show quite clearly that precision has powerful effects on retention. For example, students who receive precision training and are then transferred to new sets of sentences perform every bit as well as our successful students. Our less successful students therefore do not appear to have some general "memory deficit" that interferes with their ability to learn. Second, our students who have received precision training really enjoy the experience. This is important, because these experiences set the stage for continued efforts to help them learn to learn. The final point about our precision training is that it merely represents a small beginning. We discussed some of the limitations of our initial training (the training involving sentences), but even our more recent training involving sentences plus one or two passages is unlikely to have marked effects on classroom performance. One reason for this assumption is that students may perform effectively in a special experimental context yet fail to employ the same learning activities when confronted with classroom tasks.

In our opinion, it will be necessary to develop a relatively extensive curriculum in order to help students develop the learning skills necessary for transfer to everyday classroom activities. The important point, however, is that we see no reason why this could not be accomplished. We find that our students are very receptive to the general concept of "the need for precision," and that they are interested in learning about themselves as learners. A curriculum developed along these lines might help students to a considerable degree.

Note

1. The research reported in this paper was supported, in part, by grant NIE-G-79-0117. We are especially indebted to Mrs. T. Rucker, the principal of Head School in Nashville, and to Mrs. E.R. Johnson, a teacher at Head School who has provided invaluable assistance and advice.

A Positive Approach to Assessment and Correction of Reading Difficulties in Middle and Secondary Schools

Joan Nelson-Herber
SUNY at Binghamton
Harold L. Herber
Syracuse University

Corrective reading instruction in middle and secondary schools has taken on a decidedly negative character over the years for a variety of reasons. Both the assessments and the instruction provided in corrective reading classes are primarily based on students' weaknesses rather than on their strengths. Further, assessment and instruction in these classes bear little relationship to the reading tasks presented in other instructional settings where reading is required. Consequently, one can find scant evidence of positive transfer of gains purportedly made in corrective reading classes to regular classroom reading performance.

It is our intent in this paper to examine the roots of this negative approach to corrective reading and to present an alternative: a positive, nondeficit approach to reading instruction in middle and secondary schools. This approach is based on the contention that a better understanding of the nature of reading comprehension processes and of the sophisticated reading tasks required of students at this level will lead to a new conceptualization of reading strengths and weaknesses. Our position is based on considerable experience working with teachers and students in real classroom situations, on the growing body of research evidence that supports an interactive model of reading comprehension, and on consensual intuitions regarding instructional processes to support such a model.

Back to Basics: A Nonprofessional Solution to a Nonexistent Problem

In spite of increasing evidence that today's elementary school students are reading as well as or better than their counterparts of 10,

20, and 30 years ago (Farr, Tuinman, and Rowls, 1975; Farr, Fay and Negley, 1978; Farr and Blomenberg, 1979; Micklos, 1980; NAEP, 1981), the media event of a reading crisis persists. Increasing public criticism tends to make reading educators very nervous—so nervous, in fact, that many have ignored what is really needed in reading instruction at middle and secondary school levels in order to continue to do, and then redo with greater urgency, what they are already doing well. Though there is ample evidence that students are learning the *basic* decoding and comprehension skills, the data from the National Assessment for Educational Progress (NAEP, 1981) suggests a need for concern regarding the performance of middle and secondary students on higher level inferential reading-reasoning processes. Yet, educators willingly consign a whole nation of students "back to basics" without professional consideration of the complexities of reading comprehension and of the kind of instruction that is really needed to enhance students' reading achievement.

Make no mistake; the authors are not against basic reading instruction (although we are sometimes troubled by the way it is conducted). What we are against is the persistent recycling of large numbers of students through basic word recognition and literal comprehension skills because of a misinterpretation of the difficulties students encounter in reading their content area texts.

This deficit recycling is especially evident in corrective reading classes. Reading teachers, most of whom were trained to teach elementary reading skills, tend to lock middle and secondary school students into a skills-deficit model. This type of instruction is based on a skills-sufficiency theory that promotes the idea that if a certain set and sequence of skills are learned sufficiently, comprehension will take care of itself. The extent to which such instruction persists is a measure of how the profession has ignored the recent body of evidence indicating that reading comprehension occurs as a complex interaction among all the knowledge systems operating within the reader—conceptual, social, linguistic, experiential, etc.—and all the linguistic systems operating in the text—grapho-phonemic, syntactic, semantic (Adams & Bruce, 1980; Adams & Collins, 1979; Anderson et al., 1977; Kamil, 1978; Rumelhart, 1977; Santa & Hayes, 1981). The very nature of the more sophisticated reading tasks required of students in middle and secondary schools creates problems not amenable to the simple application of sets and sequences of skills. The fact that many of our students survive the transition from learning to read to reading to learn without appropriate supportive instruction is testimony to their intelligence and their reading-reasoning power.

Basic Premises for Positive Reading Improvement

There are two premises that help in developing the rationale for a positive approach to middle and secondary school reading instruction:

1. The majority of students who seem to need corrective reading instruction in middle and secondary schools *don't*.
2. The majority of students who *do* need corrective reading instruction *don't* need the kind they're getting.

The first premise is based on the conviction that *all* students should have the benefit of reading instruction in every classroom where reading is required, and that reading strategies should be taught simultaneously with the content of the subject being taught. If this were done, very few students would need corrective instruction. Unfortunately, we generally abandon the teaching of reading at the very point where students need to integrate the skills gleaned from basic reading instruction with their knowledge, their experience and their reasoning power to address more complex reading comprehension tasks (Nelson, 1980).

The easiest way to illustrate the problem is to compare the direct teaching of reading skills as it is done in the majority of elementary schools with the functional teaching of the reading proccess as it should be done in middle and secondary schools. (It must be noted that this dichotomy cannot be drawn where reading is taught as a functional holistic process from the outset.) The comparison will be made on three dimensions: 1) separation vs. integration of skills; 2) word recognition vs. word acquisition; and 3) reconstruction of meaning vs. construction of new meanings.

Separation vs. Integration

Elementary school reading programs generally separate reading into a multiplicity of skills. This fragmentation is based on the notion that students can learn to read better if the whole process is broken into separate pieces and each of those pieces carefully taught. It is assumed that when students have learned all of the parts they will be able to reassemble them into a holistic reading process. It is interesting to note that there is no set or sequence of reading skills that can be supported on the basis of research. Most skill sequences are based on common sense considerations; however, when both materials and tests are constructed around these skill sequences, the results in terms of students' basic reading achievement are reasonably good.

Nelson-Herber and Herber

In middle and secondary schools, reading tasks are holistic in nature, requiring the simultaneous use of many skills. The content of the material determines how skills must be integrated to comprehend it. Students need a different kind of reading instruction that provides strategies for integrating and applying previously acquired skills to new content. Because some students have difficulty in making this transition, it is assumed that they lack the basic skills. As a result, they are repeatedly recycled through separate skills instruction. This process, though it may lead to increased scores on skill oriented reading tests, generally fails to solve the problem of integrating and transferring skills to the increasingly sophisticated reading tasks assigned in content area reading classrooms.

In some cases, this "corrective" reading process exacerbates the problem it is intended to solve. First, it labels students as "problem readers" causing them new problems with self-concept and social relationships. Second, it takes time away from content classes causing students to fall further behind their peers. Finally, and most important for reading comprehension, it leads to heavier and heavier reliance on graphic data to the detriment of the necessary integration of graphic and experiential data that is required for creative construction of meaning.

Word Recognition vs. Word Acquisition

Elementary schools concentrate on word recognition skills so that students can *re-cognize* words that are already in their own lexicons. For example, students are taught phonics so that they can attempt to pronounce, in left to right sequence, the sounds of a word to gain clues to its recognition as a word they already know. Given that this process has questionable efficacy even for known words, it seems too obvious to set in print that students will have difficulty using their phonics skills to recognize words that they would not recognize even if they could pronounce them.

Take the sentence, *As we rode the old-fashioned carousel, the sounds of the calliope surrounded us.* If the word *calliope* were not in the students' personal lexicons, they would not only fail to recognize it, they would most likely mispronounce it as well. While the context provides some support for the meaning of the word, it could as easily mean *crowd, engine, carnival, amusement park, children.* Further, the presence of the word *calliope* in the text would probably cause students, reading orally, to also miscue on other words in the sentence because of the anxiety produced by anticipation of the unknown word.

Failure on the part of teachers to recognize the reasons for the students' difficulties at this point could lead to incorrect assessment of the problem as a lack of decoding skills. While students may appear to lack these basic reading skills, they are simply unable to apply the skills they possess to the more difficult reading tasks required of them in content area textbooks which contain new concept words and technical vocabulary that may be entirely unfamiliar to them. It should be no surprise, then, that some students have difficulty reading these texts independently. What is needed is not a recycling through skill-drill word recognition activities, but a program of instruction in each content classroom that 1) provides experience with the new vocabulary of the content *before* students are expected to *re-cognize* it in their reading, and 2) provides positive strategies for acquisition of new vocabulary within the context of the content.

Reconstruction vs. Creative Construction

Meaning resides in the experiences of the reader. What the reader brings to the text, both in terms of linguistic experience and of world experience, determines, to a large extent, what the reader takes from the text. The importance of the reader's background has been noted by Adams and Bruce (1980, p. 38):

> To say that background knowledge is often used, or is useful in comprehending a story is misleading. It suggests that a reader has the option of drawing on background knowledge to enhance the comprehension process, but that he or she might just as well do without such frills—as if there were a reading process separate from the drawing-on-background-knowledge process.
>
> In fact, reading comprehension involves the construction of ideas out of preexisting concepts. A more concrete statement of the role of background knowledge would be that comprehension is the use of prior knowledge to create new knowledge. Without prior knowledge, a complex object, such as a text, is not just difficult to interpret; strictly speaking, it is meaningless. (p. 38)

Elementary school reading programs recognize the importance of background knowledge in reading when they almost invariably use text materials containing vocabulary, facts, concepts, and values that operate within the conceptual framework of the elementary pupils' experience. Stories about home, family, pets, play, and domestic animals are the mainstay of elementary readers. Pupils are taught word recognition and comprehension skills so that they can reconstruct, from the text, ideas and meanings already within the realm of their experience.

By the end of the elementary grades, with good instruction, most pupils can successfully use their reading skills to recognize common words and to reconstruct familiar meanings. The mistake lies in the assumption that they can automatically transfer these skills to the reading of textbooks that contain uncommon vocabulary, unknown facts, unfamiliar concepts, and unusual values. That some students do make this transfer with apparent ease is testimony to their intelligence and reasoning power; that many have difficulty should be no surprise to educators.

It's sometimes necessary, however, to use very unusual illustrations to help proficient adult readers to recognize the difficulty. Take, as an example, the following sentence: *There's a bear in a plain brown wrapper doing flip-flops around 78 and passing out green stamps.* This is a perfectly good English sentence. It has nouns, verbs, adjectives, phrases, clauses, etc. Even the words are all familiar. However, anyone not familiar with CB radio language would be very unlikely to comprehend the author's message, no matter how well he or she had learned the basic reading skills. To understand the message, both the context of the message and the technical vocabulary must reside in the experience of the reader. The reader must recognize the sentence as a CB communication, both experientially and syntactically, and must recognize the special and unusual meanings of the words when used within this context. The reader who can tap this experience can readily comprehend the message as meaning: *A state trooper in an unmarked car is cruising back and forth on the highway around mile marker 78 and issuing tickets to speeders.* The reader without this CB experience cannot comprehend no matter how well he or she applies decoding or basic comprehension skills.

The same kind of thing happens when students encounter content area text materials containing facts, concepts, and values that are outside the realm of their experience. They have difficulty comprehending, not because they lack decoding and comprehension skills, but because they lack the experience necessary to bring meaning to the text. Even where concepts are somewhat familiar to students, they may lack enough elaboration of the experience to comprehend fully. In reading the sentence, *After finishing our mousse, Jean went to the checkroom and I passed out tribute to all the outstretched palms*, most adults would immediately recognize the setting as a restaurant and the action as finishing dessert, retrieving the wraps, and tipping the waiters. They have developed full and elaborate restaurant schemata from many restaurant experiences and can tap these experiences to bring meaning to the message. But what about the student whose only experience of a restaurant is McDonald's or Burger King? Will this student recognize the word *mousse* or even be able to pronounce it? Will he or she be able to answer comprehension questions such as: *What does "tribute" mean in this sentence?* or *What are the characters in the story doing?* Will the student even recognize that the action is occurring in a restaurant? To make matters worse, when students are asked to read aloud from a text that they are having difficulty comprehending, they tend to miscue and stumble, even on familiar words, giving the impression that word recognition skills are lacking. Consequently, both students and teachers become frustrated, and students are consigned to "corrective" classes where they are again recycled through the skills.

Advanced Instruction is the Key

What reading educators must recognize is that the transition from reading materials containing common words and familiar concepts to content area text books containing uncommon vocabulary and unfamiliar concepts involves a change in the reading process from recognition of known words to acquisition of new words, from reconstruction of meaning out of experience to creative construction of new meanings and new experience. This process involves reasoning, reasoning from what is known to what is new, reasoning in, around, and beyond the text material (Herber, 1978).

The key to easing the transition is instruction—not instruction in special reading classes where students are recycled through decoding and comprehension skills, but instruction that occurs in every class where reading is required: in literature, in science, in mathematics, in the social sciences, and in other subjects as appropriate.

Premises Revisited

Returning to the first premise, that *the majority of students who seem to need corrective reading instruction in middle and secondary schools don't*, it is our contention, based on the previous discussion, that if, instead of abandoning the teaching of reading at the end of the elementary grades, advanced instruction in reading-reasoning processes were provided in each content classroom, the majority of students would be able to integrate the skills they possess, access new vocabulary, and grow in the creative construction of meaning. Such advanced instruction would include the following:
1. Strategies that tap pupils' experience related or analogous to new concepts to provide conceptual frameworks for integrating new ideas with prior experience.

2. Strategies that build new concepts or examine conflicting values before students are expected to comprehend them in reading.
3. Strategies that provide students' experience with the technical or uncommon vocabulary of the content area before they are expected to recognize that vocabulary in their reading.
4. Feed-forward strategies that emphasize predicting and anticipating meanings on the basis of prior experience.
5. Strategies that guide and support students' reading at the literal, interpretive, and applied levels of comprehension (Herber, 1978).
6. Strategies that build positively on students' skills instead of recycling them.
7. Strategies that provide opportunities for interaction among students for pooling of experience; discussion of ideas; clarification of concepts; multiple recitation of vocabulary, facts, concepts, and values; and to take advantage of the benefits of peer-tutoring (Nelson, 1980).
8. Strategies that guide and support creative reasoning through and beyond the text material.

As teachers provide instructional support during students' transition from learning to read to reading to learn, middle and secondary schools find far fewer students who need corrective reading instruction. This leads to our second premise, *the majority of students who do need corrective reading instruction in middle and secondary schools don't need the kind they're getting.*

Assume for a moment that subject teachers are trained in methods and strategies for teaching reading simultaneously with the content of their subject area and are providing such instruction. Even so, a few of their students may need additional help in reading. It is for these students that a corrective reading program is established. It serves as a supplement to the instruction they receive in the regular content area classrooms. As a supplement, it should be consistent in purpose, function, and definition. Unfortunately, much of what goes on in corrective reading classes bears little relationship to the reading tasks required in regular classrooms. Once again, there seems to be a lack of application of what we know about reading comprehension to the instructional setting.

Comprehension is the primary objective in reading; all other objectives have to do with accomplishing comprehension—phonics, structural analysis—or with using comprehension—summarizing, outlining—(Goodman, 1970). As stated earlier, comprehension occurs as a complex interaction of all knowledge systems operating within the reader and all the linguistic systems operating in the text. Why, then, do corrective reading programs focus so heavily on a skills deficit model wherein students' weaknesses become the center of interest while the strengths are virtually ignored? Even more disturbing is the tendency to concentrate the students' attention on graphic cues without the necessary integration of graphic and experiential data required for construction of meaning.

Examine, for example, the oral reading protocol shown.

Oral Reading Protocol
(David N.)

TOM AND NED LIVE NEAR [Liver nea] A LARGE CITY PARK [PACK]. THEY OFTEN VISIT [visitor] IT WITH THEIR PLAYMATES. IN THE PARK ARE MANY SHADY [shades] MAPLE TREES. THERE IS A PLEASANT [forest] PICNIC GROUND ON THE HILL, AND THE VALLEY BELOW HAS A PRETTY LITTLE POND [pound]. THE GIRLS ALWAYS ENJOY WATCHING THE BOYS WHILE THEY SAIL THEIR TINY BOATS IN THE WATER. MOTHER AND FATHER ENJOY [s] PICNICS IN THE PARK.

Paragraph 4, Gilmore Oral Reading Test, John V. Gilmore, Harcourt Brace Jovanovich. New York, 1951 (out of print).

It represents the oral reading of a fifth grade boy we'll call David. After listening to a tape recording of David's reading of this and several other paragraphs with similar miscues, thirty-two reading teachers were given a checklist with items of suggested corrective options ranging from heavy decoding emphasis to heavy meaning emphasis items. Not surprisingly, the most checked item was: *A structured review of phonics with emphasis on blending sounds in the middle of words.* Among the least checked items was: *Lessons that stress anticipation of meaning from experience.* The teachers seemed so attuned to reading as a

Nelson-Herber and Herber

decoding or word calling process that they failed to notice the most disturbing element of David's oral reading—that he does not recognize that reading is a process of creating meaning from print. Consequently, many of the teachers would engage David in an iatrogenic process, one that makes the problem worse by treating it. David is already relying too heavily on graphic cues. Another recycling through phonics will only exacerbate the problem. When David fails to stop at the end of the first sentence to express confusion or make corrections, it should be recognized at once that he is not in touch with the primary objective in reading—comprehension.

What the teachers did not know was that David, according to his records, had been recycled through phonics at least three times and had developed the learned helplessness that one so often sees in long term corrective reading students (Thomas, 1979). Once his phonics knowledge was viewed as a strength rather than as a weakness, and he began to work on exercises that stressed reading for meaning using his strength in phonics as a tool (e.g., using cloze process with phonic clues), he began to make rapid progress.

It is recognized, of course, that some students do have skill deficiences. What is being suggested is that skills are not sufficient to meet the reading needs of middle and secondary school students. Consistency between the corrective reading program and the regular reading program calls for instruction not only to correct real skill deficiencies, but to integrate the skills with the use of strategies that parallel instruction in content classrooms—instruction that focuses on students' strengths rather than on their presumed weaknesses.

There are several sources of strength in students who have need for corrective reading: experience, language facility, decoding skills, curiosity, and capacity to reason.

Experience. By the time students reach the middle and secondary school grades, they have accumulated a rich store of experiences. This experiential strength may not be literally and directly related to what is studied in school. However, if analyzed in reference to broadly based concepts and principles that are worthy of study, students' experiences have a high degree of relevance.

A positive approach to corrective reading utilizes students' experiential strength in the study of important ideas. Instructional strategies are available to help students make connections between their own experiences and what they are studying in school. They learn that there are many dimensions to a single experience and their own experience can enrich others even as, through reading, their own can be enriched.

Language facility. Students have linguistic strengths. They understand language and can use it to communicate with others. At least intuitively, they recognize that language communication is not just the product of a set of specific skills but is a unified process used as a means to an end rather than as an end in itself.

A positive approach to corrective reading brings on this familiarity with language and the ability to communicate with language. Instructional strategies are available to help students to understand that each subject has its own special language and that once they learn the vocabulary they can communicate as easily in that language as in their more familiar, general language. These strategies acquaint students with special language from different disciplines and support its use as students discuss ideas that are central to an understanding of those disciplines.

Decoding skills. By the time students reach middle and secondary schools they usually have had considerable exposure to phonics. They recognize that there is a relationship between sounds and symbols and can use their phonetic knowledge to pronounce phonetically regular words in meaningful context. Further intensive phonics instruction at this level does not appear to be as beneficial as the use of a whole language approach that places emphasis on the use of syntactic and semantic cues as well as on graphic cues (Otto, 1979). Indeed, there is evidence of a more dominant use of semantic and grammatical cues by high achieving, comprehending readers. According to Otto in a review of approaches to remedial reading for adolescents, instruction which optimizes student use of syntactic and semantic cues appears to facilitate student achievement more consistently than isolated phonics instruction. This is probably because basic phonics skills lose their efficacy as reading materials advance in difficulty, containing words and concepts beyond the realm of student experience (Spache, 1976).

A positive approach to corrective reading acknowledges the decoding skills that students bring to middle and secondary schools and builds on those skills rather than overemphasizing them. Instructional strategies are available to help students realize that decoding is only a means to an end and that the purpose of reading is to comprehend the intended message.

Curiosity. Students are naturally curious and inquisitive beings and with that curiosity comes an ability to speculate, to hypothesize, and to set purposes. This curiosity motivates students to explore their personal environments and themselves more than to explore the unknown concepts presented in the various curricula studied in middle

Nelson-Herber and Herber

and secondary schools. Teachers, focusing on the latter rather than the former, conclude that students "are not interested in learning."

A positive approach to corrective reading draws heavily on students' natural curiosity. Instructional strategies are available to tap into their ability to hypothesize or predict, their interest in problem solving, their motivations for confirmation of their speculations, their need to know about concurring opinions. Through these strategies students develop a need for reading to satisfy their need to know.

Capacity to reason. While we recognize that students are not equally endowed with the capacity to reason, we believe the basic capacity is present in all. It is not our function as teachers to teach our students "to think." They already can do that. Rather, it is our function to teach them "how to think," how to use their reasoning powers to the maximum. Even students who have difficulty comprehending what they are reading have the ability to reason about the information once they acquire it—either through reading or by alternate means. Lack of reading skill does not automatically mean lack of reasoning skill. Indeed, the latter can be used to promote the former.

A positive approach to corrective reading builds on students' ability to reason and does not withhold the utilization of this natural capacity until the more unnatural act of reading is fully developed. Instructional strategies are available to stimulate students' reasoning power. Coupled with their natural curiosity about the world around them, this reasoning power creates in them a need to know that makes reading a natural and productive means to an end rather than an end in itself.

Conclusion

A positive approach to corrective reading is one that builds on students' strengths, several of which have been identified. As must be clear, these strengths are present in all students, not just in those who need corrective reading. Logically, then, these strengths should be the basis for instruction in all areas, not solely in corrective reading.

Recall that we mentioned the need for a parallel between reading instruction in content-area classrooms and in corrective reading classes. When the latter instruction is a supplement to the former, there is consistency both in the reading processes stressed and the instructional strategies utilized. For that reason, we regularly repeated the statement that "Instructional strategies are available..." to build on students' strengths in corrective reading (Nelson, 1980; Herber, 1978; Herber & Nelson, 1975).

These instructional strategies are demonstrably successful[1] when integrated, in content-area classrooms, with instruction in the subject matter of the related curricula. They are equally applicable in corrective reading classes for students who truly need additional reading instruction. While concentrating on the integration of skills, while focusing on students' strengths, and while guiding the study of important concepts, reading teachers can provide corrective reading instruction that is positive in its approach, consistent with students' needs, and lasting in its value.

Note

1. The authors direct a Network of Secondary School Demonstration Centers for Teaching Reading in Content Areas, funded by the National Basic Skills Program, U.S. Department of Education. Information and materials are available upon request.

Selecting Vocabulary to Teach in the Intermediate and Secondary Grades

Michael F. Graves
University of Minnesota

From about 1910 to 1950, vocabulary study represented an important thrust of educational research (Clifford, 1978; Lorge & Chall, 1963). In contrast, from about 1950 to the mid 1970s, very little research on vocabulary was conducted (Calfee & Drum, 1978). More recently, however, vocabulary has once again become a topic of interest to educational researchers. In 1977, Becker suggested that lack of vocabulary is one of the most potent factors affecting disadvantaged students' problems with reading comprehension and proposed that the schools should undertake a massive, long term program to systematically teach students a basic vocabulary. This suggestion has not met with universal acceptance. In particular, Anderson and Freebody (1979) have suggested that vocabulary knowledge may not be causally related to reading comprehension and that direct instruction in vocabulary might not promote comprehension. Some research appears to support Anderson and Freebody's position. A study by Jenkins, Pany, and Schreck (1978) has been widely cited as presenting evidence against the hypothesis that vocabulary instruction can improve comprehension. However, the results on several measures of that study showed positive effects of vocabulary instruction. Moreover, several other studies have indicated that vocabulary instruction can improve reading comprehension. Draper and Moeller (1971) have improved comprehension as measured by a standardized test with a program that taught a large number of words over a school year. My colleagues and I have increased comprehension of a specific selection by preteaching the vocabulary of that selection (Graves & Bender, 1980) and increased reading comprehension as measured by a standardized test by teaching science and social studies terms in a one semester reading course (Barrett & Graves, 1981). And Beck, Perfetti, and McKeown (in press) achieved both specific and general comprehension gains with an intensive five month program that thoroughly taught students a small body of words.

Questions of whether or not and under just what circumstances vocabulary instruction improves comprehension are not, of course, fully answered in a few studies. Nevertheless, it is my opinion and that of others (Beck, 1982; Becker, 1977; Calfee, 1981; O'Rourke, 1974; Stotsky, 1976) that after the primary grades most American children pass through school without receiving substantial instruction in vocabulary and that rigorous and systematic programs of vocabulary instruction that extend beyond the primary grades need to be developed. At the very least, vocabulary instruction which is more rigorous and more systematic than that most children currently receive in the intermediate and secondary grades ought to be considered.

In the remainder of the paper, I describe a system for classifying new reading vocabulary in terms of the learner's knowledge of the word or concept being taught. I believe that this system is useful in selecting words to teach and in deciding just what teaching a certain word entails. I believe that the system may also be useful in considering what it means to know a word. Finally, I am hopeful that the system can be useful in promoting consideration of rigorous and systematic vocabulary programs.

The System for Classifying Vocabulary

As I have noted, the system classifies vocabulary in terms of the learner's knowledge of the word or concept being taught. It was originally proposed by Goodman (1970). More recently, it has been modified and described in greater detail by several of my colleagues (Boettcher, 1979; Palmer, 1979; Ryder, 1978) and myself (Graves, 1978). In its more recent form, the system identified four types of vocabulary.

> Type One Words—words which are in the students' oral vocabulary but which they cannot read.
>
> Type Two Words—new meanings for words which are already in the students' reading vocabulary with one or more other meanings.
>
> Type Three Words—words which are in neither the students' oral vocabulary nor their reading vocabulary and for which they do not have an

available concept but for which a concept can be easily built.

Type Four Words—words which are in neither the students' oral vocabulary nor their reading vocabulary, for which they do not have an available concept, and for which a concept cannot be easily built.

Before each of the types is considered in detail, some general characteristics of the system should be noted. First, the order in which the types are listed generally parallels the difficulty of the teaching and learning task. Teaching students to read words which are already in their oral vocabularies and teaching them new meanings for words they already know with another meaning are relatively simple tasks. Teaching new words which represent easily available concepts is a more difficult endeavor. Finally, teaching new words which represent new and difficult concepts is a still more difficult task.

A second general characteristic of the system is that because it classifies words and concepts according to an individual's prior knowledge of those words and concepts, the system is relative rather than absolute. What is a Type One word for one student may be a Type Four word for another.

The third general characteristic of the system is a qualification on the second. The fact that words and concepts are classified according to individual students' prior knowledge of them does not mean that most words will be differentially classified in a particular classroom. Rather, within reasonably homogeneous classes, the relationship between the word or concept being taught and students' prior knowledge will be similar for most of the students.

The fourth general characteristic of the system, and the last one I will note here, is that the four categories are not mutually exclusive.

I turn now to identifying words of each type.

Type One Words

Learning to read Type One words, words which are in their oral vocabularies, is the major vocabulary learning task of students when they enter school. Children enter first grade with relatively large oral vocabularies; estimates range from about 2,000 words to about 25,000 words (Lorge & Chall, 1963). Even if the lower estimate is more accurate, this is an impressive number of words. However, most beginning first graders can read very few words. Primary grade texts introduce words slowly; and in order to simplify the learning task, they deal almost exclusively with words that are in students' oral vocabularies. Thus, primary grade teachers' main task is to teach such words. Over the first three years of school, students will encounter in the neighborhood of 2,000 to 3,000 such words in their readers and additional ones in their other texts. Examples of words appearing in primers are *fast, home*, and *two*. Additional ones appearing in first grade readers might be *got, many*, and *surprise*. Additional ones appearing in second grade readers might be *job, quite*, and *stretch*; and additional ones appearing in third grade readers might include *amaze, machine*, and *weigh* (Harris & Jacobson, 1972). These words can be further classified as decodable or not decodable, using the phonics skills that students have. Of course, what is decodable and what is not will change as the students' phonics skills mature. Each year, primary grade students learn to deal with additional spelling patterns. Still, there are some words that will never be readily decodable using phonics because they contain irregular and seldom occurring letter-sound correspondence. *Language* and *laughter* are such words.

With beginning readers, then, teachers need to teach the majority of Type One words students encounter, but as students' phonics skills and other word identification skills increase, teachers need to teach fewer and fewer of them. By the time most students get to fourth grade or so, they will have become quite proficient at using phonics skills and at least somewhat skilled in using structural analysis and context clues and can use these skills to identify most of the Type One words they encounter. A recent study in which we compared competent fourth grade students' reading and oral vocabularies indicated that they could read about 96% of the words they could understand orally (Graves, 1980).

The situation is very different with many poor readers in the intermediate and secondary grades. These students have not acquired the phonics and other word recognition skills that would enable them to identify the Type One words they encounter in their reading. They recognize a limited number of words on sight. Moreover, they are forced to ponder over many of the words they do recognize on sight, identifying them only with conscious attention. Having to identify words in this fashion interferes with comprehension. Students need to process the vast majority of words they encounter without conscious attention, instantaneously and automatically (LaBerge & Samuels, 1974; Perfetti & Hogaboam, 1975). Thus, these poor readers need to be taught a set of basic words which will include the majority of the words they encounter while reading, and they need to reach a level of automaticity in processing these words.

For students who read primarily in a particular reading series, the basic vocabulary used in that series is the most appropriate source of words to teach. Identifying just which words need to be taught in such a situation is straightforward. The words that need to be taught first are those that are most useful to students, those that occur most frequently in their reading materials. By and large, these more frequent words will be introduced early in a series. Thus, identifying what words to teach can be accomplished by starting with the word lists in the earliest readers, testing students' ability to pronounce the words on those lists, and then teaching the words they can not pronounce. Testing, I should repeat, can consist merely of asking students to pronounce the words. They already know the meaning of these words. Also, students' knowledge of words at any particular level can often be tested with a subset of the words used at that level. If students can identify a randomly selected set of 20 words taken from the 200 word vocabulary used in a particular first reader, it is a good bet that they will know most of the other 180 words, and further testing at that level is not necessary. If, on the other hand, they can identify only 15 of the 200 words, then they probably need to be tested on all the words to determine which ones they need to be taught.

After words at a lower level are mastered, the teacher can proceed by testing words at successively higher levels, teaching the words not known at one level before going on to select those needing to be taught at the next. Exactly how many words should be screened and then taught if necessary is difficult to determine. However, it seems reasonable to eventually deal with the basic vocabulary of series up through the third grade readers. In *Ginn 720* (Ginn, 1976) this means about 2,600 words, while in *Pathfinder* (Allyn & Bacon, 1978) it means about 2,200 words.

For students who read in a variety of materials, sources of words other than their reading series must be found. Fortunately, a number of lists of frequent words are useful here. The shortest, easiest, and probably best known list is the Dolch List of 220 Basic Sight words (Dolch, 1945). The majority of students will have learned the Dolch words by about the end of second grade. But they occur extremely frequently. It has been estimated, for example, that they make up 60 percent of the words in intermediate grade texts (Bond & Tinker, 1973). Thus, it is crucial that older students who do not know all of these words learn them.

More extensive lists include Dale's List of 769 Easy Words (Dale, 1931), Stone's Revision of the Dale List of 769 Easy Words (Stone, 1956) and the Spache Revised Word List (Spache, 1974) of approximately 1,100 words. Each of these lists contains nearly all of the 220 Dolch words and, of course, a number of additional words. Each of them contains a great number of the same words. And for reasons I have explained elsewhere (Graves, 1978), a good deal of primary grade materials and much of the high interest, easy reading material written for older youngsters who do not read well (see Graves, Boettcher, & Ryder, 1979) employ these words exclusively or nearly exclusively. If, then, teachers can guarantee that students know the words on these lists, they are in a position to identify a number of books in which the vocabulary will not be a stumbling block for students.

Exactly just which of these lists one chooses to use or whether one uses a combination of them probably is not that important. However, I believe that it would be extremely useful for a school or district to identify a list of about 1,000 words and to make every effort to insure that *all* students in a school could respond automatically to them by a certain grade level. Such a list would be basically a list of the 1,000 or so most frequent words in the language. Insuring that all students could read these words would again consist of two steps. First, all students would need to be screened to identify those few who could not read some of them. Second, students who did not know some of the words would need to be taught them.

It should be possible for an elementary school staff to insure that virtually all students have mastered the words by the end of the sixth grade or for a junior high staff to insure that virtually all students had mastered them by the end of the seventh grade. Knowledge that their students had *all* mastered a specific basic vocabulary should be extremely useful to teachers in selecting materials to use with their lower performing students.

Whether direct instruction in a general body of Type One words much larger than 1,000 words ought to be attempted is definitely a question, but I believe it is a question worth asking. As with the smaller word list, the purpose of insuring that all students could read the words in a larger list would be to see that they knew the majority of words they would come across in their reading and to let teachers know what they knew. If insuring that students could read all of the words on a larger list were desirable, two sources suggest themselves. One is the Harris-Jacobson list (1972). This is based on a frequency count of words appearing in basal readers and other materials used in grades 1-6. It lists about 6,000 words by the grade level at which they are first widely used, and it would be easy to select a subset of these, say the 3,000 easiest words. The other source is the Carroll, Davies, and Richman *Word Frequency Book* (1971). This is based on a frequency count of words used in third through ninth grade materials and lists the words by frequency. As with the Harris-Jacobson list, a subset of 3,000 or so of the more frequent words listed in the Carroll et al. text could be selected for instruction.

The process of identifying words from these larger lists would be the same as that for the smaller lists, and as with the smaller lists relatively few students would need to be taught the words. These lists as long as 3,000 words or so would probably be most useful at the junior high level. Junior high staffs might attempt to insure that all students have mastered them by the end of ninth grade.

In concluding this section on teaching Type One words, I want to reiterate three points. First, while the recommendation is to insure that all students can read a set of basic words, relatively few intermediate or secondary grade students will need to be taught these words. Most have already learned them. Second, the words need to be taught so that students' responses to them are automatic; too frequent analysis of words will thwart fluency and retard comprehension. Third, although a variety of lists have been mentioned, no suggestion is being made that teachers work with all of them. Rather, the suggestion is to insure that all students master a set of about 1,000 words by the sixth or seventh grade and perhaps an additional set of 2,000 words by the ninth grade.

Type Two Words

Learning to deal with Type Two words, words which they can already read with one or more meanings but for which they now need to learn another meaning, is important to both intermediate and secondary grade students. However, there are two kinds of multiple meaning words, and the two kinds are differentially important to the two age groups. On the other hand, there are words that have more than one common meaning. It is frequently pointed out, for example, that the word *run* has a large variety of meanings. One can run a race, run to the store, run a store, or run the rapids. What is not as frequently pointed out is the fact that a great many English words have multiple meanings. The research of Dale and O'Rourke (1981) indicates that perhaps a third of the relatively common English words have multiple common meanings.

Dealing with the secondary meaning of such words can indeed prove difficult (Mason, 1979). To overcome this difficulty, students need to learn that words have multiple meanings and that the particular meaning a word has is determined by the context in which it occurs. Two sources are useful in identifying words having a number of common meanings. One is the students' reading material. Intermediate grade teachers can scan selections students are about to read looking for words that are used with their less common meanings.

The other source is Dale and O'Rourke's *The Living Word Vocabulary* (1981). *The Living Word Vocabulary* (LWV) is a word list containing 43,000 entries. Each entry consists of a word and one of its meanings, a word meaning combination. For each word meaning combination, the LWV indicates the percentage of children at a certain grade level who, through testing, demonstrated their ability to read the word and assign it the meaning given. In most cases, the grade level for which data is provided is that at which between 67 percent and 84 percent of the students tested correctly identified a particular word meaning combination. Shown below are four entries for the word *line*.

Grade	Score	Word	Word Meaning
4	83%	line	a stretched string
6	80%	line	a boundary
8	77%	line	descent, ancestry
10	72%	line	kind of business

The entries indicate, for example, that 83 percent of the fourth graders tested knew the meaning of *line* as "a stretched string" but that only 72 percent of the tenth graders tested knew the meaning of *line* as a "kind of business."

Whether identified from students' readings or from the LWV, once identified, multiple meaning words can be used in exercises and discussions aimed at helping students to become better able to deal with the many words with multiple common meanings that they will encounter. Note that because the purpose of this instruction is to teach students to become generally able to deal with words with multiple common meanings rather than to teach them the multiple meanings of specific words, the specific words used in these exercises are more important for what they demonstrate about multiple meaning words than they are in themselves.

Graves

At the beginning of this section, I noted that there are two kinds of multiple meaning words. The second kind of multiple meaning word has one common meaning, usually the more frequent meaning, and then another restricted meaning that is unique to a specific subject area, usually a less frequent meaning. *Legend* is a good example of such a word. Most intermediate grade students know that a legend is an old story. And although these students will probably learn more about legends in the literature classes they take (for example, they are likely to learn that legends are often believed to be true), they probably learned this original, common meaning without formal instruction. However, even in the secondary grades, many students do not know that a legend is a key to an illustration or map. Most students will learn this meaning of *legend* only if their teacher, probably their history or geography teacher, points it out. Moreover, knowing the more common meaning of *legend* is of little help in figuring out this restricted meaning.

How many of this type of multiple meaning words are there? There certainly are not a great number of them. But in secondary grade materials there are enough of them that teachers should be concerned with identifying those that may hinder students' understanding. Unlike the other kind of multiple meaning words, words having a specialized meaning in a particular subject should probably be chosen exclusively from subject matter reading materials. Students need to be taught the specialized meanings of words used in the material they are studying.

In summary, there are two kinds of multiple meaning words—those that have multiple common meanings and those that have both a common meaning or meanings and a meaning specific to a particular subject area. Learning to deal with words having a variety of common meanings is particularly important for intermediate grade students. *The Living Word Vocabulary* is a convenient list for identifying this sort of multiple meaning words to teach. Learning to deal with words having a specialized meaning in a particular subject area is particularly important for secondary students. This kind of multiple meaning word can be identified in subject matter texts.

Type Three Words

Learning to deal with Type Three words, words which are in neither their oral vocabulary nor their reading vocabulary, but for which they have an available concept, is the largest word learning task intermediate and secondary students face. Estimates of vocabulary size vary tremendously. Kirkpatrick (1891) estimated that the average college undergraduate has a recognition vocabulary of about 19,000 words, while Seashore and Eckerson (1940) estimated that the average college undergraduate has a recognition vocabulary of about 160,000 words. However, whatever the exact number of words they will eventually learn, the majority of the new words intermediate and secondary grade students face will be Type Three words.

Also, whatever the exact number of Type Three words students need to learn during the intermediate and secondary grades, it is almost certainly larger than the number that can reasonably be taught (Nagy & Anderson, 1982). However, the fact that not all the words students need to learn can be taught does not argue that none of them should be taught. Rather, it suggests that teachers need to employ some judicious combination of 1) insuring that students have strategies that will enable them to deal with Type Three words independently, 2) allowing and encouraging them to use these strategies whenever possible, and 3) identifying and teaching those Type Three words which students would have problems dealing with independently or which are particularly important for a variety of reasons.

Teaching students general strategies for dealing with unknown words is not my concern here. However, the following discussion is undertaken with the assumption that students either already have or are being taught the use of context, structural analysis, and the dictionary to determine word meanings. It also relies on the assumption that students need to continually practice using these strategies.

There are three steps in identifying Type Three words. The first is getting some idea of just which words intermediate and secondary grade students are likely to know. The second is setting up criteria for selecting the words, and the third is actually identifying the words.

There is not a lot of information about teachers' ability to identify words students do and do not know. However, in one recent study (Graves & Gebhard, in press), a colleague and I found that teachers vary greatly in their accuracy in predicting which words their students do and do not know.

There are several ways that teachers can sharpen their perception of what words their students do and do not know. One is to consult *The Living Word Vocabulary*. As I noted in the section on multiple meaning words, this text lists words, their meanings, the grade level at which between 67 percent and 84 percent of the students tested knew the word, and the exact percentage of students at that grade level that knew the word. It answers the question, "What percent of my students are likely to know this word with this meaning?" Moreover, the predictions appear to be quite accurate (Graves & Gebhard, in press).

Another source that teachers can use to sharpen their perception of the words students are likely to know is the Carroll, Davies, and Richman *Word Frequency Book*. As noted, this lists 86,000 words by frequency. Although the relationship between word frequency as defined in the Carroll et al. text and word knowledge is not a strong one (Graves, Boettcher, Peacock, & Ryder, 1980), students are certainly more likely to know very frequent words than very infrequent ones. Moreover, the book contains other information—for example, data indicating the frequency of words in texts from various subject areas—that teachers may find useful.

The other source of information about what words students know is the students themselves. Teachers can identify the words in upcoming selections that they think will be difficult for students and build multiple-choice or matching tests to find out whether or not the words are difficult. Of course, constructing such tests is time consuming. However, it need not be done for every selection. Several experiences of identifying words that they think will be difficult and then checking students' performance to see just what was difficult will sharpen teachers' general perceptions of which words do and do not cause students' problems. Teachers can also take the opportunity to ask students which words they find troublesome. However, some students are not very good at this task, and asking students to select difficult vocabulary ought to be part of a broader program of determining students' vocabulary strengths and weaknesses.

Once potentially difficult vocabulary is identified, the next step is to determine just which words are worth teaching. Very often, selections contain more difficult vocabulary than can be taught. Consequently, criteria for identifying the most important vocabulary to teach need to be established. The answers to four questions will be helpful in establishing these criteria.

The first question to ask is "Is understanding the word important to understanding the selection in which it appears?" If the answer is "No," then other words would usually take precedence for teaching.

The second question is "Are students likely to be able to assign the word a meaning using the context or structural analysis skills?" If the answer here is "Yes," then they probably ought to be allowed to do so. Having students use their word attack skills when they can will both help them to cement these skills and reduce the number of words that need to be taught.

Another question to ask is "Can this word be used to further students' contextual, structural analysis, or dictionary skills?" If the answer here is "Yes," then dealing with the word can serve two purposes. It can aid students in learning the word, and it can help them acquire a generative skill.

The final question I would suggest asking is "How useful is this particular word outside of the selection being currently taught?" By and large, the answer to this question will depend on the word's frequency. The more frequent a word in the materials students will be dealing with in the future, the more useful it is for them to know it. Moreover, the more frequent the word, the greater the chances that students will retain it once it is taught. The Carroll et al. list is, of course, useful in identifying more and less frequent words.

A further matter regarding frequency deserves consideration here. Many commercial vocabulary programs, programs that teach specific sets of words, err in that they teach rather obscure words when they should be teaching relatively common ones; that is, they teach less frequent words rather than more frequent ones. This is unfortunate. The student who does not know such words as *thrive, tremble,* and *span* needs to learn to deal with such words before spending much time learning such obscure words as *temerity* and *somatic*.

As a final note on the four questions to be used in deciding which difficult words to teach, I should note that the four questions are not independent. In fact, the answer to one question may suggest that a word should be taught, while the answer to another suggests that it should not. Just what to do in such cases is a matter of teacher judgment, but the answers to the questions can inform this judgment.

My summary to this section on teaching Type Three words can be brief. New words which represent available or easily taught concepts represent the largest set of words intermediate and secondary grade students need to learn. Teachers need to learn to identify Type Three words that are likely to be difficult for their students. There are several ways to do this. Once having identified potentially difficult Type Three words, teachers need to decide just which ones to teach.

Type Four Words

Learning to deal with Type Four words, words which represent new and difficult concepts, is the most difficult vocabulary learning task that intermediate and secondary grade students face. The concept of Type Four words is also difficult, or at least somewhat elusive. This is true for two reasons. First, as I noted in the introductory section, the distinction between Type Three words and Type Four words is sometimes a fine one. More specifically, words and the concepts they represent form a continuum in which some words very definitely represent familiar concepts and can be easily explained, others represent somewhat familiar concepts and can be fairly easily explained (at least if they do not have to be explained too fully), and still others represent distinctly new concepts and require a good deal of time and effort to explain (particularly if they need to be explained fully). The other reason that the concept of Type Four words is somewhat elusive is suggested by the parenthetical comments above. That is, the difficulty of teaching a word or concept is influenced by the depth or precision of meaning that needs to be developed. *Fascism*, for example, would represent a new and potentially difficult concept for most 6th graders. However, teaching students that fascism is "a type of dictatorship" is certainly radically easier than teaching the full blown concept.

A word of caution is in order here. Neither the fact that Type Three and Four words represent a continuum of difficulty nor the fact that difficult concepts can sometimes be taught at a simple level should be taken to mean that Type Four words really are not very difficult. In fact, I have included the notion of Type Four words here largely to enable me to distinguish word learning tasks—the kind of task necessary to deal with Types One, Two, and Three words—from concept learning tasks—the kind of task necessary to deal with Type Four words.

In the next few pages, I will deal with identifying Type Four words by presenting examples of words falling at several points on the continuum of Type Three and Four words. Following this, I will discuss selecting Type Four words to teach.

The word *persevere* is a good example of a word that is near the Type Three end of the continuum. Consider the case for eighth grade students. *Persevere* would be unknown to many eighth grade students; *The Living Word Vocabulary* indicates that it was known by only 69 percent of the twelfth graders tested. To be sure, eighth grade students probably have an available concept close to that represented by *persevere*, something like CONTINUE TRYING. And a part of teaching *persevere* consists of telling the students that it means to continue trying. Having learned this meaning, students could interpret "The members of the expedition vowed to persevere until they reached the peak" as "The members of the expedition vowed to continue trying until they reached the peak." This interpretation would be basically correct, but only basically correct. The gloss does not capture the richness and power of the word. "Continue trying" is rather flat. It does not suggest the strength and courage implied by *persevere*. Teaching students the full meaning of the word would consist of more than defining it with a short phrase; for at least some students, learning the full meaning of *persevere* would require first gaining the concept of PERSEVERANCE.

The word *fulcrum* represents another point on the continuum. Consider the case with 6th grade students. *Fulcrum* would be a Type Four word for many of them. One dictionary defines fulcrum as "the support or point of support on which a lever turns in raising or moving something." Unless they have been taught it, this notion will be totally foreign to most sixth graders. It simply is not the sort of thing that one would spontaneously think about. And the definition by itself is not going to be much help in getting students to think about it. For one thing, the definition can be understood only if one understands the concept LEVER. More importantly, both FULCRUM AND LEVER are best explained if students are given models to manipulate. To understand the principles involved, students need to move fulcrums back and forth, try levers of various lengths, and put different weights on the levers. There are, of course, a variety of other matters that might be dealt with in teaching these concepts, but I believe the point has been made. Teaching *fulcrum* definitely involves teaching a concept or set of concepts, and teaching this set of concepts is an involved and time consuming task.

Mores is an example of a much more difficult Type Four word, one that might be introduced in senior high classes. *Mores* is also a good example of a word which can be taught at various levels. The teacher could, for example, define mores as "customs," in which case it would represent an available concept. Such a definition might serve some purposes, although these would be unambitious ones, merely allowing students to get through a piece of material which included the word. As defined by William Sumner, who introduced the term and developed the concept in the late 1800s, mores are certain sorts of customs—"customs that are regarded by general agreement as highly important and obligatory as evidenced by strong sentiments against deviation and by severe punishment for violation" (Williams, 1968, p. 205). Obviously, mores are not simply customs. Less obviously, the concept MORES is not at all fully defined by the above definition. Fully understanding a concept involves being able to identify specific instances and non-instances of the concept and distinguishing between that concept and other related concepts. Thus, one who understands the concept MORES should be able to answer such questions as "Is armed robbery against the mores of our society?" or "Are folkways the same as mores?" The answer to the first question is "Not really." Armed robbery is against a specific law. Mores are not formally prescribed laws. The answer to the second question is also negative. Folkways are the customary acts of society. Unlike mores, they are not necessarily considered vital to the society or enforced by the threat of severe punishment. Of course, there is much more to be said about the concept of mores and the difference between mores and a variety of related concepts. And that is just the point. Knowing the definition of mores given above, even understanding it, does not prepare students to answer even the above two questions, let alone provide them with a fully formed concept of mores. One might well devote a week to a concept such as MORES.

I turn now to the matter of selecting Type Four words to teach, and this is another topic about which I can be brief. There is only one source of Type Four words. This is the subject matter being taught. Those Type Four words that need to be fully developed are the major concepts of the subject matter. Type Four words that need to be less fully developed are those that are less central to the subject matter.

I cannot add much about determining what is more and less important in various subject areas. This is the task of content teachers. What I can say though, and what I have tried to illustrate in this section, is that as one moves increasingly toward teaching words that represent new and difficult concepts, the teaching task becomes radically more difficult and time consuming. Thus, while it may make sense to talk about taking 10-15 minutes to teach ten Type Three words before students read a selection in which they are used, it makes no sense to talk about teaching ten Type Four words in anything like this period of time. Teaching a single concept may take days, and attempting to teach new concepts as if they were merely new words will only confuse students.

Concluding Remarks

Thus far I have discussed the system for classifying reading vocabulary in terms of the learners' knowledge of the word or concept that is being taught in some detail. I have also discussed the difficulties involved in teaching the various types of words. However, I have said almost nothing about methods of teaching the various types. Explaining teaching methods was not the purpose of this paper. At the same time, I do want to emphasize one point about instruction.

The point is that the relationship between a word and the concept it represents and the learners' knowledge of that word and concept determines the teaching strategies that can appropriately be used with the word. With Type One words, for example, the basic task for students is to associate what is unknown, the written word, with what is already known, the spoken word. To establish this association, students need to see the word at the same time that it is pronounced. Then, students need to repeatedly encounter the word in context so that they become automatic in responding to it. There is no question of teaching meaning here, and activities focused on meaning are misdirected. By definition, students know the meaning of Type One words.

The situation is very different with Type Three words. Here, students must be taught a meaning, not just taught to recognize the printed form of a known word. Teaching a word's meaning may include giving students a synonym for the word, defining it, modeling its use, having them use it, having them manipulate it in various ways, and a host of other procedures. In fact, a discussion of procedures for teaching Type Three words could occupy another paper at least the length of this one. But I believe the point has been made. Methods appropriate for teaching Type Three words are very different from those appropriate for teaching Type One words. Similarly, methods for teaching Type Two and Four words differ from those appropriate for teaching the other sorts.

In conclusion, I will mention several sources of teaching suggestions. A set of papers by my colleagues and me (Boettcher, 1979; Graves, 1978; Palmer, 1979; Ryder, 1978) deals specifically with teaching each word type. Also, Beck, McKeown, McCaslin, and Burkes (1979) and Calfee (1981) present some very useful suggestions for teaching Type Three and Type Four words.

There are certainly other good sources of teaching methods. Again, though, the major purpose of this paper was not to suggest teaching methods or sources of methods. Its purpose has been to present a rather thorough discussion of the various relationships that exist between the words and concepts to be taught and the words and concepts students already know and of how words representing various relationships might be selected. Armed with this knowledge, teachers should be in a good position to select appropriate words to teach and appropriate methods with which to teach them.

Comprehending and the Teacher of Reading

John Chapman
The Open University

There can be little doubt that if teachers wish to improve their pupils' reading comprehension, then the more they know about what happens when children are actually comprehending the more effective their instruction is likely to be. Yet, paradoxically, over the years teachers have been concerned, almost exclusively, with the end product or the results of reading a passage. More often than not this end product is measured by a series of questions after the reading, thereby drawing attention away from the process of comprehending to its results. For most teachers, comprehension involves both understanding and answering questions, which may or may not reveal what happens while the child is reading.

In the literature on reading instruction both product and process have been referred to as comprehension. To redress the balance, therefore, and to emphasis the distinction, I propose to retain the term comprehension for the end product and to introduce the term comprehending for the active process.

Moving attention to comprehending, however, is not without problems. Pearson and Johnson (1978), for example, have warned that,

> Comprehension as a process is an elusive entity. It is what happens to readers as they read. It is what keeps them going when they read. . . . However, when we get down to the bottom line, most of us would probably agree that processes are either totally or mostly inaccessible.

Elusive or not, inaccessible or not, the process of comprehending is the crucial one for the teacher (and the reader for that matter) for it is during that process, when individual readers are actively interpreting the text according to their knowledge and purpose, that learning is taking place. It is, furthermore, when teachers might judiciously intervene for the betterment of the process.

Intervention

Before going on to discuss teaching comprehending, I would like to make a few comments so as to allay doubts about the wisdom of teachers intervening in children's reading. For those who might object to the notion of teacher intervention, it should be remembered that intervention is no new thing during reading instruction, as witness the behavior of most teachers of beginning readers. It appears almost intuitive to give support while listening to beginning readers. For instance, first letter sounds are gently prompted, and when a word is not recognized, especially when that word is proving a stumbling block to fluency, then the actual word itself is given. With more fluent children, some teachers carry the process further and interpose questions that require inferences to be made to promote understanding. Teachers seem compelled to intervene to back up the readers, sometimes to the extent of virtually reading parts of the passage to the child. And this, according to Smith (1979), is no bad thing. Children, he suggests, learn to read by reading, and if they can't recognize enough words to learn, then someone else must read for them.

However, while intervention is typical of early reading instruction, caution needs to be expressed as to the timing and extent of that intervention. Clay's studies of children's behavior during oral reading (Clay, 1969), for example, have drawn attention to the growing ability of young readers to monitor their own reading behavior and to correct themselves. Too early or badly timed intervention at this stage may retard the growth of reading independence. Teachers need to know a great deal about the process and the child so as to intervene at the most propitious time.

To return to comprehending, while it is true that the comprehending process is mostly inaccessible, nonetheless it is possible to infer something of its nature, perhaps more nowadays than previously. The well-known work of Goodman (1967) with miscues provides an illustration of this. Using miscue analysis, he shows what goes on during reading, revealing those points where a misperceived word, or part thereof, can cause confusion in the reader. The analysis provides, as he puts it, a window on the reading process.

But what is the difference between comprehending and what many would call quite simply, reading? Reading has come to mean many things to many people and this is hardly surprising for if we have come to appreciate anything over the past decade or two, it is the extent of its complexity. Because of this increasing awareness, definitions of

Chapman

reading have multiplied and continue to, as its study becomes increasingly eclectic (Chapman, 1980) drawing on many disciplines. An example of this is given in the Bullock Report (Department of Education and Science, 1975), where three definitions of reading, those of Fries (1962), Goodman (1970), and Gray (1956) are combined in the following manner.

Table 1

1.	2.	3.
A response to graphic signals in terms of the words they represent.	(plus) A response to text in terms of the meanings the author intended to set down.	plus: A response to the author's meanings in terms of all the relevant previous experience and present judgments of the reader.

A child is often said to be able to read when his response to graphic signals is satisfactory from the teacher's point of view, or, to put it another way, when he has become a proficient decoder. This is the burden of definition one in the table above. When we add the skills required by the second definition, that is when the detection of the author's intended meaning is involved, then the tendency among reading teachers is to prefer the term comprehension. Yet, for many, this is still what they understand as reading. I would suggest, however, that the third definition includes a learning element. Most teachers would undoubtedly use the term comprehension for this, that is, something has been learned as a result of reading the passage. However, one could say that reading is the combination of all three definitions, for such a usage as three survives, for example, when the practice of acquiring knowledge by undergraduates is known as "reading for a degree."

It is clear that reading has to be retained as a very general term. To examine specific functions and areas, therefore, we should use other terms and restrict their usage. Comprehension, then, as indicated earlier, can be used for what has been learned from reading, while comprehending can be employed for what goes on while the reader is responding in the three ways indicated in Table 1. I want to go on to outline some of the factors involved in this response.

First, when and where does the process begin? A probable answer from most would be, "When the reader has opened the book at the first page and begun to respond to the graphic signals on that page." Yet this is now readily acknowledged to be an oversimplification. It may come as a surprise to some, however, to realize that comprehending could be said to begin *before* readers actually open a book, for they can only understand the text in terms of what is already known.

Prior Knowledge

Children bring to school stores of knowledge that differ considerably in amount, kind and quality. The extent of these individual variations in knowledge in any class of children, no matter the grade or geographical location of the school district, is truly remarkable. However, while this is widely appreciated, teachers often do not realize that their prior knowledge differs widely from that of their pupils, and that this should be taken into account in their classroom practice.

To understand what is involved in comprehending, it is convenient to consider what is covered by prior knowledge along three dimensions: 1) text-bound, 2) real world, and 3) specific content knowledge. Text-bound knowledge involves all that is covered by modern work in text linguistics (Chapman [1979a] and the references cited there for an introduction). Real world knowledge includes both knowledge gained from real life experience and that gained vicariously, from books and television. Specific content prior knowledge includes the amount of the reader's familiarity with the subject(s) of whatever text is to be read. While each of these will be looked at in turn, it is important to remember that they cannot be isolated in practice. The teacher, however, needs to keep each aspect in mind during reading instruction.

1. *Text-bound Prior Knowledge*

Recently, attempts have been made to gather together many of the facts known about texts into text grammars (e.g., Werlich, 1976) or as text linguistics, which according to van Dijk (1978) can be thought of as a domain or a series of interrelated or interdisciplinary studies. These studies both add to and include the classical sentence grammars. Text grammars are not, as yet, unified theoretical grammars like transformational grammar, for instance, but rather collections of facts about texts which in some cases are unified only by the author's cataloguing. While many would find this lack of theoretical unity problematic (whether it is possible to construct a grammar of texts is yet to be demonstrated), a look down the contents lists of such collections serves to remind us of how much prior knowledge an adult has of linguistic features compared with that of a child, and how much of this is taken for granted and left implicit for the child in school. Take, for example, some of the following characteristics of texts: the features which mark the difference between expository and narrative texts and between fact and fiction; the ordering of material and abbreviations typical of dictionaries, encyclopaedias and directories, and the choice of words and other textual characteristics that distinguish, say, a mathematical treatise from a sermon and, more narrowly, a biography from an autobiography. Recently too, notions of coherence and cohesion in texts, that is ways in which texts are said to 'hang together', have become prominent. Beyond the text itself, there is much prior knowledge about authors, both general and specific, which a teacher or other educated adult would 'know' so that without being conscious of it he or she knows what differences to expect of a work by Dickens or Salinger.

This prior knowledge of texts allows us to begin to anticipate what is to come when we read and that anticipation allows the comprehending process to begin. Our expectations are then confirmed or otherwise by a multitude of clues based on previous knowledge.

Take, for instance, an adult's expectations of a novel. Here the characters, a setting, and a plot provide the well-known structure underlying the actual words for the text. Look, for example, at the second and third sentences on the first page of *David Copperfield* by Charles Dickens, Chapter 1, "I am Born."

> To begin my life with the beginning of my life, I record that I was born (as I have been informed and believe) on a Friday, at twelve o'clock at night. It was remarked that the clock began to strike, and I began to cry, simultaneously.

Contrast this with the beginning of *Catcher in the Rye* by J.D. Salinger:

> If you really want to hear about it, the first thing you'll probably want to know is where I was born, and what my lousy childhood was like. . . . and all that David Copperfield kind of crap. . . .

Here Salinger knows that his readers will expect him to make such an introduction at the beginning of a work of fictional autobiography, and while he denies that he is going to follow in Dickens' footsteps, he nonetheless gives his reader a considerable amount of information about his character and begins to set the scene. Adult readers have these expectations from a detailed knowledge of texts, and in the same way as they would expect a novel to have a certain format, so they would anticipate nonfiction to have a different expository-type structure. The reader would anticipate information to be presented in a certain organized fashion.

How then is this text knowledge of importance to comprehending? Researchers have shown (Stein & Glenn, 1978) that children's understanding of a story is related to the underlying structure of that story. It is probable that this story grammar of event structures, episodes, and so on, is so well known as to give support to comprehending. The story grammar has, with time, become internalized. It is not difficult to imagine that, extrapolating from these findings, readers' comprehending will also be affected by text type differences.

In this way a prior knowledge of texts, their forms, and authors' predilections, provides readers with the basis for their expectations. So it is that the facilitating effect of their familiarity with texts is involved before the first words are met. Comprehending could be said to begin when a reader considers such things as the cover of the book. What text type does this indicate? Cues such as where the book was located in the library or in the bookshop will begin to build expectations. And again, what prior knowledge have we of the author? What style might we expect? A glance at the first pages of Dickens' and Salinger's novels mentioned above indicated the extent of stylistic variation that can be met.

It is important, therefore, as a first teaching strategy, to find out what children already know about the texts in general. Often in discussion the combined knowledge of a group of readers can advance that of the individual. However, the teacher will need to fill in the gaps in the group's knowledge. This is by way of preparation for reading, for the teacher will provide the focus for the discussion.

2. Cohesion and Coherence

Another important textual characteristic that has recently entered the literature on reading is the notion of cohesion or coherence, or the way in which a text hangs together. It is this characteristic that makes a text a text rather than a haphazard collection of sentences. That texts have such a property has been known for some time, and it can be demonstrated to be present by the simple expedient of taking a text, cutting it up into the sentences that compose it, jumbling them, and then asking a group of skilled readers individually to reassemble the text. It does not take long for them to put the text together again in its original order. Furthermore, when asked, skilled readers can rank cohesion or coherence of texts, saying whether one is more cohesive than another (Barnard, 1974).

When skilled readers are asked how they accomplished these tasks, it becomes clear that there is a series of clues, some hardly noticeable to skilled adult readers, that helps them to order or reconstruct the text. For instance, a theme or story line or a logical progression provides texts with coherence. However, before the theme is established, a series of linguistic features provides linkages between sentences in such a way as to build up that theme or story line. These are words within sentences which as well as playing their part in the syntax of the sentence, also have a further function which ties the meaning of one sentence or smaller meaning element to that of a previous or following sentence. These linguistic elements are called cohesive ties by Halliday and Hasan (1976) who have arranged them in five groups.

The first group of cohesive ties is the reference group which are anaphoric in their action. This is to say that they directly relate something that has already been read to what is being read now, an important feature in comprehending. Look at this occurring in the following simple passage for example (Neale, 1966):

> A black cat came to my house. She put her kitten by the door. Then she went away. Now I have her baby for a pet. (p. 3)

Notice the simple pronoun connections in this early reading passage, "cat"....."She"....."her"....."she"....."her." In the second sentence, the identity of "she" can only be found by relating back to the previous sentence and we know that it must refer to "cat" as this is the only animate (female) noun available with which to match the pronoun. In this way the relationship between anaphor and antecedent provides cohesion between sentences. "She" is next connected by "her" and then to "she" again in the following sentence. In the final sentence "her" occurs again. In this simple anaphoric pronoun sequence the main character is referred to throughout. The reader can maintain the identity of "cat" while at the same time following the action. Notice also that "my" in sentence one and "I" in the last sentence are similarly related.

Here various teaching strategies can be adopted. In the case of an early reading text as in the passage above, the teacher may intervene with simple questions to check that the identity chain of cohesive ties is being maintained. This intervention, like all such procedures, needs to be carried out very sensitively because most children learning to read, as we have noted above, soon begin to monitor their reading, self-correcting where necessary. Indeed, the actual self-corrections can be analyzed for awareness of this detail of cohesion.

As well as this, more direct teaching can be employed to alert children to the way in which these linguistic features work. Simple activities can be prepared to enable children to trace the chains through a passage. Sometimes ambiguity surrounds the pronoun and such events present useful teaching points. There are occasions also when the same pronoun is being used for much of the text though the antecedents are changing. The identity of the group which is referred to as "they," for example, can alter during a narrative as the action ebbs and flows. Tracing the antecedents can provide illuminating work for children.

There are other cohesive ties in the passage, and two of these are the conjunctions *then* and *now*. They do not operate in the same way as the anaphoric pronouns, but perform another function which is also cohesive. In this case a simple time linkage is involved. There are, of course, other types of conjunction, the additive, the adversative, and the causal. Conjunctions clearly link or confirm the meaning contained in one sentence with that of the next. In this instance they signal the progress of time.

As well as the anaphoric and conjunction types, there is a further group known as the lexical cohesive ties. As the term implies, these involve linguistic relationships that exist between the actual words chosen by the writer. Consider, for example, the cohesive effect of "come" in the first sentence and "went away" in sentence three. These are antonyms or opposites, and because of this basic lexical association have the effect of contributing to cohesion. There are further semantic associative relationships of this kind; those between "house" in sentence one and "door" in sentence two, and those between "cat," "kitten," "baby" and "pet."

Here again there are opportunities for teaching to assist children's understanding of this important textual characteristic. Activities can be prepared that require pupils to provide associations between words by way of vocabulary extension. With careful guidance pupils can be alerted to the relationships to be met in the text, so as to provide a basis for comprehending. Depending on the reading ability of the pupils, questions concerning style and register can be introduced.

Even in this simple passage of four sentences (which is,

incidentally, part of a test of reading ability), there are many cohesive ties which create textual cohesion. The words are performing their syntactic function in the structure of the sentence as well as providing cohesion as the overall meaning of the passage is built up. This dual-level functioning is important, for teachers tend to assist the limited syntactic process, that is, they encourage the reader to concentrate on the sentence without drawing attention to the build-up of the overall meaning which occurs across sentence, and indeed paragraph, boundaries. Cohesion then operates at the semantic level, often spanning many sentences to bring together the meanings they carry. The pronoun "she," for example, in sentences two and three, acts as a subject of the verb "put" and "went away." At the same time it maintains the link with "black cat." This anaphoric process has been called backward acting, and in a way it is, for the identity of "she" can only be decided by referring back in the passage to the antecedent. However, during comprehending, the reader is working forwards and probably only literally refers back when an ambiguous pronoun is reached. (See Carpenter & Just, 1977, for eye movement data on this topic.) The identity of the referent, which may change while the pronoun remains the same, has to be maintained in working memory (see Chapman, 1979b).

It is not clear at the moment how the equality and quantity of cohesive ties affect comprehension. The number of ties and the different types and their various combinations appear to be directly related to the register of the text. That this itself is also important is evident, but a great deal of research is needed to provide a clear picture. However, while research is probing this question, the concept gives a fresh way of looking at texts providing teachers with new insights to assist their understanding of comprehending. How the various groups of ties function in different texts is dealt with more fully in Chapman (1981).

It is important to remember that during comprehending, the three levels of language proposed by linguists are at work, the phonological or sound system, the syntactic (word ordering) and the semantic or meaning elements. As the reader moves further into, or becomes more proficient at, silent reading, processing of sounds becomes automatic and the domination of sound recedes. This leaves more cognitive capacity available for the processing of syntax and semantics and the subtle relationships between them.

This area of the reading process is probably one of the most important for the teacher and contains much that has been left implicit so far.

3. Real World Knowledge

It is not only our prior knowledge of texts that is involved in comprehending, but our knowledge of the world as it has been built up by direct experience and learning. There are many occasions during reading when the comprehending process, or the growth of understanding of a text, is hindered or aided by the amount and/or quality of the reader's prior knowledge of the world. This knowledge can be said to be organized into personal knowledge banks of scenes or frames (Fillmore, 1979). It includes many everyday examples, such as "restaurant behavior," "catching a train," "painting a door," or "birthday parties."

It is always surprising to look at the extent of the information that is available to us in our stores of personal knowledge. Look at one of the examples above, which might well vary considerably from adult to adult, that of restaurant behavior. Most people will be able to predict the type of action that will take place in a restaurant. The word "restaurant" itself will have predisposed you to think of a certain type of public eating place where food and service can be obtained for money, probably with waiter or waitress service. You will have distinguished, virtually unconsciously, a restaurant from a cafe or hot-dog stand. The behavior in a restaurant will be of a particular type, and while already distinguished from that in other eating-out places will have further refinements according to levels of sophistication and its attendant expense. The greater the experience, either direct or through reading, the more prepared the reader will be, for example, to understand a story that is set in a specific type of restaurant.

The particular scene begins to be established early in the text, and as the reader proceeds through it, more and more information is filled in. This information is cross-referenced in the memory store so that the mention of one word or series of words will prompt many associations within the reader's personal scene or frame. Such associations help in correcting miscues or in filling in larger areas of meaning. For example, "mucking out" and "mucking about" are less likely to be confused in a story about horses read by a pupil with some horse management experience: "mucking out" being the term usually applied to cleaning out stables, and "mucking about," which is probably the more familiar term generally speaking, being idle mischievous behavior. Similarly, understanding of larger passages and the concepts they contain will be influenced by prior knowledge.

A strategy for determining the extent of the knowledge already available before reading has been supplied by Langer (1980). This can be employed to gauge the starting point for the individual or group of readers. The advantage of the system is that the teacher can ensure it fits both children and the texts to be read. To adapt the maxim, start the children's reading where the children are.

Comprehending then can be thought of as a combination of the general knowledge of the world in which we live and of technical text linguistic knowledge. The latter, although complex, is becoming more and more accessible to the teacher of reading.

4. *Specific Content Prior Knowledge*

The third dimension along which prior knowledge varies can be found in the content or subject areas. Here the level of reading skill required by content area teachers, and indeed parents, is considerable, but often not supported by continuing reading instruction.

The demands of the school curriculum increase in specificity as children get older and move through the school system. To many this will appear self-evident, but it is often wise when considering school situations which can be taken for granted to spell out their implications for reading. And here two major interrelated points need making.

First, because of the step-by-step organization of most content area teaching, the increase in specificity of that content is gradual. Yet the load on reading which accompanies this increasing specificity is not of the same incremental order. A fundamental change takes place in the attitude of the teacher to reading and this must be discerned by the pupil, often without guidance. It takes some time for children to appreciate that the nature of their reading has changed from that which characterized their early reading, such as the enjoyment of a story, to one in which reading is used to instruct. The change that is implicit is from learning to read to reading to learn. Reading a story now becomes part of a study of literature and reading itself a tool for learning about other school subjects. In other words the learning element, which in a way has always been present, now assumes a different and greater priority. Furthermore, although the change in specificity is gradual, the change in text type is often immediate. As noted above, the teacher of reading will appreciate that the skills required to comprehend narrative are different from those required to cope with expository texts, and the reader more often than not is taken unaware by this and the change in the attendant teaching style.

A cautionary tale in this respect can be found in the research findings of a recent School Council Project in the United Kingdom.

This study, *The Effective Use of Reading* (Lunzer & Gardner, 1979), indicates that

> for average and above average pupils the experience of meaningful reading across the curriculum becomes stabilized, or even regresses, at first year secondary level and has low priority throughout the pre-examination years. . . . A fundamental necessity is to provide the pupils with a meaningful experience of reading in science, social studies, mathematics and English.

The second major point to be made is that the writers of content area texts anticipate specific content prior knowledge. In order to learn from those texts it is necessary for readers to have received sufficient preparation of such things as vocabulary items special to them. This does not mean oral preparation only but a visual display of the words to be encountered and examples of the types of syntactical structures and cohesive elements that are typical of the text.

Topic familiarity has been shown to improve comprehension. It follows, therefore, that during the comprehending process its influence must be functioning in order to produce the final effects. It is possible that there is a threshold of prior knowledge required for the reader to learn efficiently from the text.

When specific content areas are involved, the two facets indicated above are interrelated during comprehending. The first is the distinction to be made by the teacher of reading concerning change in text type compared with the gradual increase in topic specificity. The second is the threshold of prior knowledge of the topic required in pupils to enable them to acquire further knowledge of specific content from textbooks.

The Development of Comprehending

The aim of this paper is to draw attention to much that is implicit or taken for granted by teachers that should be made explicit by the teacher of reading. The central issue is that of comprehending, which is distinguished from comprehension with its attendant problems of measurement. Comprehending is seen to be influenced by three dimensions of the prior knowledge which is brought to reading by each individual reader and which varies according to the stage of development. These are text linguistic knowledge, real world knowledge and specific content knowledge. In each of these areas there are implications for the work of the reading teacher, both in preparation and in sensitive intervention, for this is the teachable component of the reading process as a whole.

Promoting Reading Comprehension: Instruction Which Ensures Continuous Reader Growth

Diane Lapp
James Flood
San Diego State University

The following statements were recently made by teachers in a large public school district.

> How can I teach comprehension? I never really seem to "get a handle" on what the skills are. I have a hard time deciding what the differences are between literal, inferential, and critical comprehension skills. I rely on skill materials to help me.
>
> I do a lot better teaching word recognition and structural analysis skills than I do with comprehension skills. I have students from various ethnic backgrounds with various abilities in speaking and reading the English language and it's hard for me to teach comprehension.
>
> I know I should be concentrating on teaching inferential and critical reading skills but I'm not sure of the exact differences, and most of the materials in my classroom seem to stress the development of word recognition and literal comprehension skills.

These statements seem to reflect the confusion experienced by many teachers when attempting to:

1. Define comprehension.
2. Teach a reader to comprehend written discourse.

The purpose of this article is an exploration of these areas.

Defining Comprehension

Reading is *comprehension*. If students can decode letters of words and name those words, they have made a good start; but they have not *read* until they can understand what those strings of words mean. We as teachers must be careful not to confuse *word calling* with *reading.* So often we teachers confuse word calling and comprehension because it has been a long time since we have experienced any difficulty comprehending printed materials ourselves. The following paragraph may help us to differentiate word calling and comprehension.

> Rigging the Mainsail
>   Bend to boom and attach outhaul. Secure tack to gooseneck and attach main halyard. Hoist mainsail while making sure battens are in their pockets. Sail will not go to the masthead if vang, mainsheet, or outhaul are not loose.

If after reading this paragraph you were asked to rig the mainsail or to answer a series of questions related to the information you had comprehended from this paragraph, how would you perform?

As an experienced mariner this paragraph wouldn't offer any difficulty, however, those of us who have not experienced the sport of sailing may be unfamiliar with the meaning of the terms even though we can sound them out and pronounce them.

As this paragraph about sailing helps to clarify, *comprehension* occurs when the reader extracts meaning from the written text rather than when he merely names the words in the text. The meaning that is extracted from written discourse can be acquired from explicit text information, from implicit relationships in the text, and from knowledge and experience of the world. Because many students have limited world experiences, teachers aid the development of comprehension abilities every time they provide alternate world experiences. Life experiences cannot all be learned vicariously; therefore, the classroom must provide a common base for all. Such experiences are often accomplished through language experience activities, show and tell, or any other activity which provides the experiential base a reader must have in order to fully understand the text which is about to be read.

Stop for a second and think about the activities of your mind when you are "really" reading. Are you passive? Is your mind at rest? Of course not. You are actively engaged because reading is a process which involves active participation. The reader who comprehends a story, poem, essay, or other form of written text is actively involved with that text. Readers must decode, scan their schematic memory and *think* while processing a text. Support for the theory that passivity and successful reading comprehension are mutually exclusive is conveyed by Jenkins (1974) who states: "I think we will eventually conclude that the mind remembers what the mind *does*, not what the word does. That is, experience is the mind at work, not the active world impinging on a passive organism—and experience is what will be remembered."

The *proficient* reader performs many mental operations when

Lapp and Flood

processing written discourse. Such processing, which involves an interaction between the reader's mind and the text, is an indivisible whole. The following example serves to clarify this interaction.

THE TEXT SAYS:

1. The men drove away in the hot car.

3. These car thieves were being pursued by the police in at least three states.

THE READER THINKS:

2. "I see an ambiguity!"
Possibility #1:
The men were driving a *stolen car*.
Possibility #2:
The car radiator or other mechanical part was malfunctioning and causing the engine to overheat.
"I wonder which meaning is correct. I had better look at more of the text before I decide."

4. The reader must process the missing connective (car thieves of sentence 2) and disambiguate "hot car" of sentence 1 because the lexical item "hot" is used to describe stolen goods. Further, the reader calls upon his/her semantic knowledge to tie thieves to stolen goods.

This type of processing happens quickly in the mind of a proficient reader. The amount of time that is required for text processing may not be the critical element. The critical element may be the *active participation* of the reader. The ability to interact with the text and process information in this manner may be defined as the strategies employed by the *proficient reader*. However, there is a period of development which occurs prior to the *proficient reading* period which we will call the *learning to read period*. It is during this *learning to read period* that the learner acquires and practices the strategies needed for the *proficient reading* stages. Whenever the reader engages in reading difficult, unfamiliar text he may use the strategies of the learning to read period. Proficient readers apply appropriate strategies that have been acquired and practiced during the learning to read period.

The quality of the reader-text interaction will be dependent on whether the reader is at the *learning to read* or *proficient reading* period of development. While these periods are not age dependent as was demonstrated by the earlier paragraph, *Rigging the Mainsail*, the proficient reader will be able to apply the necessary strategies to ensure comprehension. For example, since most of us are proficient readers we would use a dictionary or skilled sailor to help supply word meaning which is prerequisite for comprehension. Therefore, reading strategies are applied by the proficient reader to ensure a successful experience.

Active participation during either the learning to read or proficient reading period may be encouraged if:

1. Strategies that aid readers in comprehending stories and texts are taught prior to reading.
2. Activities which foster and encourage concentration and observation by the reader are explained as part of the reading processing.
3. Goals which are clearly discernible are made apparent to the reader.
4. Materials which provoke reader interest are available in the environment.

Based on this discussion we may conclude that reading is an active interaction between the text and the reader.

Now that we have established a general definition of reading, let us further delineate the cognitive processes which constitute the act of comprehending in an attempt to better understand the types of knowledge that must be contained in the mind of the reader in order to facilitate a successful text/reader interaction during either period of reading development.

Teaching Comprehension Strategies

Teaching comprehension strategies during either period of development involves an initial preparation (getting ready tasks) before the information presentation (teaching tasks) is begun.

A. Getting Ready Tasks

1. Analyzing the Tasks of Comprehension

The getting ready task may be accomplished by determining the specific reading comprehension strategies which will have to be learned or applied by the reader who is at the *learning to read period* and the *proficient reading period* of development. Next you will need to determine if your readers are at the initial *learning to read period* or at the *proficient reading period* of development. Once you have made this diagnosis you will be ready to proceed.

Pearson and Johnson (1978) discuss reading tasks at the concept level and at the proposition level. At the *concept* level of understanding they suggest that the reader will be required to understand simple associations which may include synonyms, antonyms, classification, and complex associations, which include the understanding of analogies, ambiguous words, multiple meanings, homographs, and homophones. At the *propositional* level of understanding the reader must be able to process paraphrase, figurative language, analogies, sequence, main idea, supporting details, and multiple meanings.

If you experience difficulty when analyzing the tasks of comprehension in this manner it may be because you are used to discussing a three part division of literal, inferential and critical comprehension. As Lapp and Flood (1983) suggest, there are two major objections to a three-level (literal, inferential, and critical comprehension) classification scheme:

a. It is assumed by some educators that there is a linear progression of difficulty in these three levels of comprehension, and it is assumed that tasks that measure comprehension can be correctly labeled as literal, inferential, or critical.

b. This three part schema takes only the source of comprehension into consideration. It does not take into account the dynamic, active process of comprehension in which the reader participates during the *learning to read* or *proficient reading periods*. In short, the *operations of the learner* during the reading process are ignored in this three-level scheme.

It is extremely important to begin to unravel some of the processes involved in proficient comprehension. An appropriate way to begin this unraveling is to examine the operations of the reader during reading episodes. We know the following facts about readers:

1. A reader processes propositions and not sentences. A proposition is a relational structure established by a predicate term and one or more argument terms. For example, in the

sentence, "Mary's daughter, Denise, is an intelligent girl," there are at least six propositions:

Mary is a mother.
Mary has a daughter.
The daughter is Denise.
Denise has a mother.
Denise is a girl.
Denise is intelligent.

These propositions are not consciously articulated by the proficient reader. In this view of reading, it is suggested that the reader is ready to accept anything that follows logically from these propositions, such as "Denise can answer questions," but the reader is also prepared to carefully examine new information that does not logically follow from these propositions, such as, "Denise got an *F* on her report card."

2. A second fact we know about reading is that all readers process (infer) regardless of memory demands (Flood and Lapp, 1977).

3. Readers attend to certain semantic and/or syntactic elements in the initial propositions of texts (Flood, 1978; Trabasso, 1972). An example of this phenomenon was reported by Flood (1978) when he asked proficient readers to supply the second sentence for two passages that began in the following ways:

Passage A	Passage B
Christmas always meant going to Grandma's house.	One of the oldest drinks known to man is milk.

In Passage A, all readers wrote in a personal narrative (reminiscent) style, supplying a second highly descriptive sentence about the event of Christmas. In Passage B, all readers supplied a second data-filled sentence using a formal, non-narrative style.

All proficient readers seem to participate in similar operations during comprehension. Most proficient readers, after being exposed to the following two sentences

Daryl is laughing, smiling, and squealing.
He is hugging the Master of Ceremonies.

Lapp and Flood

will probably infer something like "Daryl is happy because he won the prize." If you attempted to delineate the operations in which the reader participates when reading this sentence, your analysis might include:

Type	Example
a. Clarification of anaphoric referent.	he = Daryl
b. Superordination of strings of lexical items.	laughing, smiling, squealing = happy
c. Inferring causality.	Daryl is laughing, smiling, and squealing and hugging the Master of Ceremonies *BECAUSE* he won the prize.

Although we are only at the threshold of our understanding of reading comprehension, we are coming to some agreement that we need to specify the operations that the readers must perform at the *learning to read* and *proficient reading* periods. When thinking about your instructional planning, think about *processes* engaged in by the reader and you will eleminate any difficulties you may be having in analyzing the tasks of comprehension.

Once this analysis has been completed you will be ready to proceed to the next *getting ready* task.

2. *Analyzing the Texts Used by Your Students*

To accomplish this getting ready task, ask yourself:

"Are the passages clearly written; do they make sense?"

"Are there frequent illustrations, offering clues to the meaning of the passage?"

"Is the text's vocabulary appropriate to the language knowledge of the readers?"

"Is the text structure appropriate to the concept formation and genre knowledge of the readers?"

"Do these passages contain characters and information that are similar to the knowledge of the world of the reader?"

If you think the storybook or textbook is too difficult, you can do the following:

a. Abandon the book and select an alternate one that is more appropriate for your students.

b. Rewrite the text, correcting it to clarify potentially troublesome areas.

For example, if the text says, "Bill and Ben are playing basketball, but Bob is not. Bob and Bea are roller skating," you may want to:
   a. Change the names to avoid confusion.
   b. Make the unclear reference to Bob in the second sentence less ambiguous. The reader could rightly wonder if the Bob in the second sentence is the Bob in the first sentence.
A corrected, more readable version of the text that adheres closely to the original might be: "Mike and Patti are playing basketball, but Anthony is not, because he is roller skating with Linda."

Once you have analyzed the text to determine its instructional appropriateness, you are ready for the third getting ready task.

3. *Planning an Integrated Language Arts Curriculum*
   It is critical to integrate the language arts into an interactive instructional program. Students at both the elementary and secondary levels should be asked to listen, discuss, read, and write in order to maximize their involvement and understanding of the strategies that are involved in reading comprehension. In addition to answering questions about texts, students should be asked to rewrite or paraphrase texts. For example, students might be asked if the following sentence could have two meanings:
   The chicken is ready to eat.
If yes, they might be asked to rewrite the sentence twice to convey the two meanings.
   1. We are ready to eat the chicken for dinner.
   2. The chicken is hungry, and he is ready to eat.
This activity involved resolving ambiguity. A similar activity would involve asking the student to read the sentence, "Pat is dancing and singing, so is Mary," and answer the question, "What is Mary doing?" Answer: Mary is dancing and singing. To answer this question the student evidenced an understanding of ellipsis. Other activities might involve the student in writing a sentence that means the same thing.
   (Lexical Transform) The mechanical woman shot the poisonous ray.
   e.g., The robot shot the poisonous ray.
   (Syntactic Transform) The Cheshire cat chased the toy poodle.
   e.g., The toy poodle was chased by the Cheshire cat.
Students might also be asked to create writing samples that demonstrate their comprehension of a specific text, e.g., "If you were the girl in the story, what would you say to the baker?"

The intent of this approach would be to demonstrate the interrelatedness and interdependence of the language arts. Each lesson could simultaneously contain exercises in several comprehension strategies. Such lessons might show that vocabulary skills, comprehension skills, and study skills are necessary for the total acquisition of meaning.

A model lesson of this type might resemble the following:

Lesson Understanding Words in Context
Exercise 1 Goal: Disambiguating ambiguous lexical items within sentences
Read the following sentences and explain the meaning of the word "crew."
The crew arrived.
The crew arrived to paint the house.

Exercise 2 Goal: Understanding multiple meanings
Write as many examples for the meaning of "crew" as you know:
The crew rowed the boat.
The wrecking crew tore the house down.
The whole crew (gang) was there.

Exercise 3 Goal: To improve writing skills
Compose a story using one of the following as your starter.
1. The crew staggered out of the smoking car....
2. "I never had a worse crew," shouted....
3. The rains kept coming as we watched the crew....

Exercise 4 Goal: Understanding multiple meanings
Write two examples of each of these multiple meaning words.
bomb
lemon
star

Exercise 5 Goal: Understanding words in context
Read these sentences and tell the meanings that each word has in the sentences below.
1. He bought a used car. What a lemon.
2. That play was a bomb.
3. I want to be a star.

As well as planning an Integrated Language Arts Curriculum, you will also need to provide experiences which ensure the integration of literacy skills and life encounters.

B. *Teaching Tasks*

    1. *Exposing Students to Various Types of Genre Diversified Types of Writing*

As early as possible children should be encouraged to develop comprehension strategies in several contexts. This may be accomplished by exposure to many types of writings. The following types of writing should be part of your instructional program:

a. Narrative Writings	-tales, fables, short stories, novelettes
b. Poetry Writings	-poetry, song lyrics, nursery rhymes, proverbs
c. Textual Writings	-textbooks; science, social studies
d. Dramatic Writings	-dramas, plays
e. Editorial Writings	-magazines, newspapers, diaries, journals
f. Representational Writings	-charts, graphs, tables, figures, maps
g. Functional Literacy Writings	-cartoons, propaganda, advertisements, applications, schedules

The emphasis at each level should reflect each child's developmental stage and should address his specific needs, e.g., the acquisition of comprehension strategies in narrative writings should be emphasized for very young children.

    2. *Exposing Students to a Variety of Response Modes*

The texts you select for instruction should contain several response modes as a motivating element as well as a sound instructional procedure. Appropriate response modes include: true/false, multiple choice, cloze, short answers, paraphrase, Wh questions, drawing a picture, matching, manual (manipulating written comprehension).

    3. *Utilizing an Effective Questioning Program*

In addition to clarifying unclear texts, you can develop your students' reading abilities by developing comprehension tasks. The most commonly used directive task is *questioning*. Questions are useful tools for stimulating thinking and learning, however, you must remember that questions do not automatically produce a certain type of thinking on the part of the respondent. Reading is performed by readers as they activate their thinking processes; reading is not performed by a question. Unfortunately, we as teachers have spent a great deal of time and effort labeling questions as literal, inferential, and critical (evaluative). Much of this time and effort has been futile. Instead, if we wish to understand the effect of our questions, we should turn our attention to examining the *processes* that are involved *during* reading as the direct result of the questions that we ask. We may find that what we labeled as an evaluative question became a literal question for the student who had experiences other than we had anticipated. Thus we realize the futility of the question labeling process. Therefore, since teacher-generated questions can stimulate a student's thinking, it is important to analyze the questions that we ask. When attempting this, remember that students interpret questions in many different ways. It is possible for students to give different answers than those that teachers had intended. For example:

Lynne Turner, rushing through the door, expecting to find a surprise party, found a quiet meeting taking place.

Question: What did Lynne Turner expect to find?

Intended answer: A surprise party.

Possible answers: 1. Her birthday celebration.
2. Friends.
3. She was the laughingstock of the meeting.

Each of the possible answers is relatively correct. Although each seems to stray further from the text and the actual question (What did Lynne Turner expect to find?), it is important to appreciate an interpretive answer such as, "She was the laughingstock of the meeting," if we want to fully understand the ways in which students make sense of texts.

We may also consider questions as a tool for ordering thinking, for putting together many pieces of a puzzle. When a student misinterprets or miscomprehends a question, what do we know? We only know that something went wrong. We need to go back to the passage and discover, with the student, the pieces of the puzzle that were misunderstood or forgotten. As Lapp and Flood (1983) suggest, this retracing procedure can be performed through systematic questioning that is based on the logical propositions within the text or story. Consider, for example, the beginning of the book, *Where the Wild Things Are* by Maurice Sendak:

1. The night Max wore his wolf suit and made mischief of one kind
2. and another
3. his mother called him "Wild Thing!"
4. and Max said, "I'll eat you up!"
5. so he was sent to bed without eating anything.

Let us suppose that you asked your children to answer one question: Why did Max's mother send him to bed without eating? The answer that you might expect from your students would be similar to the following:

Max was sent to bed without eating

cause	because he was fresh to his mother
effect 1	and she got angry with him
effect 2	and she sent him to bed.

In order to give you such a response, the child has to attend to the text and perform numerous mental processes. For example, the child has to do the following:

Text
and Max said, "I'll eat you up!"

his mother called him "Wild Thing" and (so, therefore) Max said

"I'll eat you up" (to her) (his mother)

(So his mother said "Go to your room without eating anything.") so he was sent to bed without eating anything.

Processes
1. Understand synonyms—
   Max was "fresh"

   "Fresh" means the reader has been able to understand:

   a. tone (Max's intent)
   b. dialogue rules between his mother and him
   c. his mother's intention in her reply

2. Understand conjunctions—and, so, or therefore, there is a cause-and-effect relationship

3. Understand that Max was speaking to his mother

4. Understand cause-and-effect inferences

If your students are unable to answer the question correctly, you can retrace their steps by asking logically ordered questions that require them to process one bit of information at a time. A set of questions like the following may help your children.

Question 1: What did Max's mother call him on the night he made mischief of one kind and another?

Text source: 1. The night Max wore his wolf suit and made mischief of one kind
2. and another
3. his mother called him "Wild Thing!"

Operation: syntactic transformation of questions to subject-verb-object sentence, i.e., Max's mother called him "Wild Thing!"

Question 2: Why did Max's mother call him "Wild Thing"?

Text source: 1. The night Max wore his wolf suit and made mischief of one kind
2. and another
3. his mother called him "Wild Thing!"

Operation: syntactic deletion—...Max...made mischief of one kind and another

inferred causality—(so) his mother called him "Wild Thing."

Question 3: What did Max say to his mother when she called him "Wild Thing"?

Text source: 4. and Max said "I'll eat you up!"

Operation: elongation—I'll eat you up (to her)

Question 4: What do you think Max's mother thought of that?

Text source: 5. so he was sent to bed without eating anything.

Operation: extracting Max's purpose/tone
application of world knowledge

Question 5: Then what did Max's mother say/do?

Text source: 5. so he was sent to bed without eating anything.

Operation: passive to active transformation→he was sent _____ sent Max to bed; syntactic substitution (elongation—Mom sent Max to bed; world knowledge of (rule)—Mom's turn to talk—"I send you to bed without dinner" deleted imperative—Go to bed.)

Leading children through the text in this step-by-step manner may be a productive procedure for helping them to understand the interrelatedness of the entire text.

Another teaching task which you may wish to use will help you to extend the concept formation strategies of your students.

4. *Providing Activities Which Extend Your Students' Concept Formation Strategies*

As well as remembering that by asking questions you are helping children to develop their comprehension strategies, it is also important to remember that learning to read or proficient reading comprehension is an interactive process that takes place as the reader interprets the text. This interpretation is based on the experience and background of each child. You have to help your students to develop knowledge and experiences that will enhance their reading. One way to develop this background is through instruction in *concept formation*. In helping children learn how to form concepts, you are helping them to develop their critical thinking skills.

An appropriate way to help children to form a concept is by sharing with them a broad general experience. With relatively inexperienced younger students, you may wish to involve them in an activity they have never done before (for instance, making homemade ice cream, a short introduction to modern dance movements, or visiting a nearby store or factory). This can be followed by organizing the many details of the experience into a workable grouping of simple "research topics." The following process will help you to develop strategies for each grouping:

a. Ask students, "What did you see?" "What did you hear?" "What did you smell?" This line of questioning will stimulate your young students' awareness of their senses. An excellent method for increasing sensory awareness is the "blindfold walk." It was first popularized by nature guides who wanted to increase their students' capacity for absorbing the whole realm of their environment. The "blindfold walk" is carried out in the following manner:

Divide your students into pairs.

Each pair receives a blindfold from the teacher.

Each member of the pair takes a turn at being blindfolded and led through by the hand. The partner who is not blind-

Lapp and Flood

folded does the leading through the environment (nature trail, school grounds, school corridors). It is the leader's job to guide the blindfolded person carefully and to ask questions like, "What does this feel like? Can you guess what it is? What can you smell?"

In addition to being a useful group activity, the "discoveries" of a "blindfold walk" can easily be turned into a classroom writing exercise.

b. As students begin to group the items of their experience, they will be engaged in the process of identifying common properties. They will be beginning to engage in abstraction processing.

c. After they have established categories, ask students, "How would you label these groups?" As students begin this labeling process, they are involved in hierarchical ordering or superordinates and subordinates. The acquisition of each of these processing skills is extremely important in the development of beginning or proficient reading comprehension skills.

A fifth teaching task which has been incorporated throughout this article focuses on language development.

5. *Extending the Language Skills of Students*

This may be accomplished through the language experience approach which includes all of the activities thus far discussed as getting ready and teaching tasks.

A final teaching task involves the evaluative skills of your students.

6. *Extending the Problem Solving and Problem Finding Abilities of Your Students*

Although the processes involved in critical thinking have been clearly outlined for decades, many people still make faulty evaluations, exhibit a lack of problem-solving strategies, and are unable to detect propaganda. It might be said that these are higher-level skills that need not be taught until children have mastered the basic processes of reading. Such is not the case; critical thinking must be taught in connection with beginning reading skills. In a consumer-oriented world, we must *all* possess critical reading/thinking skills if we are to be considered literate.

This may be accomplished by exposing your students to the various types of consumer propaganda which is part of their daily experiences.

Summary

Once you have defined comprehension, delineated the cognitive tasks of comprehension, and assessed the levels of functioning of your students you will be ready to begin the very important task of classroom implementation for all beginning and proficient readers. Only when theory and practice are so entwined will James Allen's dream "that every student shall have the right to read" become a reality.

References

Aaron, I., et al. *Dragonwings* (Basics in Reading, Primer Level). Glenview, Illinois: Scott, Foresman, 1978.

Ackerman, B.P. Children's comprehension of presupposed information: Logical and pragmatic inferences to speaker belief. *Journal of Experimental Child Psychology*, 1978, *26*, 92-114.

Adams, M., & Bruce, B. Background knowledge and reading comprehension. 1980. (ED 101 431)

Adams, M., & Collins, A. A schema-theoretic view of reading. In R. Freedle (Ed.), *New directions in discourse processing*. Norwood, New Jersey: Ablex, 1979.

Allington, R. Teacher interruption behaviors during primary grade oral reading. *Journal of Experimental Psychology*, in press.

Allington, Richard L., Chodos, L., Domaracki, J., & Truex, S. Passage dependency: Four diagnostic oral reading tests. *Reading Teacher*, 1977, *30*, 369-375.

Allyn & Bacon. *Pathfinder*. Boston, 1978.

Anderson, A.B., Teale, W.H., & Estrada, E. Low income children's preschool literacy experiences: Some naturalistic observations. *Quarterly Newsletter of the Laboratory of Comparative Human Cognition*, 1980, *2*, 59-65.

Anderson J.P. *Language, memory, and thought*. Hillsdale, New Jersey: Erlbaum, 1976.

Anderson, P., & Lapp, D. *Language skills in elementary education*, third edition. New York: Macmillan, 1979.

Anderson, R., Evertson, C., & Brophy, J. An experimental study of effective teaching in first grade reading groups. *Elementary School Journal*, 1979, 193-222.

Anderson, R., Spiro, R., & Montague, W. (Eds.). *Schooling and the acquisition of knowledge*. Hillsdale, New Jersey: Erlbaum, 1977.

Anderson, R. Schema-directed processes in language comprehension. In A. Lesgold, J. Pelligreno, S. Fokkema, & R. Glaser (Eds.), *Cognitive psychology and instruction*. New York: Plenum, 1978.

Anderson, R.C. The notion of schemata and the educational enterprise: General discussion of the conference. In R.C. Anderson, R.J. Spiro, & W.E. Montague (Eds.), *Schooling and the acquisition of knowledge*. Hillsdale, New Jersey: Erlbaum, 1977.

Anderson, R.C., & Freebody, P. Vocabulary knowledge and reading. Center for the Study of Reading, University of Illinois, Reading Educational Report No. 11, 1979.

Anderson, R.C., Goldberg, S.R., & Hiddle, J.L. Meaningful processes of sentences. *Journal of Educational Psychology*, 1971, *62*, 395-399.

Anderson, R.C., & Pichert, J.W. Recall of previously unrecallable information following a shift in perspective. *Journal of Verbal Learning and Verbal Behavior*, 1978, *17*, 1-12.

Anderson, R.C., Pichert, J.W., & Shirey, L.L. *Effects of the reader's schema at different points in time.* Urbana: Center for the Study of Reading, University of Illinois, Technical Report No. 119, April 1979. (ED 169 523)

Anderson, R.C., Reynolds, R.E., Shallert, D.L., & Goetz, E.T. Frameworks for comprehending discourse. *American Educational Research Journal*, 1977, *14*, 367-382.

Anderson, T.H. *Study skills and learning strategies.* Urbana: Center for the Study of Reading, University of Illinois, Technical Report No. 104, September 1978. (ED 161 000)

Applebee, A.N. *The child's concept of story.* Chicago: University of Chicago Press, 1978.

Aristotle. *The rhetoric of Aristotle.* L. Cooper, Translator. New York: Appleton-Century-Crofts, 1960.

Armbruster, B.B., & Anderson, T.H. *The effect of mapping on the free recall of expository text.* Urbana: Center for the Study of Reading, University of Illinois, Technical Report No. 160, 1980.

Atwater, J. Toward meaningful measurement. *Journal of Reading*, 1968, *11*, 429-434.

Au, K.H. *A test of the social organization hypothesis: Relationships between participation structures and learning to read.* Unpublished doctoral dissertation, University of Illinois, April 1980.

Au, K.H. Using the experience text relationship method in minority children. *Reading Teacher*, 1979, *32*, 677-699.

Aulls, M.W. Expository paragraph properties that influence literal recall. *Journal of Reading Behavior*, 1975, *7*, 391-400.

Austin, M.C., & Morrison, C. *The first R.* New York: Macmillan, 1963.

Austin, M.C., & Morrison, C. *The torchlighters.* Cambridge: Harvard Graduate School of Education, 1961.

Avery, R. Adolescents' use of the mass media. *American Behavioral Scientist*, 1979, *23*, 53-70.

Baker, L., & Brown, A.L. Comprehension monitoring and critical reading. In J. Flood (Ed.), *Understanding reading comprehension: Cognition, language, and the structure of prose.* Newark, Delaware: International Reading Association, 1983.

Baker, L., & Stein, N.L. Development of prose comprehension skill. In C.M. Santa & B.L. Hayes (Eds.), *Children's prose comprehension: Research and practice.* Newark, Delaware: International Reading Association, 1981.

Bantley, H., & Keating, T. Don't fight TV: Use it. *Massachusetts Teacher*, 1978, *57*, 20-21.

Barnard, P.J. *Structure and the content in the retention of prose.* Unpublished doctoral dissertation, University College, London, 1974.

Barr, R. Instructional pace differences and their effect on reading acquisition. *Reading Research Quarterly*, 1973-1974, *9*, 526-554.

Barr, R. The effect of instruction on pupil reading strategies. *Reading Research Quarterly*, 1974-1975, *10*, 555-582.

Barr, R.C. The influence of instructional conditions on word recognition errors. *Reading Research Quarterly*, 1972, *7*, 509-529.

Barrett, M.T., & Graves, M.F. A vocabulary program for junior high school remedial readers. *Journal of Reading*, 1981, *25*, 146-151.

Bartlett, B.J. *Top-level structure as an organizational strategy for recall of classroom text.* Unpublished doctoral dissertation, Arizona State University, 1978.

Bartlett, F.C. *Remembering.* Cambridge, England: Cambridge University Press, 1932.

Baumer-Mulloy, M. *A study of the relationship of certain home environmental factors to high or low achievement in reading among black primary school age pupils of low socioeconomic status.* Unpublished doctoral dissertation, University of Maryland, 1977.

Beck, I.L. *Comprehension instruction in the primary grades.* Paper presented at the Wingspread Conference. Relating Reading Research to Classroom Instruction, Racine, Wisconsin, March 1982.

Beck, I.L., McKeown, M.G., McCaslin, M.S., & Burkes, A.M. *Instructional dimensions that may affect reading comprehension: Examples from two commercial reading programs.* Pittsburgh: University of Pittsburgh Learning Research and Development Center, 1979. (LRDC publication 1979/20)

Beck, I.L., Perfetti, C.A., & McKeown, M.G. The effects of long term vocabulary instruction on lexical access and reading comprehension. *Journal of Educational Psychology,* in press.

Becker, W.C. Teaching reading and language to the disadvantaged—what we have learned from field research. *Harvard Educational Review,* 1977, *47,* 518-543.

Becker, W.C., & Carnine, D. *Direct instruction: A behaviorally based model for comprehensive educational intervention with the disadvantaged.* Unpublished manuscript, University of Oregon, 1978.

Berger, N.S., & Perfetti, C.A. Reading skill and memory for spoken and written discourse. *Journal of Reading Behavior,* 1977, *9,* 7-17.

Berkovich, B. Personal communication, December 1979.

Bieger, G.R., & Dunn, B.R. *Sensitivity to developmental differences in children's recall of prose: A comparison of two prose grammars.* Paper presented at the annual meeting of the American Educational Research Association, Boston, April 1980.

Biemiller, A. Changes in the use of graphic and contextual information as functions of passage difficulty and reading achievement level. *Journal of Reading Behavior,* 1979, *11,* 307-318.

Biny, E. Effect of child rearing practices on development of differential cognitive abilities. *Child Development,* 1963, *34,* 631-648.

Blatt, B., & Garfunkel, F. Teaching the mentally retarded. In R.M.W. Travers (Ed.), *Second handbook of research on teaching.* Chicago: Rand McNally, 1973.

Boettcher, J.A. New concept vocabulary: What is it, and what do I do with it when I find it? *Minnesota English Journal,* 1979, *10,* 33-48.

Bogdan, R., & Taylor, S.J. *Introduction to qualitative research methods.* New York: Wiley, 1975.

Boggs, S. The meaning of questions and narratives to Hawaiian children. In C. Cazden, V. John, & D. Hymes (Eds.), *Functions of language in the classroom.* New York: Teachers College Press, 1972.

Bond, G.L., & Tinker, M.A. *Reading difficulties: Their diagnosis and correction,* third edition. Englewood Cliffs, New Jersey: Prentice-Hall, 1973.

Bower, G.H. Experiments on story comprehension and recall. *Discourse Processes,* 1978, *1,* 211-231.

Brainerd, C.J. Cognitive development and concept learning: An interpretative review. *Psychological Bulletin,* 1977, *84,* 919-939.

Brandt, D.M. *Prior knowledge of the author's schema and the comprehension of prose.* Unpublished doctoral dissertation, Arizona State University, 1978.

Bransford, J. *Children's comprehension and learning.* Presentation at National Council for Research on English workshop, Boston, 1980.

Bransford, J.D. *Human cognition: Learning, understanding, and remembering,* Belmont, California: Wadsworth, 1979.

Bransford, J.D., Franks, J.J., Morris, C.D., & Stein, B.S. Some general constraints on learning and memory research. In L.S. Cermak & F.I.M. Craik (Eds.), *Levels of processing in human memory.* Hillsdale, New Jersey: Erlbaum, 1979.

Bransford, J.D., & Johnson, M.K. Contextual prerequisites for understanding: Some investigations of comprehension and recall. *Journal of Verbal Learning and Verbal Behavior,* 1972, *11,* 717-726.

Bransford, J.D., Stein, B.S., Shelton, T.S., & Owings, R.A. Cognition and adaptation: The importance of learning to learn. In J. Harvey (Ed.), *Cognition, social behavior, and the environment*. Hillsdale, New Jersey: Erlbaum, in press.

Bridgman, P.W. Operationism. In W.G. Hardy (Ed.), *Language, thought, and experience*. Baltimore, Maryland: University Park Press, 1978.

Britton, B.K., Meyer, B.J.F., Glynn, S., & Penland, M. Use of cognitive capacity in reading text: Effects of variations in surface features of text with underlying meaning held constant. *Journal of Educational Psychology*, in press.

Bronfenbrenner, U. Toward an experimental ecology of human development. *American Psychologist*, 1977, *32*, 513-531.

Brophy, J., & Evertson, C. *Learning from teaching: A developmental perspective*. Boston: Allyn & Bacon, 1976.

Brophy, J.E., & Good, T.L. Teachers' communication performance: Some behavioral data. *Journal of Educational Psychology*, 1970, *61*, 365-374.

Brown, A.L. Knowing when, where, and how to remember: A problem of metacognition. In R. Glaser (Ed.), *Advances in instructional psychology*, vol. 1. Hillsdale, New Jersey: Erlbaum, 1978.

Brown, A.L. Metacognitive development and reading. In R.J. Spiro, B.C. Bruce, & W.F. Brewer (Eds.), *Theoretical issues in reading comprehension*. Hillsdale, New Jersey: Erlbaum, 1980.

Brown, A.L. Recognition, reconstruction, and recall of narrative sequences by preoperational children. *Child Development*, 1975, *46*, 156-166.

Brown, A.L. Theories of memory and the problems of development: Activity, growth, and knowledge. In L.S. Cermak & F.I.M. Craik (Eds.), *Levels of processing in human memory*. Hillsdale, New Jersey: Erlbaum, 1979.

Brown, A.L., Campione, J.C., & Day, J. Learning to learn: On training students to learn from texts. *Educational Researcher*, 1980.

Brown, A.L., & DeLoache, J.S. Skills, plans, and self-regulation. In R. Siegler (Ed.), *Children's thinking: What develops*. Hillsdale, New Jersey: Erlbaum, 1978.

Brown, A.L., & Smiley, S.S. Rating the importance of structural units of prose passages: A problem of metacognitive development. *Child Development*, 1977, *48*, 1-8.

Brown, J.S., & Burton, R.R. Diagnostic models for procedural bugs in basic mathematical skills. *Cognitive Science*, 1978, *2*, 155-192.

Brown, R. *A first language: The early stages*. Cambridge, Massachusetts: Harvard University Press, 1973.

Bruce, B. *What makes a good story?* Urbana: Center for the Study of Reading, University of Illinois, Reading Education Report No. 5, June 1978. (ED 158 222)

Bruce, D.J. The analysis of word sounds by young children. *British Journal of Educational Psychology*, 1964, *31*, 158-169.

Bruner, J. On prelinguistic prerequisites of speech. In R. Campbell & P. Smith (Eds.), *Recent advances in the psychology of language*. New York: Plenum Press, 1976.

Calfee, R.C. *The book: Components of reading instruction*. Unpublished paper, Stanford University, 1981.

Calfee, R.C., & Drum, P.A. Learning to read: Theory, research, and practice. *Curriculum Inquiry*, 1978, *8*, 183-249.

Campbell, D.T., & Stanley, J.C. Experimental and quasiexperimental designs in educational research. In N.L. Gage (Ed.), *Handbook of research on teaching*. New York: Rand McNally, 1963.

Carpenter, P.A., & Just, M.A. Reading comprehension as eyes see it. In M.A. Just & P.A. Carpenter (Eds.), *Cognitive processes in comprehension*. Hillsdale, New Jersey: Erlbaum, 1977, 109-140.

Carroll, J.B., Davies, P., & Richman, B. *The American heritage word frequency book*. Boston: Houghton Mifflin, 1971.

Carver, R.P. Reading as reasoning: Implications for measurement. In W.H. MacGinitie (Ed.), *Assessment problems in reading*. Newark, Delaware: International Reading Association, 1973.

Carver, R.P. Reading tests in 1970 versus 1980: Psychometric versus edumetric. *Reading Teacher*, 1972, *26*, 299-302.

Cazden, C. Peekaboo as an instructional model: Discourse development at home and at school. In *Papers and reports on child language development*, No. 17. Stanford University Department of Linguistics, 1979.

Cazden, C.B. Language assessment: Where, what, and how. *Anthropology and Education Handbook*, 1977, *8*, 83-91.

Cazden, C.B. Learning to read in classroom interaction. In L.B. Resnick & P.A. Weaver (Eds.), *Theory and practice in early reading*, vol. 3. Hillsdale, New Jersey: Erlbaum, 1979.

Chafe, W.L. *Meaning and the structure of language.* Chicago: University of Chicago Press, 1970.

Chall, Jeanne. *Reading 1967-1977: A decade of change and promise.* Bloomington, Indiana: Phi Delta Kappan Educational Foundation, 1977.

Chapman, L.J. *Some developments in textlinguistics: Implications for the teacher of reading.* Paper presented at the First UKRA Anglo-Scandinavian Conference, Leeds, 1979. (ED 173 767)

Chapman, L.J. *The perception of language cohesion during fluent reading.* P. Kolers, M. Wrolstad, & H. Bouma (Eds.). New York: Plenum Publishing, 1979.

Chapman, L.J. Presidential address. In L.J. Chapman (Ed.), *The reader and the text.* Proceedings of the Seventeenth UKRA Course and Conference. London: Heinemann, 1981.

Chapman, L.J. *Developing reading.* London: Heinemann, 1981.

Cherry, L.J. A sociolinguistic approach to the study of teacher expectations. *Discourse Processes*, 1978, *1*, 373-394.

Chi, M.T.H. Knowledge structures and memory development. In R.S. Siegler (Ed.), *Children's thinking: What develops?* Hillsdale, New Jersey: Erlbaum, 1978.

Chiesi, H.L., Spilich, G.J., & Voss, J.F. Acquisition of domain related information in relation to high and low domain knowledge. *Journal of Verbal Learning and Verbal Behavior*, 1979, *18*, 257-273.

Chomsky, N. *Aspects of the theory of syntax.* Cambridge, Massachusetts: MIT Press, 1965.

Christie, D.J., & Schumacher, G.M. Developmental trends in the abstraction and recall of relevant versus irrelevant thematic information from connected discourse. *Child Development*, 1975, *46*, 598-602.

Christina, R. Do illustrations hinder or assist sight vocabulary acquisition? In P.L. Nacke (Ed.), *Diversity in mature reading: Theory and research.* Twenty-second yearbook of the National Reading Conference, 1973, 185-189.

Cicourel, Aaron V. (Ed.). *Language use and school performance.* New York: Academic Press, 1974.

Cirilo, R.K., & Foss, D. Text structure and reading time for sentences. *Journal of Verbal Learning and Verbal Behavior*, 1980, *19*, 96-109.

Clark, H.H., & Haviland, S.E. Comprehension and the given-new contract. In R.O. Freedle (Ed.), *Discourse production and comprehension*, vol. 1. Norwood, New Jersey: Ablex, 1977.

Clark, M. *Young fluent readers.* London: Heinemann, 1976.

Clay, M.M. Reading errors and self-correction behaviour. *British Journal of Educational Psychology*, 1969, *39*, 47-56.

Clifford, G. Words for schools: The application in education of the vocabulary researches of Edward L. Thorndike. In P. Suppes (Ed.), *Impact of research on education: Some case studies.* Washington, D.C.: National Institute of Education, 1978.

Clymer, T. What is reading: Some current concepts. In H.M. Robinson (Ed.), *Innovation and change in reading instruction.* Sixty-seventh yearbook of the National Society for the Study of Education. Chicago: University of Chicago Press, 1968.

Clymer, T., et al. *Helicopters and gingerbread* (720 Reading Series, Level 4). Lexington, Massachusetts: Ginn, 1976.

Clymer, T., et al. *The dog next door and other stories* (720 Reading Series, Level 7). Lexington, Massachusetts: Ginn, 1976.

Cofer, C.N. A comparison of logical and verbatim learning of prose passages of different lengths. *American Journal of Psychology*, 1941, *54*, 1-20.

Cohen, M.W., & Mosenthal, P. The relationship between teacher-student interaction and students' reading comprehension. In M.L. Kamil & A.J. Moe (Eds.), *Reading research: Studies and applications*. Twenty-eighth yearbook of the National Reading Conference. Clemson University, South Carolina: National Reading Conference, 1979.

Cohen, P.R., & Perrault, C.R. Elements of a plan-based theory of speech acts. *Cognitive Science*, 1979, *3*, 177-212.

Colby, B.N. A partial grammar of Eskimo folktales. *American Anthropologist*, 1973, *75*, 645-662.

Cole, M., Hood, L., & McDermott, R. *Ecological niche picking: Ecological validity as an axiom of experimental cognitive psychology* (Working Paper 14). New York: Rockfeller University, Laboratory of Comparative Human Cognition and the Institute of Comparative Human Development, 1978.

Collins, A., Brown, J.S., & Larkin, K.M. Inference in text understanding. In R.J. Spiro, B.C. Bruce, & W.F. Brewer (Eds.), *Theoretical issues in reading comprehension*. Hillsdale, New Jersey: Erlbaum, 1980.

Collins, J., & Michaels, S. The importance of conversational discourse strategies in the acquisition of literacy. *Proceedings of the sixth annual meeting of the Berkeley Linguistics Society*. Berkeley, California: 1980.

Collins, W.A. Effect of temporal separation between motivation, agression, and consequences: A developmental study. *Developmental Psychology*, 1973, *8*, 215-221.

Collins, W.A. The developing child as viewer. *Journal of Communication*, 1975, *25*, 35-44.

Cook, D.A. Some structural approaches to cinema: A survey of models. *Cinema Journal*, 1975, *14*, 41-54.

Cook-Gumperz, J. *Social-ecological perspectives for studying children's use of persuasive arguments*. Paper presented at the Sociology Seminar, Indiana University, November 1977.

Cousert, G.C. *Six selected home reading environment factors and their relationship to reading achievement at third grade*. Unpublished doctoral dissertation, Indiana University, 1978.

Craik, F.I.M., & Lockhart, R.S. Levels of processing: A framework for memory research. *Journal of Verbal Learning and Verbal Behavior*, 1972, *11*, 671-684.

Crane, S. *The red badge of courage*. In S. Crane, *The red badge of courage and four great stories*. New York: Dell, 1966.

Crapper, D.A., Meck, D.S., & Ash, M.J. The relation between formal operations and a possible fifth stage of cognitive development. *Developmental Psychology*, 1977, *13*, 517-518.

Cromer, W. The difference model: A new explanation for some reading difficulties. *Journal of Educational Psychology*, 1970, *61*, 471-488.

Dale, E. A comparison of two word lists. *Educational Research Bulletin*, 1931, *18*, 484-488.

Dale, E., & O'Rourke, J. *The living word vocabulary*, third edition. Chicago: World Book-Childcraft International, 1981.

D'Angelo, F.J. Paradigms as structural counterparts of *topoi*. In D. McQuade (Ed.), *Linguistics, stylistics, and the teaching of composition*. Akron, Ohio: University of Akron Press, 1979, 41-51.

Danner, F.W. Children's understanding of intersentence organization in the recall of short descriptive passages. *Journal of Educational Psychology*, 1976, *68*, 174-183.

Dansereau, D.F., et al. Development and evaluation of a learning strategy training program. *Journal of Educational Psychology*, 1979, *71*, 64-73.

Dave, R.H. *The identification of environmental process variables that are related to educational achievement.* Unpublished doctoral dissertation, University of Chicago, 1963.

Davies, W.J.F. *Teaching reading in early England.* London: Pitman, 1973.

Davis, F. Psychometric research on comprehension in reading. In F. Davis (Ed.), *The literature in reading with emphasis on models.* Washington, D.C.: Targeted Research and Development Program in Reading, Office of Education, National Center for Educational Research and Development, Department of Health, Education and Welfare, 1971.

Davis, F.B. Fundamental factors of comprehension in reading. *Psychometrika,* 1944, *9,* 185-197.

Davis, F.B. Research in comprehension in reading. *Reading Research Quarterly,* 1968, *3,* 499-545.

Dawes, R.N. Memory and distortion of meaningful written material. *British Journal of Psychology,* 1966, *57,* 77-86.

Day, J.D. *Training summarization skills: A comparison of teaching methods.* Unpublished doctoral dissertation, University of Illinois, 1980.

DeBeaugrande, R. *Text, discourse, and process.* (In publication; manuscript prepared 1979).

DeBoer, J.J., & Dallmann, M. *The teaching of reading.* New York: Holt, Rinehart & Winston, 1960, 135-136.

DeFord, D. *Written language acquisition: After instruction.* Paper presented at the annual convention of the International Reading Association, Atlanta, 1979.

Department of Education and Science. *A language for life* (Bullock Report). London: HMSO, 1975.

Desjardins, M. Reading and viewing: A survey. *School Librarian,* 1972, *21,* 26-30.

De Stefano, J.S. *Awareness in the reading process: Linguistic and extralinguistic.* Paper presented at the International Seminar on Linguistic Awareness and Learning to Read, University of Victoria, June 1979.

Dolch, E.W. *A manual for remedial reading.* Champaign, Illinois: Garrard, 1945.

Dooling, D.J., & Christiansen, E.E. Episodic and semantic aspects of memory for prose. *Journal of Experimental Psychology: Human Learning and Memory,* 1977, *3,* 428-436.

Dooling, D.J., & Lachman, R. Effects of comprehension on retention of prose. *Journal of Experimental Psychology,* 1971, *88,* 216-222.

Dore, J. Requestive systems in nursery school conversations: Analysis of talk in its social context. In R. Campbell & P. Smith (Eds.), *Recent advances in the psychology of language.* New York: Plenum Press, 1976.

Dore, J. Children's illocutionary acts. In R. Freedle (Ed.), *Discourse production and comprehension,* vol. 1. Norwood, New Jersey: Ablex, 1977.

Dore, J. The structure of nursery school conversation. In K. Nelson (Ed.), *Children's Language,* vol. 1. New York: Gardner Press, 1978.

Downing, J. Children's concepts of language in learning to read. *Educational Research,* 1970, *12,* 106-112.

Downing, J. *Cognitive clarity and linguistic awareness.* Paper presented at the International Seminar on Linguistic Awareness and Learning to Read, University of Victoria, June 1979.

Downing, J., & Leong, C. *Psychology of reading.* New York: Macmillan, 1982.

Doyle, W. Making managerial decisions in classrooms. In the seventy-eighth yearbook, part II of the National Society for the Study of Education. Chicago: University of Chicago Press, 1979.

Draper, A.G., & Moeller, G.H. We think with words (therefore to improve thinking, teach vocabulary). *Phi Delta Kappan,* 1971, *52,* 482-484. (ED 036 207)

Drum, P.A. Prose recall responses and categories for scoring. In P.D. Pearson & J. Hansen (Eds.), *Reading: Disciplined inquiry in process and practice.* Clemson, South Carolina: National Reading Conference, 1978.

Dumont, R.V. Learning English and how to be silent: Studies in Sioux and Cherokee classrooms. In C. Cazden, D. Hymes, & V. Johns (Eds.), *Functions of language in the classroom.* New York: Teachers College Press, 1972.

Durkin, Dolores. After ten years: Where are we now in reading? *Reading Teacher,* 1974, *28,* 262-267.

Durkin, D. *Children who read early.* New York: Teacher's College Press, 1966.

Durkin, D. *Do basal reader manuals provide for reading comprehension instruction?* Paper presented at the Center for the Study of Reading Publishers' Conference, Tarrytown, New York, February 1981.

Durkin, D. *What classroom observations reveal about reading comprehension instruction.* Urbana: Center for the Study of Reading, University of Illinois, Technical Report No. 106, 1978.

Durkin, D. What classroom observations reveal about reading comprehension instruction. *Reading Research Quarterly,* 1979, *14,* 481-533.

Eddy, L.K. *Conventional and naturalistic inquiry in educational research.* Paper presented at the Annual Meeting of the American Educational Research Association, Boston, April 1980.

Educational Testing Service. *Cooperative English tests.* Menlo Park, California: Addison-Wesley, 1960.

Elkonin, D.B. The psychology of mastering the elements of reading. In B. Simon & J. Simon (Eds.), *Educational psychology in the U.S.S.R.* London: Routledge & Kegan Paul, 1963.

Elliott, S.N. *Effect of prose organization on recall: An investigation of memory and metacognition.* Unpublished doctoral dissertation, Arizona State University, 1980.

Emig, J. Writing as a mode of learning. *College Composition and Communication,* 1976, *10,* 122-128.

Engelman, S. *Sequencing cognitive and academic tasks.* Unpublished paper, University of Oregon, 1977.

Erickson, F., & Mohatt, G. *The social organization of participation structures in two classrooms of Indian students.* Paper presented at the American Educational Research Association, New York, April 1977.

Erickson, F., & Shultz, J. When is a context?: Some issues and methods in the analysis of social competence. In J. Green & C. Wallat (Eds.), *Ethnographic approaches to face-to-face interaction.* Norwood, New Jersey: Ablex, in press.

Erman, L.D., Hayes-Roth, F., Lesser, V.R., & Reddy, D.R. The hearsay-II speech-understanding system: Integrating knowledge to resolve uncertainty. *Computing Surveys,* 1980, *12,* 213-253.

Evans, E.D. A study of what Chicanos and Anglos remember about stories they read and hear. *Reading Research Quarterly,* 1978-1979, *14,* 272-276.

Fareed, A.A. Interpretive responses in reading, history, and biology: An exploratory study. *Reading Research Quarterly,* 1971, *6,* 493-532.

Farr, R. *Measurement of reading achievement.* ERIC/IRA Reading Research Profiles. Newark, Delaware: International Reading Association, 1971.

Farr, R. Measuring reading comprehension: An historical perspective. In Frank P. Greene (Ed.), *Reading: The right to participate.* Twentieth yearbook of the National Reading Conference, 1971.

Farr, R. Standardized reading tests. In R. Karlin (Ed.), *Reading for All.* Newark, Delaware: International Reading Association, 1973.

Farr, R., & Blomenberg, P. Contrary to popular opinion. *Early Years,* 1979, 52-53, 68.

Farr, R., Fay, L., & Negley, H. *Then and now: Reading achievement in Indiana.* Bloomington: Indiana University, 1978.

Farr, R., Tuinman, J., & Rowls, M. *Reading achievement in the United States: Then and now.* Report for Educational Testing Service. (Contract OEC-71-3715 USOE) Washington, D.C.: U.S. Government Printing Office, 1975.

Feuerstein, R. *Instrumental enrichment.* Baltimore, Maryland: University Park Press, 1980.

Fillmore, C. The case for case. In E. Bach & R. Harms (Eds.), *Universals in linguistic theory.* New York: Holt, Rinehart and Winston, 1968, 1-81.

Fillmore, C.J. Scene and frame semantics. In A. Zampoli (Ed.), *Linguistic structures processing, Vol. 5: Fundamental studies in computer science.* Amsterdam: North Holland Publishing, 1979, 55-81.

Fillmore, C.J. Some problems for case grammar. In R.J. O'Brien (Ed.), *Report of the twenty-second annual round table meeting of linguistics and language studies.* Washington: Georgetown University Press, 1971.

Fisher, C., et al. Teaching behaviors, academic learning time, and student achievement: An overview. In C. Denham & A. Lieberman (Eds.), *Time to learn.* Washington, D.C.: NIE, 1978.

Fisher, C., et al. *Teaching behaviors, academic learning time, and student achievement: Final report of phase 111-B, beginning teacher evaluation study* (Technical Report V-1). San Francisco: Far West Laboratory for Educational Research and Development, June 1978.

Fisher, D., & Ford, P.C. *Comprehension and the competent reader: Interspeciality views.* New York: Praeger, 1981.

Flood, J. The effects of first sentences on reader expectations in prose passages. *Reading World,* May 1978.

Flood, J., & Lapp, D. In search of the 'perfect question': Questioning strategies for developing story comprehension in young children. *Principal,* 1980, *56,* 20-23.

Flood, J., & Lapp, D. *Language/reading instruction for the young child.* New York: Macmillan, 1981.

Flood, J., & Lapp, D. *Prose analysis and the effects of staging on prose comprehension.* Paper presented at the Second Annual Reading Association of Ireland Conference, Dublin, 1977.

Flood, J., and Salus, P. *Language and the language arts.* Englewood Cliffs, New Jersey: Prentice-Hall, 1984.

Flower, L. Writer-based prose: A cognitive basis for problems in writing. *College English,* 1979, *41,* 19-37.

Frederiksen, C.H. Effects of task-induced cognitive operations on comprehension and memory processes. In J. Carroll & R.O. Freedle (Eds.), *Language comprehension and the acquisition of knowledge.* Washington, D.C.: W.H. Winston, 1972.

Frederiksen, C.H. *Inference and structure of children's discourse.* Paper presented at the Society for Research, in Child Development meeting, New Orleans, 1977.

Frederiksen, C.H. Representing logical and semantic structure of knowledge acquired from discourse. *Cognitive Psychology,* 1975, *7,* 371-458.

Frederiksen, C.H. Semantic processing units in understanding text. In R.O. Freedle (Ed.), *Discourse production and comprehension,* vol. 1. Norwood, New Jersey: Ablex, 1977.

Freedle, R.O. *Children's recall of narrative and expository prose: The acquisition of an expository schema.* Presentation at the meeting of the American Educational Research Association, Boston, April 1980.

Freedle, R.O., & Hale, G. Acquisition of new comprehension schemata for expository prose by transfer of narrative schema. In R.O. Freedle (Ed.), *New directions in discourse processing.* Norwood, New Jersey: Ablex, 1979.

Fries, C.C. *Linguistics and reading.* New York: Holt, Rinehart and Winston, 1962.

Gallant, R.A. The garbage collectors of the sea. In I. Asimov & R.A. Gallant, *Ginn science program* (Intermediate Level C). Lexington, Massachusetts: Ginn, 1975.

Gardner, H. *The quest for mind: Piaget, Levi-Strauss, and the structuralist movement.* New York: Knopf, 1973.

Gentner, D.R. The structure and recall of narrative prose. *Journal of Verbal Learning and Verbal Behavior,* 1976, *15,* 411-418.

Getzels, J.W. Theoretical research and school change. In R. Glaser (Ed.), *Research and development and school change.* Hillsdale, New Jersey; Erlbaum, 1978.

Gibson, E.J., & Levin, H. *The psychology of reading.* Cambridge, Massachusetts: MIT Press, 1975.

Ginn 720. Lexington, Massachusetts: Ginn, 1976.

Glenn, C.G. The role of episodic structure and of story length in children's recall of simple stories. *Journal of Verbal Learning and Verbal Behavior*, 1978, *17*, 229-247.

Glenn, C., & Stein, N. Syntactic structures and real world themes in stories generated by children. Urbana: Center for the Study of Reading, University of Illinois, 1978, mimeographed.

Goetz, E.T. Inferring from text: Some factors influencing which inferences will be made. *Discourse Processes*, 1979, *2.*

Golinkoff, R.M. A comparison of reading comprehension processes in good and poor comprehenders. *Reading Research Quarterly*, 1975-1976, *11*, 623-659.

Gomulicki, B.R. Recall as an abstractive process. *Acta psychologica*, 1956, *12*, 77-94.

Good, T., Grouws, D.A., & Beckerman, T.M. Curriculum pacing: Some empirical data in mathematics. *Journal of Curriculum Studies*, 1979.

Goodman, K.S. Behind the eye: What happens in reading. In *Reading: Process and program*. Urbana, Illinois: National Council of Teachers of English, 1970.

Goodman, K.S. Psycholinguistic universals in the reading process. In F. Smith (Ed.), *Psycholinguistics and reading*. New York: Holt, Rinehart & Winston, 1973.

Goodman, K.S. Reading: A psycholinguistic guessing game. *Journal of the Reading Specialist*, May 1967.

Goodman, Y. *A study of the development of written language literacy in preschool children*. Tucson, Arizona: University of Arizona, NIE Research Grant Proposal, 1976.

Goodman, Y., & Burke, C. *Reading miscue inventory: Evaluation form*. Bloomington: Indiana University, 1976 (mimeographed).

Goodman, Y., & Burke, C. *Reading miscue inventory*. New York: Macmillan, 1971.

Gordon, C.J. *The effects of instruction in metacomprehension and inferencing on children's comprehension abilities*. Unpublished doctoral dissertation, University of Minnesota, 1980.

Gough, P. One second of reading. In J.P. Kavanagh & I.G. Mattingly (Eds.), *Language by eye and by ear*. Cambridge, Massachusetts: MIT Press, 1972.

Gough, P.B. One second of reading. In H. Singer & R.B. Ruddell (Eds.), *Theoretical models and processes of reading*. Newark, Delaware: International Reading Association, 1976, 509-535.

Grabe, M., & Prentice, W. The impact of reading competence on the ability to take a perspective. *Journal of Reading Behavior*, 1979, *19*, 21-25.

Graesser, A.C., Higginbotham, M.W., Robertson, S.P., & Smith, W.R. A natural inquiry into the *National Enquirer*'s self-induced versus task-induced reading comprehension. *Discourse Processes*, 1978, *1*, 355-372.

Graesser, C., Hoffman, N., & Clark, L.F. Structural components of reading time. *Journal of Verbal Learning and Verbal Behavior*, 1980, *19*, 135-151.

Grant, A.K. *I rode with the epigrams*. Dunedin, New Zealand: John McIndoe, 1979.

Graves, M.F. Types of reading vocabulary to teach. *Minnesota English Journal*, 1978, *9*, 2-17.

Graves, M.F. *A quantitative and qualitative study of students' vocabularies*. Paper presented at the American Educational Research Association Convention, Boston, April 1980.

Graves, M.F., & Bender, S.D. Preteaching vocabulary to secondary students: A classroom experiment. *Minnesota English Journal*, 1980, *10*, 27-34.

Graves, M.F., Boettcher, J.V., Peacock, J.L., & Ryder, R.J. Word frequency as a predictor of students' reading vocabularies. *Journal of Reading Behavior*, 1980, *12*, 117-127.

Graves, M.F., Boettcher, J.V., & Ryder, R.J. *Easy reading: Book series and periodicals for less able readers*. Newark, Delaware: International Reading Association, 1979.

Graves, M.F., & Gebhard, D.V. Content teachers' predictions of students' knowledge of specific words. *Reading Psychology*, in press.

Gray, W.S. The importance of intelligent silent reading. *Elementary School Journal,* 1924, *24,* 348-356.

Gray, W.S. *The teaching of reading and writing: An international survey.* Paris: Unesco, 1956.

Greene, J., & Wallat, C. *Sociolinguistic ethnography.* Paper presented at the Annual Convention of the International Reading Association, Houston, May 1978.

Gregg, L.W. (Ed.). *Knowledge and cognition.* Hillsdale, New Jersey: Erlbaum, 1974.

Grice, H. Logic and conversation. In P. Cole & J. Morgan (Eds.), *Syntax and semantics, III: Speech acts.* New York: Academic Press, 1975, 41-58.

Grimes, J.E. *The thread of discourse.* The Hague, Holland: Mouton, 1975.

Halliday, M.A.K. *Explorations in the functions of language.* New York: Elsevier, 1973.

Halliday, M.A.K. *Language as a social semiotic: The social interpretations of language and meaning.* Baltimore, Maryland: University Park Press, 1978.

Halliday, M.A.K. *Learning to mean.* London: Edward Arnold Limited, 1975.

Halliday, M.A.K., & Hasan, R. *Cohesion in English.* London: Longman, 1976.

Hansen, J. *An instructional study: Improving the inferential comprehension of fourth grade good and poor readers.* Urbana: Center for the Study of Reading, University of Illinois, Technical Report, in press.

Hansen, J. The effects of inference training and practice on young children's reading comprehension. *Reading Research Quarterly,* 1981, *16,* 391-417.

Hansen, J., & Pearson, P.D. *The effects of inference training and practice on young children's comprehension.* Urbana: Center for the Study of Reading, University of Illinois, Technical Report No. 166, 1980. (ED 186 839)

Haring, M.J. *The effect of pictures on reading comprehension.* Unpublished doctoral dissertation, Arizona State University, 1978.

Harris, A.J. *Effective teaching of reading.* New York: David McKay, 1962.

Harris, A.J., & Jacobson, M.D. *Basic elementary reading vocabularies.* New York: Macmillan, 1972.

Harris, A.J., & Serwer, B.L. The CRAFT project: Instructional time in reading research. *Reading Research Quarterly,* 1966, *2,* 27-56.

Heap, J.L. *Rumpelstiltskin: The organization of preference in a reading lesson.* Paper presented at the Annual Meeting of the Canadian Sociology and Anthropology Association, London, Ontario, June 1978.

Hempel, C.G. *Philosophy of natural science.* Englewood Cliffs, New Jersey: Prentice-Hall, 1966.

Hendry, L.D., & Patrick, H. Adolescents and television. *Journal of Youth and Adolescence,* 1977, *6,* 325-336.

Herber, H. *Teaching reading in content areas.* Englewood Cliffs, New Jersey: Prentice-Hall, 1978.

Herber, H., & Nelson, J. Questioning is not the answer. *Journal of Reading,* 1975, *18,* 512-517.

Hildyard, A. Children's production of inferences from oral texts. *Discourse Processes,* 1979, *2,* 33-56.

Hildyard, A., & Olson, D.R. Memory and inference in the comprehension of oral and written discourse. *Discourse Processes,* 1978, *1,* 91-117.

Hoskins, K.F. *The effects of home reading experiences on academic readiness for kindergarten children.* Unpublished doctoral dissertation, University of Missouri at Columbia, 1976.

House, E.R., Glass, G.V., McLean, L.D., & Walker, D.F. No simple answer: Critique of the follow through evaluation. *Harvard Educational Review,* 1978, *48,* 128-160.

Huey, E.B. *The psychology and pedagogy of reading with a review of the history of reading and writing and of methods, texts, and hygiene in reading.* Cambridge: MIT Press, 1908, 1973.

Hunt, L.C., Jr. Can we measure specific factors associated with reading comprehension? *Journal of Educational Research*, 1957, *51*, 161-172.

Insfield, J.H. What students read outside of class: Underground literature. *English Education*, 1977, *8*, 90-94.

Irwin, J.W. The effects of explicitness and clause order on the comprehension of reversible causal relationships. *Reading Research Quarterly*, 1980, *15*, 477-488.

Jackson, N. *The nature of procedure discourse.* Paper presented to Title IV-C Evaluation Committee, Poolesville, Maryland, May 1979.

Jenkins, J.J. Can we have a theory of meaningful memory? In R.L. Solso (Ed.), *Theories in cognitive psychology: The Loyola symposium.* Hillsdale, New Jersey: Erlbaum, 1974.

Jenkins, J.J. Four points to remember: A tetrahedral model of memory experiments. In L.S. Cermak & F.I.M. Craik (Eds.), *Levels of processing in human memory.* Hillsdale, New Jersey: Erlbaum, 1979.

Jenkins, J.R., Pany, O., & Schreck, J. *Vocabulary and reading comprehension: Instructional effects.* Urbana: Center for the Study of Reading, University of Illinois, Technical Report No. 100, 1978. (ED 160 999)

Just, M.A., & Carpenter, P.A. *Cognitive processes in comprehension.* Hillsdale, New Jersey: Erlbaum, 1977.

Kamil, M. Models of reading: What are the implications for instruction in comprehension? In S. Pflaum-Conner (Ed.), *Aspects of reading education.* Berkeley, California: McCutcheon, 1978.

Kean, M., Summers, A., Rauietz, M., & Farber, I. *What works in reading.* Philadelphia: School District of Philadelphia, 1979.

Kingston, A.J. The measurement of reading comprehension. In O.S. Causey and E.P. Bliesmer (Eds.), *The ninth yearbook of the National Reading Conference.* Fort Worth: Texas Christian University Press, 1960, 88-93.

Kintsch, W. On comprehending stories. In M. Just & P. Carpenter (Eds.), *Cognitive processes in comprehension.* Hillsdale, New Jersey: Erlbaum, 1977.

Kintsch, W. *The representation of meaning in memory.* Hillsdale, New Jersey: Erlbaum, 1974.

Kintsch, W., & Greene, E. The role of culture-specific schemata in the comprehension and recall of stories. *Discourse Processes*, 1978, *1*, 1-13.

Kintsch, W., & Keenan, J.M. Reading rates as a function of number of propositions in the base structure of sentences. *Cognitive Psychology*, 1973, *6*, 257-274.

Kintsch, W., et al. Comprehension and recall of text as a function of context variables. *Journal of Verbal Learning and Verbal Behavior*, 1975, *14*, 196-214.

Kintsch, W., & van Dijk, T.A. Toward a model of text comprehension and production. *Psychological Review*, 1978, *85*, 383-394.

Kintsch, W., & Vipond, D. Reading comprehension and readability in educational practice and psychological theory. In L.G. Nilsson (Ed.), *Perspectives on memory research.* Hillsdale, New Jersey: Erlbaum, 1979.

Kirkpatrick, E.A. The number of words in an ordinary vocabulary. *Science*, 1891, *18*, 107-108.

Kochman, T. *Rippin and runnin.* Urbana: University of Illinois Press, 1972.

Kosoff, T. Personal communication. September 1979.

LaBerge, D., & Samuels, S.J. Toward a theory of automatic information processing in reading. *Cognitive Psychology*, 1974, *6*, 293-323.

Labov, W. The relation of reading failure to peer group status. In W. Labov (Ed.), *Language in the innercity.* Oxford: Blackwell, 1977.

Langer, J.A. *Prior knowledge and its effect on comprehension.* Paper presented at the seventeenth annual UKRA Course and Conference, University of Warwick, 1980.

Langer, S.K. Philosophy and a new key, third edition. Cambridge, Massachusetts: Harvard University Press, 1971.

Lapp, D. (Ed.). *Making reading possible through effective classroom management.* Newark, Delaware: International Reading Association, 1980.

Lapp, D., & Flood, J. *Teaching reading to every child.* New York: Macmillan, 1978; second edition, 1983.

Larrick, N. *A parent's guide to children's reading.* Garden City, New Jersey: Doubleday, 1958.

Leifer, A.D., et al. Developmental aspects of variables relevant to observational learning. *Child Development,* 1971, *42,* 1509-1516.

Levenstein, P., & Sunley, R. Stimulation of verbal interaction between disadvantaged mothers and children. *American Journal of Orthopsychiatry,* 1968, *38,* 116-121.

Levin, H., & Williams, J.P. (Eds.), *Basic studies on reading.* New York: Basic Books, 1970.

Lieven, E. Turntaking and pragmatics: Two issues in early child language. In R. Campbell & P. Smith (Eds.), *Recent advances in the psychology of language.* New York: Plenum Press, 1976.

Lorge, I., & Chall, J. Estimating the size of vocabularies of children and adults: An analysis of methodological issues. *Journal of Experimental Education,* 1963, *32,* 147-157.

Lunzer, E., & Gardner, K. *The effective use of reading.* London: Heinemann, 1979.

Mandler, J.M. A code in the node: The use of a story schema in retrieval. *Discourse Processes,* 1978, *1,* 14-35.

Mandler, J.M., & DeForest, M. Is there more than one way to recall a story? *Child Development,* 1979, *50,* 886-889.

Mandler, J.M., & Johnson, N.S. Remembrance of things parsed: Story structure and recall. *Cognitive Psychology,* 1977, *9,* 111-151.

Marshall, N. *The structure of semantic memory for text.* Unpublished doctoral dissertation, Cornell University, 1976.

Marshall, N. *Framework for evaluation.* Paper presented at the National Reading Conference, St. Petersburg, December 1978.

Marshall, N. *The effects of discourse type upon comprehension.* Paper presented at the National Reading Conference, San Antonio, December 1979.

Marshall, N., & Glock, M.D. Comprehension of connected discourse: A study into the relationships between the structure of text and information recalled. *Reading Research Quarterly,* 1978-1979, *14,* 10-56.

Mason, J. Prereading: A developmental perspective. In P.D. Pearson (Ed.), *Handbook of research in reading.* New York: Longman, in press.

Mason, J.M. Effects of polysemous words on sentence comprehension. *Reading Research Quarterly,* 1979, *15,* 49-65.

Mathews, Mitford. *Teaching to read: Historically considered.* Chicago: University of Chicago Press, 1966.

Mattingly, I.G. *Reading, linguistic awareness, and language acquisition.* Paper presented at the Internation Seminar on Linguistic Awareness and Learning to Read, University of Victoria, June 1979.

Mattingly, I.G. Reading, the linguistic process, the linguistic awareness. In J.F. Kavanagh I.G. Mattingly (Eds.), *Language by ear and by eye.* Cambridge, Massachusetts: MIT Press, 1972.

McClure, E., Mason, J., & Barnitz, J. An exploratory study of story structure and age effects on children's ability to sequence stories. *Discourse Processes,* 1979, *2,* 213-249.

McDermott, R. Achieving school failure: An anthropological approach to illiteracy and social stratification. In G.D. Spindler (Ed.), *Education and cultural processes: Toward an anthropology of education.* New York: Holt, Rinehart & Winston, 1974.

McDermott, R. *Kids make sense.* Unpublished doctoral dissertation, Stanford University, 1976.

McDermott, R. Social relations as contexts for learning in school. *Harvard Educational Review,* 1977, *47,* 198-213.

McDermott, R., & Aron, J. Pirandello in the classroom: On the possibility of equal educational opportunities in American culture. In M.C. Reynolds (Ed.), *Futures of exceptional students: Emerging structures.* Reston, Virginia: Council for Exceptional Children, 1978.

McDermott, R.P. The ethnography of speaking and reading. In R. Sharp (Ed.), *Linguistic theory.* Newark, Delaware: International Reading Association, 1977.

McNamee, G.D. The social interaction origins of narrative skills. *The Quarterly Newsletter of the Laboratory of Comparative Human Cognition,* 1979, *1,* 63-68.

Mehan, H. *Learning lessons: Social organization in the classroom.* Cambridge, Massachusetts: Harvard University Press, 1979.

Mehan, H. Structuring school structure. *Harvard Educational Review,* 1978, *48,* 32-64.

Mehan, H., & Wood, H. *The reality of ethnomethodology.* New York: Wiley Interscience, 1975.

Meyer, B.J.F. *Idea units recalled from prose in relation to their position in the logical structure, importance, stability, and order in the passage.* Unpublished master's thesis, Cornell University, 1971.

Meyer, B.J.F. *The organization of prose and its effect on memory.* Amsterdam: North-Holland Publishing, 1975.

Meyer, B.J.F. Basic research on prose comprehension: A critical review. In D.F. Fisher & C.W. Peters (Eds.), *Comprehension and the competent reader: Interspecialty perspectives.* New York: Praeger, 1981.

Meyer, B.J.F. Identification of the structure of prose and its implications for the study of reading and memory. *Journal of Reading Behavior,* 1975, *7,* 7-47.

Meyer, B.J.F. Organizational patterns in prose and their use in reading. In M.L. Kamil & A.J. Moe (Eds.), *Reading research: Studies and applications.* Clemson, South Carolina: National Reading Conference, 1979, 109-117.

Meyer, B.J.F. *Research on prose comprehension: Applications for writing instruction.* Presentation at the Conference on College Composition and Communication, Minneapolis, April 1979.

Meyer, B.J.F. *Signaling in text and its interaction with reader strategies.* Paper presented at a meeting of the American Educational Research Association, Boston, April 1980.

Meyer, B.J.F. The structure of prose: Effects on learning and memory and implications for educational practice. In R.C. Anderson, R. Spiro, & W.E. Montague (Eds.), *Schooling and the acquisition of knowledge.* Hillsdale, New Jersey: Erlbaum, 1977.

Meyer, B.J.F. What is remembered from prose: A function of passage structure. In R.O. Freedle (Ed.), *Discourse production and comprehension,* vol. 1. Norwood, New Jersey: Ablex, 1977.

Meyer, B.J.F., Brandt, D.M., & Bluth, G.J. *Use of author's schema: Key to ninth graders' comprehension.* Paper presented at the meeting of the American Educational Research Association, Toronto, March 1978.

Meyer, B.J.F., Brandt, D.M., & Bluth, G.J. Use of the top level structure in text: Key for reading comprehension of ninth grade students. *Reading Research Quarterly,* 1980, *16,* 72-103.

Meyer, B.J.F., & Freedle, R.O. *The effect of different discourse types on recall.* Department of Educational Psychology, Arizona State University, Technical Report No. 6, 1979.

Meyer, B.J.F., Haring, M.J., Brandt, D.M., & Walker, C.H. Comprehension of stories and expository text. *Poetics,* 1980, *9,* 203-211.

301

Meyer, B.J.F., & McConkie, G.W. What is recalled after hearing a passage? *Journal of Educational Psychology*, 1973, *65*, 109-117.

Meyer, B.J.F., & Rice, G.E. *Signaling in text.* Paper presented at a meeting of the American Psychological Association, Montreal, September 1980.

Meyer, B.J.F., & Rice, G.E. *The amount, type, and organization of information recalled from prose by young, middle, and old adult readers.* Paper presented at a meeting of the American Psychological Association, Montreal, September 1980.

Meyer, B.J.F., Rice, G.E., Bartlett, B.J., & Woods, V. *Facilitative effects of passages with the same structure and different content on prose recall.* Unpublished manuscript, Arizona State University, 1979.

Meyer, B.J.F., & Walker, C.H. *Effects of discourse type on the recall of retired adults.* Unpublished manuscript, Arizona State University, 1978.

Michaels, S. *Sharing time: An oral preparation for literacy.* Paper presented at the Ethnography in Education Research Forum, University of Pennsylvania, March 1980.

Michaels, S. *Sharing time revisited.* Paper presented at the University of Pennsylvania, Ethnography in Education Research Forum, March 1981.

Micklos, J. The facts, please, about reading achievement in American schools. *Journal of Reading*, 1980, *24*, 44-45.

Milner, E. A study of the relationship between reading readiness in grade one school children and patterns of parent-child interaction. *Child Development*, 1951, *22*, 95-112.

Mishler, E.G. Meaning in context: Is there any other kind? *Harvard Educational Review*, 1979, *49*, 1-19.

Moeser, S.D. Inferential reasoning in episodic memory. *Journal of Verbal Learning and Verbal Behavior*, 1976, *15*, 193-212.

Monteith, Mary K. Schemata: An approach to understanding reading comprehension. *Journal of Reading*, 1979, *22*, 368-371.

Morine-Dershimer, G., Galluzzo, G., & Fagal, F. *Participant perspectives of discourse, classroom status, pupil participation, and achievement in reading: A chaining of relationships*, part 3. Final report, grant NIE-G-78-0161, Research Foundation, California State University at Hayward, August 1980.

Mosenthal, P. Children's strategy preferences for resolving contradictory story information under two social conditions. *Journal of Experimental Child Psychology*, 1979, *28*, 323-343.

Mosenthal, P. The new and given in children's comprehension of presuppositive negatives in two modes of processing. *Journal of Reading Behavior*, 1978, *10*, 267-278.

Mosenthal, P. Three types of schemata in children's recall of cohesive and noncohesive text. *Journal of Experimental Child Psychology*, 1979, *27*, 129-142.

Mosenthal, P., Davidson-Mosenthal, R., & Krieger, V. How fourth graders develop point of view in classroom writing. *Research in the teaching of English*, in press.

Mosenthal, P., & Na, T.J. Classroom competence and children's individual differences in writing. *Journal of Educational Psychology*, in press.

Mosenthal, P., & Na, T.J. Quality in children's recall under two classroom testing tasks: Toward a sociopsycholinguistic model of reading comprehension. *Reading Research Quarterly*, 1980, *15*, 504-528.

Mosenthal, P., & Na, T.J. Quality of text recall as a function of children's classroom competence. *Journal of Experimental Child Psychology*, 1980, *30*, 1-21.

Mosenthal, P., & Na, T.J. *Taking a perspective; From the perspective of a classroom competence model.* Paper presented at the Annual Meeting of the American Educational Research Association, Boston, April 1980.

Mosenthal, P., Walmsley, S., & Allington, R. Word recognition reconsidered: Toward a multicontext model. *Visible Language*, 1978, *12*, 448-468.

Nagy, W.E., & Anderson, R.C. *The number of words in printed school English.* Urbana: Center for the Study of Reading, University of Illinois, Technical Report, 1982.

National Assessment of Educational Progress. *Three national assessments of reading: Changes in performance 1970-1980,* Reading Report 11-R-01. Denver, Colorado: Education Commission of the States, 1981.

Neale, M.D. *Neale analysis of reading ability test booklet,* second edition. London: Macmillan, 1966, 3.

Neilsen, A. *The role of macrostructure and relational markers in comprehending familiar and unfamiliar written discourse.* Unpublished doctoral dissertation, University of Minnesota, 1977.

Neisser, U. *Cognition and reality.* San Francisco: W.H. Freeman, 1976.

Nelson, J. *American readers: Changing views and meeting challenges,* teachers' edition. New York: American Book Company, 1980.

Niles, O.S. Organization perceived. In H.L. Herber (Ed.), *Developing study skills in secondary schools.* Newark, Delaware: International Reading Association, 1965, 57-76.

Ninio, A. *Joint bookreading as a multiple vocabulary acquisition device.* Unpublished manuscript, 1979.

Ninio, A., & Bruner, J. The achievement and antecedents of labelling. *Journal of Child Language,* 1978, *5,* 1-15.

Norvell, George W. *The reading interests of young people.* East Lansing, Michigan: Michigan State University Press, 1973.

Olson, D.R. From utterance to text: The bias of language in speech and writing. *Harvard Educational Review,* 1977, *47,* 257-281.

Olson, G.M., Duffy, S.A., & Mack, R.L. Knowledge of writing conventions in prose comprehension. In W.J. McKeachie & K. Eble (Eds.), *New directions in learning and teaching.* San Francisco: Jossey-Bass, in press.

Omanson, R.C. An analysis of narratives: Identifying central, supportive, and distracting content. *Discourse Processes,* in press.

Omanson, R.C., Warren, W.H., & Trabasso, T. Goals, inferential comprehension, and recall of stories by children. *Discourse Processes,* 1978, *1,* 337-354.

O'Rourke, J.P. *Toward a science of vocabulary development.* The Hague: Mouton, 1974.

Ortony, A. *Figurative language: Aid or hinderance to comprehension?* Paper presented at the National Reading Conference, San Antonio, December 1979.

Otto, J., Sr. A critical review of approaches to remedial reading for adolescents. *Journal of Reading,* 1979, *23,* 244-248.

Owings, R., et al. Spontaneous monitoring and regulation of learning: A comparison of successful and less successful fifth graders. *Journal of Educational Psychology,* 1980, *2,* 250-256.

Paivio, A. On the functional significance of imagery. *Psychological Bulletin,* 1970, *73,* 385-392.

Palmer, R.J. Teaching new words for which students already have a concept. *Minnesota English Journal,* 1979, *10,* 22-34.

Paris, S.C., & Lindauer, B.K. The role of inference in children's comprehension and memory. *Cognitive Psychology,* 1976, *8,* 217-227.

Paris, S.C., & Upton, L.R. Children's memory for inferential relationships in prose. *Child Development,* 1976, *47,* 660-668.

Paris, S.G., & Carter, A.Y. Semantic and constructive aspects of sentence memory in children. *Developmental Psychology,* 1973, *9,* 109-113.

Paul, M.C. *The effect of formal preschool experiences and supportive reading behavior in the home on first grade reading readiness.* Unpublished doctoral dissertation, University of South Carolina, 1976.

Pearson, P.D. Methodological concerns in comprehension research. In R.F. Carey & J.C. Harste (Eds.), *New perspectives on comprehension.* Bloomington, Indiana: Publications Office, School of Education, Monograph in Reading and Thinking Series, 1979.

Pearson, P.D. *The text and the task in reading comprehension.* Paper presented at the Twenty-Third Annual Convention of the International Reading Association, Houston, May 1978.

Pearson, P.D., Hansen, J., & Gordon, C. The effect of background knowledge on young children's comprehension of explicit and implicit information. *Journal of Reading Behavior,* 1979, *11*, 201-210.

Pearson, P.D., & Johnson, D.D. *Teaching reading comprehension.* New York: Holt, Rinehart and Winston, 1978.

Perfetti, C.A. *Language comprehension and fast decoding: Some psycholinguistic prerequisites for skilled reading comprehension.* Paper presented at the International Reading Association seminar on the Development of Reading Comprehension, Newark, Delaware, July 1975.

Perfetti, C.A., & Hogaboam, T.W. The relationship between single word decoding and reading comprehension skill. *Journal of Educational Psychology,* 1975, *67,* 461-469.

Perfetti, C.A., & Lesgold, A.M. Discourse comprehension and sources of individual differences. In M. Just & P. Carpenter (Eds.), *Cognitive processes in comprehension.* Hillsdale, New Jersey: Erlbaum, 1977.

Philips, S. Participant structures and communicative competence: Warm Springs children in community and classroom. In C. Cazden, V. John, & D. Hymes (Eds.), *Functions of language in the classroom.* New York: Teachers College Press, 1972.

Piaget, Jean. *Psychology and epistemology.* Translated by Arnold Rosin. New York: Viking, 1972.

Pichert, J.W. *Sensitivity to what is important in prose.* Urbana: Center for the Study of Reading, University of Illinois, Technical Report No. 149, November 1979. (ED 179 946)

Pichert, J., & Anderson, R.C. Taking different perspectives on a story. *Journal of Educational Psychology,* 1977, *69,* 309-315.

Pitcher, E.G., & Prelinger, E. *Children tell stories: An analysis of fantasy.* New York: International Universities Press, 1963.

Poulsen, D., Kintsch, E., Kintsch, W., & Premack, D. Children's comprehension and memory for stories. *Journal of Experimental Child Psychology,* 1979, *28,* 379-403.

Pratt, M. *Toward a speech act theory of literary discourse.* Bloomington, Indiana: Indiana University Press, 1977.

Raphael, T.E. *The effects of metacognitive strategy awareness training on students' question answering behavior.* Unpublished doctoral dissertation, University of Illinois, 1980.

Read, C. Preschool children's knowledge of English phonology. *Harvard Educational Review,* 1971, *41,* 1-34.

Reber, H.S., & Scarborough, D.L. (Eds.). *Toward a psychology of reading.* Hillsdale, New Jersey: Erlbaum, 1977.

Resnick, D.P., & Resnick, L.B. The nature of literacy: An historical exploration. *Harvard Educational Review,* 1977, *47,* 370-385.

Rhodes, L.K. *The interaction of beginning readers' strategies and texts reflecting alternate models of predictability.* Unpublished doctoral dissertation, Indiana University, 1978.

Rice, G.E. *The role of cultural schemata in narrative comprehension.* Unpublished doctoral dissertation, University of California at Irvine, 1978.

Riegel, K.F. The structure of the structuralists. *Contemporary Psychology,* 1974, *19,* 811-813.

Robinson, H.A. *Teaching reading and study strategies: The content areas.* Boston: Allyn and Bacon, 1978.

Robinson, H.M. Insights from research: Children's behavior while reading. In W.D. Page (Ed.), *Help for the reading teacher: New directions in research.* NCRE/ERIC Clearinghouse on Research in Reading and Communication Skills, 1975, 9-21.

Rosenblatt, L.M. *Literture as exploration.* New York: Appleton-Century-Crofts, 1938.

Rosenblatt, L.M. *The reader, the text, the poem.* Carbondale, Illinois: Southern Illinois Press, 1978.

Rosenshine, B. Content, time, and direct instruction. In H. Walberg & P. Peterson (Eds.), *Research on teaching: Concepts, findings, and implications.* Berkeley, California: McCutchan, 1979.

Rosenshine, B. How time is spent in elementary classrooms. In C. Denhan & A. Lieberman (Eds.), *Time to learn.* Washington, D.C.: National Institute of Education, May 1980.

Rosenshine, B., & Berliner, D. Academic engaged time. *British Journal of Teacher Education,* 1978, *4,* 3-16.

Rosenshine, B.V., & Stevens, R. Advances in teacher education research. *Journal of Special Education,* in press.

Rosenthal, R., & Jacobson, L. *Pygmalion in the classroom: Teachers' expectations and pupils' intellectual development.* New York: Holt, 1968.

Rubin, A.D. *Hypothesis formation and evaluation in medical diagnosis,* report AI-TR-316. Cambridge, Massachusetts: Institute of Technology, Artificial Intelligence Laboratory, 1975.

Ruddell, R.B. Developing comprehension abilities: Implications from research for an instructional framework. In S. J. Samuels (Ed.), *What research has to say about reading instruction.* Newark, Delaware: International Reading Association, 1978.

Rudner, R.S. *Philosophy of social science.* Englewood Cliffs, New Jersey: Prentice-Hall, 1966.

Rumelhart, D.E. Notes on a schema for stories. In D.G. Bobrow & A.M. Collins (Eds.), *Representation and understanding.* New York: Academic Press, 1975.

Rumelhart, D.E. Toward an interactive model of reading. In S. Dornic (Ed.), *Attention and performance VI.* Hillsdale, New Jersey: Erlbaum, 1977.

Rumelhart, D.E. Toward an interactive model of reading. Technical Report No. 56, Center for Human Information Processing, University of California at San Diego, 1976.

Rumelhart, D.E. Understanding and summarizing brief stories. In D. LaBerge & S.J. Samuels (Eds.), *Basic processes in reading: Perception and comprehension.* Hillsdale, New Jersey: Erlbaum, 1977.

Rumelhart, D.E. & Ortony, A. The representation of knowledge in memory. In R.C. Andersen & W.E. Montague (Eds.), *Schooling and the acquisition of knowledge.* Hillsdale, New Jersey: Erlbaum, 1977, 99-135.

Russell, David H. *Children learn to read.* Boston: Ginn, 1949.

Ryder, R.J. Teaching new meanings for words. *Minnesota English Journal,* 1978, *9,* 29-41.

Sack, A., & Yourman, J. *The Sack-Yourman developmental reading course.* New York: College Skills Center, 1972.

Salomon, G. *Interaction of media, cognition, and learning: An exploration of how symbolic forms cultivate mental skills and affect knowledge acquisition.* San Francisco: Jossey-Bass, 1979.

Salomon, G. Shape, not only content: How media symbols partake in the development of abilities. In E. Wartella (Ed.), *Children communicating: Media and development of thought, speech, understanding.* Beverly Hills, California: Sage Publication, 1979.

Samuels, S.J. Effects of pictures in learning to read, comprehension and attitudes. *Review of Educational Research,* 1970, *10,* 397-407.

Samuels, S.J., & Turnure, J.E. Attention and reading achievement in first grade boys and girls. *Journal of Educational Psychology*, 1974, *66*, 29-32.

Santa, C., & Hayes, B. (Eds.). *Children's prose comprehension: Research and practice.* Newark, Delaware: International Reading Association, 1981.

Schank, R.C. Identifying of conceptualizations underlying natural language. In R.C. Schank & K.M. Colby (Eds.), *Computer models of thought and language.* San Francisco: W.H. Freeman, 1973.

Scollon, R., & Scollon, S. *Literacy as interethnic communication: An Athabaskan case.* Working Papers in Sociolinguistics, No. 59. Austin: Southwest Educational Development Laboratory, 1979.

Scollon, R., & Scollon, S. Literacy as focused interaction. *Quarterly Newsletter of the Laboratory of Comparative Human Cognition,* 1980, *2*, 26-29.

Scott, Foresman Basics in Reading. I.E. Aaron, D. Jackson, C. Riggs, R.G. Smith, & R. Tierney, program authors. Glenview, Illinois: Scott, Foresman, 1978.

Searle, J.R. A taxonomy of illocutionary acts. In K. Gunderson (Ed.), *Minnesota studies in the philosophy of language.* Minneapolis: University of Minnesota Press, 1975, 344-369.

Searle, J.R. What is a speech act? In J.R. Searle (Ed.), *The philosophy of language.* Oxford: Oxford University Press, 1971.

Seashore, R.H., & Eckerson, L.D. The measurement of individual differences in general English vocabularies. *Journal of Educational Psychology,* 1940, *31*, 14-38.

Shallert, D.L. *A comparison of content and structural contexts in learning from expository prose.* Paper presented at the National Reading Conference, San Antonio, December 1979.

Shields, M. Some communicational skills of young children: A study of dialogue in the nursery school. In R. Campbell & P. Smith (Eds.), *Recent advances in the psychology of language.* New York: Plenum Press, 1976.

Shultz, J., Erickson, F., & Florio, S. Where's the floor? Aspects of the cultural organization of social relationships in communication at home and at school. In D. Gilmore & A. Glathorn (Eds.), *Ethnography and education: Children in and out of school.* Philadelphia: University of Pennsylvania Press, in press.

Siders, M. How to grow a happy reader: A gardening guide for parents. Gainesville: University of Florida Resource Monograph #6, 1977.

Simons, H.D. Reading comprehension: The need for a new perspective. *Reading Research Quarterly,* 1971, *6*, 338-363.

Simons, H.D., & Gumperz, J.J. *Language at school: Its influence on school performance.* Paper presented at the Annual Meeting of the American Educational Research Association, Boston, April 1980.

Sinclair, J., & Coulthard, R. *Toward an analysis of discourse: The English used by teachers and pupils.* London: Oxford University Press, 1975.

Singer, H., & Ruddell, R.B. (Eds.). *Theoretical models and processes of reading,* second edition. Newark, Delaware: International Reading Association, 1976. Originally published, 1970.

Singer, H., Samuels, S.J., & Spiroff, J. The effect of pictures and contextual conditions on learning responses to printed words. *Reading Research Quarterly,* 1974, *9*, 555-567.

Smith, F. Making sense of reading—and of reading instruction. *Harvard Educational Review,* 1977, *47*, 386-395.

Smith, F. (Ed.). *Psycholinguistics and reading.* New York: Holt, Rinehart & Winston, 1973.

Smith, F. *Reading.* Cambridge: Cambridge University Press, 1979.

Smith, F. *Understanding reading.* New York: Holt, Rinehart & Winston, 1971.

Smith, M., & Glass, G. Meta-analysis of research on class size and its relation to attitudes and instruction. *American Educational Research Journal,* 1980, *17*, 419-434.

Smith, N.B. *American Reading Instruction.* Newark, Delaware: International Reading Association, 1965.

Smith, N.B. What have we accomplished in reading? A review of the past fifty years. In W.K. Durr (Ed.), *Reading instruction: Dimensions and issues.* Boston: Houghton Mifflin, 1967, 3-13.

Snow, C. The conversational context of language acquisition. In R. Campbell & P. Smith (Eds.), *Recent advances in the psychology of language.* New York: Plenum Press, 1976.

Snow, C. *Routines and rituals in parent-child interaction.* Paper presented at the American Educational Research Association Convention, Boston, 1980.

Snow, C.E., & Goldfield, B.A. *Turn the page please: Situation-specific language learning.* Unpublished manuscript, 1980.

Snow, C.E., & Goldfield, B.A. *Building stories: From conversation to narrative.* Paper presented at the Georgetown University Round Table on Languages and Linguistics, March 1981.

Soar, R.S. *Follow-through classroom process measurement and pupil growth (1970-1971): Final report.* Gainesville: College of Education, University of Florida, 1973.

Soar, R.S., & Soar, R.M. *Classroom behavior, pupil characteristics, and pupil growth for the school year and the summer.* Gainesville, Florida: Institute for Development of Human Resources, College of Education, University of Florida, 1973.

Soloman, D., & Kendall, H.J. *Final report: Individual characteristics and children's performance in varied educational settings.* Chicago: Spencer Foundation Project, 1976.

Spache, G.D. *Diagnosing and correcting reading disabilities.* Boston: Allyn & Bacon, 1976.

Spache, G.D. *Good reading for poor readers,* ninth edition. Champaign, Illinois: Garrard, 1974.

Speer, J.R., & Flavell, J.H. Young children's knowledge of the relative difficulty of recognition and recall of memory tasks. *Developmental Psychology,* 1979, *15,* 214-217.

Spiro, R.J. Accomodative reconstruction in prose recall. *Journal of Verbal Learning and Verbal Behavior,* 1980, *19,* 84-95.

Spiro, R.J. Etiology of reading comprehension style. In M.L. Kamil & A.J. Moe (Eds.), *Reading research: Studies and applications,* twenty-eighth yearbook of the National Reading Conference. Clemson, South Carolina: National Reading Conference, 1979.

Spiro, R.J. Remembering information from text: The "state of schema" approach. In R.C. Anderson, R.J. Spiro, & W.E. Montague (Eds.), *Schooling and the acquisition of knowledge.* Hillsdale, New Jersey: Erlbaum, 1977.

Spiro, R.J., Bruce, B.C., & Brewer, W.F. (Eds.). *Theoretical issues in reading comprehension.* Hillsdale, New Jersey: Erlbaum, 1980.

Spiro, R.J., & Tirre. W.C. Individual differences in schema utilization during discourse processing. *Journal of Educational Psychology,* 1980, *72,* 204-208.

Stallings, J. *Teaching basic reading skills in the secondary schools.* Paper presented at the annual meeting of the American Educational Research Association, 1978.

Stallings, J.A., & Kaskowitz, D. *Follow-through classroom observation evaluation 1972-1973.* Menlo Park, California: Stanford Research Institute, 1974.

Stallings, J.A., Needles, M., & Staybrook, N. *How to change the process of teaching basic reading skills in secondary schools.* Menlo Park, California: Stanford Research Institute International, 1979.

Stanovich, K.D. Toward an interactive-compensatory model of individual differences in the development of reading fluency. *Reading Research Quarterly,* 1980, *16,* 32-71.

Stauffer, R. *Directing the reading-thinking process*. New York: Harper & Row, 1975.

Steffensen, M.S., Joag-Dev, C., & Anderson, R.C. A cross-cultural perspective on reading comprehension. *Reading Research Quarterly*, 1979, *15*, 10-29.

Steig, W. *Sylvester and the magic pebble*. New York: Dutton, 1970.

Stein, B.S., & Bransford, J.D. Constraints on effective elaborations: Effects of precision and subject generation. *Journal of Verbal Learning and Verbal Behavior*, 1979, *18*, 769-777.

Stein, N.L. How children understand stories: A developmental analysis. In L.G. Katz (Ed.), *Current topics in early childhood education*, vol. 2. Norwood, New Jersey: Ablex, 1979.

Stein, N. *How children understand stories: A developmental perspective*. Urbana, Illinois: Center for the Study of Reading, University of Illinois, Technical Report No. 69, March 1978.

Stein, N., & Glenn, C. An analysis of story comprehension in elementary school children. In R.O. Freedle (Ed.), *Multidisciplinary perspectives in discourse comprehension*. Norwood, New Jersey: Ablex, 1977.

Stein, N.S., & Glenn, C.G. An analysis of story comprehension in elementary school children. In R.O. Freedle (Ed.), *New directions in discourse processing, vol. 2 in discourse processes: Advances in research and theory*. Norwood, New Jersey: Ablex, 1979.

Stein, N., & Glenn, C. *The role of structural variation in children's recall of simple stories* and *A developmental study of children's construction of stories*. Papers presented at the Society for Research in Child Development, New Orleans, 1977.

Stein, N., & Glenn, C. *The role of temporal organization in story comprehension*. Urbana, Illinois: Center for the Study of Reading, University of Illinois, Technical Report No. 71, March 1978.

Stein, N., & Nezworski, T. *The effects of organization and instructional set on story memory*. Urbana, Illinois: Center for the Study of Reading, University of Illinois, Technical Report No. 68, January 1978.

Stone, C.R. Measuring difficulty of primary reading material: A constructive criticism of Spache's measure. *Elementary School Journal*, 1956, *57*, 36-41.

Stotsky, S.L. *Toward more systematic development of children's reading vocabulary in developmental reading programs for the middle to upper elementary grades*. Unpublished doctoral dissertation, Harvard University, 1976.

Sullivan, T.G. *Predicting readiness and achievement in reading by use of socioeconomic and home reading material availability scales*. Unpublished doctoral dissertation, North Texas State University, 1965.

Summers, P.F. Personal communication, November 1979.

Swanson, C. *The effects of readability and top-level structure on ninth graders' recall of textual materials*. Unpublished doctoral dissertation, Arizona State University, 1979.

Swift, M.S. Training poverty mothers in communication skills. *Reading Teacher*, 1970, *23*, 360-367.

Taylor, B.M. Children's memory for expository text after reading. *Reading Research Quarterly*, 1980, *15*, 399-411.

Tharp, R. *The direct instruction of comprehension: Results and description of the Kamehameha Early Education Program*. Paper presented at the annual meeting of the American Educational Research Association, Boston, 1980.

Thomas, A. Learned helplessness and expectancy factors: Implications for research in learning disabilities. *Review of Educational Research*, 1979, *49*, 208-221.

Thorburn, D. Television melodrama. In R. Adler & D. Cater (Eds.), *Television as a cultural force*. New York: Praeger, 1976.

Thorndike, E.L. Reading as reasoning: A study of mistakes in paragraph reading. *Journal of Educational Psychology*, 1917, *8*, 323-332.

Thorndike, R.L. Reading comprehension education in fifteen countries, *International studies in evaluation, III.* New York: John Wiley & Sons, 1973.

Thorndyke, P.W. Cognitive structure in comprehension and memory of narrative discourse. *Cognitive Psychology*, 1977, *9*, 77-110.

Thorndyke, P.W. Knowledge acquisition from newspaper stories. *Discourse Processes*, 1979, *2*, 95-112.

Thorndyke, P.W. The role of inferences in discourse comprehension. *Journal of Verbal Learning and Verbal Behavior*, 1976, *15*, 437-446.

Tierney, R.J., Bridge, D., & Cera, M.J. The discourse processing operations of children. *Reading Research Quarterly*, 1978-1979, *14*, 539-582.

Trabasso, T. Mental operations in language comprehension. *Language comprehension and the acquisition of knowledge.* Washington, D.C.: V.H. Winston, 1972.

Trabasso, T. On the making of inferences during reading and their assessment. In J.T. Guthrie (Ed.), *Reading comprehension and teaching.* Newark, Delaware: International Reading Association, 1981.

Truby, R. Parents in reading: Parents booklet. Portland, Oregon: Northwest Regional Laboratory, 1979.

Tuinman, J.J. Determining passage-dependence of comprehension questions in five major tests. *Reading Research Quarterly*, 1973-1974, *9*, 206-223.

Vacca, R.T. A study of holistic and subskill instructional approaches to reading comprehension. *Journal of Reading*, 1980, *23*, 512-518.

van Dijk, T.A. Macrostructures and cognition. In P. Carpenter & M. Just (Eds.), *Cognitive processes in comprehension.* Hillsdale, New Jersey: Erlbaum, 1977.

van Dijk, T.A. Narrative macrostructures: Logical and cognitive foundations. *PTL: A Journal for Descriptive Poetics and Theory of Literature*, 1976, *1*, 547-568.

van Dijk, T.A. New developments and problems in textlinguistics. AILA Bulletin No. 1. In Petofi, J.S. (Ed.), *Text vs. sentence: Basic questions of textlinguistics.* Hamburg: Burske Verlag, 1978.

van Dijk, T.A. Relevance assignment in discourse comprehension. *Discourse Processes*, 1979, *2*, 113-126.

van Dijk, T.A., & Kintsch, W. Cognitive psychology and discourse: Recalling and summarizing stories. In W.U. Dressler (Ed.), *Current theories in text linguistics.* New York: de Gruyter, 1978.

Van Zandt, W. *A study of home-family-community factors related to children's achievement in reading in an elementary school.* Unpublished doctoral dissertation, Wayne State University, 1963.

Venezky, R.L. Harmony and cacophony form a theory-practice relationship. In L.B. Resnick & P.A. Weaver (Eds.), *Theory and practice in early reading*, vol. 2. Hillsdale, New Jersey: Erlbaum, 1979.

Vipond, D. Micro-and macroprocesses in text comprehension. *Journal of Verbal Learning and Verbal Behavior*, 1980, *19*, 276-296.

Vygotsky, L.S. *Language and thought.* Cambridge, Massachusetts: MIT Press, 1963.

Wackman, D.B., & Eller, W. A review of cognitive development theory and research and the implication for research on children's responses to television. *Communication Research*, 1977, *4*, 203-224.

Walker, C.H., & Meyer, B.J.F. Integrating information from text: An evaluation of current theories. *Review of Educational Research*, 1980, *50*, 421-437.

Walmsley, S.A. On the purpose and content of secondary reading programs: An educational ideological perspective. *Curriculum Inquiry*, in press.

Warren, W.H., Nicholas, D.W., & Trabasso, T. Event chains and inferences in understanding narratives. In R.O. Freedle (Ed.), *Discourse production and comprehension. Vol. 1, Advances in research and theory.* Norwood, New Jersey: Ablex, 1977.

Waters, H.F. What TV does to kids. *Newsweek*, February 2, 1977, 62-65.

Waters, H.S. Superordinate-subordinate structure in semantic memory: The roles of comprehension and retrieval process. *Journal of Verbal Learning and Verbal Behavior*, 1978, *17*, 587-597.

Weir, R. *Language in the crib*. The Hague: Mouton, 1979.

Werlich, E. *A text grammar of English*. Heidelberg: Quelle & Meyer, 1976.

Wilkinson, L.C., & Dollaghan, C. Peer communication in first grade reading groups. *Theory into Practice*, 1979, *18*, 267-274.

Willey, T.G. *Oral acts in the primitive fiction of newly literate children*. (ED 112 381)

Williams, R.M., Jr. The concept of norms. In D.L. Sills (Ed.), *International encyclopedia of the social sciences*, vol. 11. New York: Macmillan, 1968.

Woods, W.A. Multiple theory function in high-level perception. In R.J. Spiro, B.C. Bruce, & W.F. Brewer (Eds.), *Theoretical issues in reading comprehension*. Hillsdale, New Jersey: Erlbaum, 1980.

Zhurova, L.E. The development of analysis of words into sounds by preschool children. *Soviet psychology and psychiatry*, 1963, *2*, 17-27.